# Pitti Palace
### all the museums • all the works

FIRENZE
MVSEI

© 2001 Ministero per i Beni e le Attività Culturali
Soprintendenza per i Beni Artistici e Storici
di Firenze, Pistoia e Prato
Soprintendenza per i Beni Ambientali
e Architettonici di Firenze, Pistoia e Prato

Published by

s i l l a b e s.r.l.
Livorno
http://www.sillabe.it

*managing editor*: Maddalena Paola Winspeare
*graphic design*: Laura Belforte
*editor*: Bettina Müller
*translation*: Anthony Cafazzo, Richard Fowler

*photolitography*: La Nuova Lito, Firenze;
Studiolito, Città di Castello

*reproduction rights*:
Archivio Sillabe / Giuseppe d'Abruzzo, Remo Bar-
dazzi, Paolo Nannoni; Archivio fotografico SBAS Firenze / Marcello Bertoni, Foto Degli Orti, Antonio Quat-
trone; Archivio fotografico SBAA Firenze; Nicolò Orsi
Battaglini, Firenze; Foto Brogiolo, Brescia; Foto
Saporetti, Milano.

ISBN 88-8347-047-8

# Pitti Palace

## all the museums
•
*all the works*

edited by Marco Chiarini

sillabe

# Contents

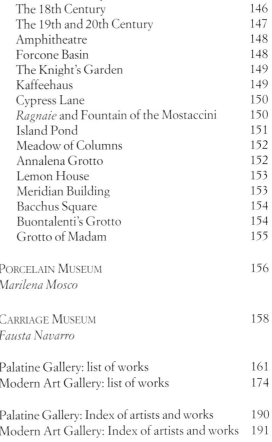

*Enough books have been written about the public museums in Florence run by the Fine Arts and Historic Works Commission to fill a large library. This is hardly surprising when one considers that the artistic heritage preserved in our museums has been famous throughout the world for centuries. For hundreds of years writer and scholars, travellers of every nationality and country have been attempting to describe all that the Florentine museums contain. They have made great efforts to explain why these museums are so fascinating, and to lead a path through paintings and sculptures for both the uninformed but willing visitor and the refined and jaded intellectual.*

*Over time, however, the museums have altered their aspect and their layout, the exhibitions have been arranged in new ways, the collections have been enriched (or impoverished). Attributions of works in the museums have also changed, restorations have transformed the appearance of many pieces, the rise and fall of aesthetic tendencies have led to reorganisation and the exhibition of differing works. All these things are constantly taking place within the public collections because museology and the history of art, like any intellectual endeavour, are in a constant state of progress and transformation. This explains why the literature surrounding the Florentine museums (like that of any of the world's great art collections) is so immense, and in a process of continual updating and change.*

*The perfect, definitive guide to a museum, any museum, does not and cannot exist.*

*The premise seems obvious, but is nonetheless necessary in order to understand the point of the publication introduced by these lines. From the moment when, in accordance with the application of the Ronchey law 4/93, the Giunti publishing house group took over the running of the support services within the Florentine museum system, it was decided to start at once on a standardised series of illustrated guides. These guides, displaying the cuneiform flower of "Firenze Musei" on the cover, guarantee that at the year of publication the state of each museum is exactly that described in the guide.*

*Certain things are obviously necessary if a museum guide is to aspire to reliability, official standing and at the same time enjoy a wide distribution: accuracy of information, high quality reproductions, an easily manageable format, a reasonable cost and – not least – a clearly written text (without, naturally, being banal or lacking in precision). Readers will judge for themselves if the guide which follows this introduction reaches these standards. I have no doubt that this will be a serious and committed judgement, just as myself and the Publisher of this guide have been serious and committed in attempting to meet the cultural needs of whoever visits our museums in the best way and with every possible care.*

Antonio Paolucci

*Head of the Fine Arts and Historic Works Commission
of Florence, Pistoia and Prato*

|  |  |
|---|---|
| ■ | Ticket office |
| B | Boboli Ticket office |
| i | Information-Bookings |
| 📖 | Bookshop |
| 📖 | Exhibition bookshop |
| ☕ | Café and snackbar |
| 👔 | Cloakroom |
| 🛗 | Lifts |
| ☎ | Telephones |
| C | Conference room |
| 🚻 | WC |
| ♿ | WC for the disabled |

**Palatine Gallery:** tel. 055.2388611-2388614, fax 055.2388613. Accessible to the handicapped. Closed: Mondays, January 1, May 1, December 25.

**Royal Apartments:** tel. 055.2388611-2388614, fax 055.2388613. Accessible to the handicapped. Closed: Mondays, January 1, May 1, December 25. From January 7 to March 31 open only for group and school visits booked in advance.

**Modern Art Gallery:** tel. 055.2388616-2388601, fax 055.2654520. Accessible to the handicapped. Closed: 1st, 3rd and 5th Monday and 2nd and 4th Sunday of each month; January 1, May 1, December 25.

**Winter Quarters or Apartments of the Duchess of Aosta:** visits by appointment only.

**Costume Gallery:** tel. 055.2388713. Accessible to the handicapped. Closed: 1st, 3rd and 5th Monday and 2nd and 4th Sunday of each month; January 1, May 1, December 25.

**Silverworks Museum:** Palazzo Pitti, piazza Pitti, tel. 055.2388709, fax 055.2388710. Accessible to the handicapped. Closed: 1st, 3rd and 5th Monday and 2nd and 4th Sunday of each month; January 1, May 1, December 25.

**Boboli Gardens:** Accessible to the handicapped. Closed: first and last Monday of each month, January 1, May 1, December 25.

**Porcelain Museum:** Closed: 1st, 3rd and 5th Monday and 2nd and 4th Sunday of each month; January 1, May 1, December 25.

For information and bookings contact Firenze Musei, tel. 055.294883, fax 055.264406, Monday to Friday 8.30-18.30, Saturday 8.30-12.30 (answer phone operative at other times).

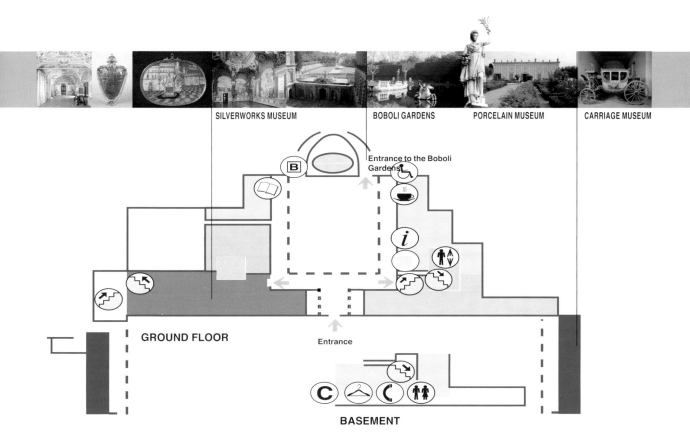

SILVERWORKS MUSEUM     BOBOLI GARDENS     PORCELAIN MUSEUM     CARRIAGE MUSEUM

Entrance to the Boboli Gardens

**GROUND FLOOR**

Entrance

**BASEMENT**

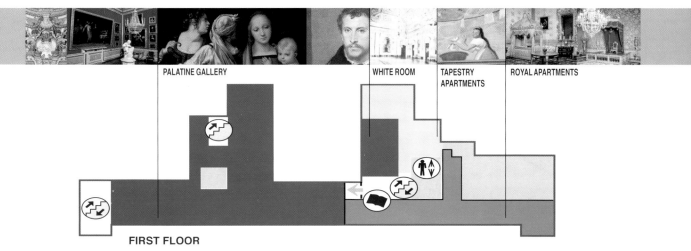

PALATINE GALLERY     WHITE ROOM    TAPESTRY APARTMENTS    ROYAL APARTMENTS

**FIRST FLOOR**

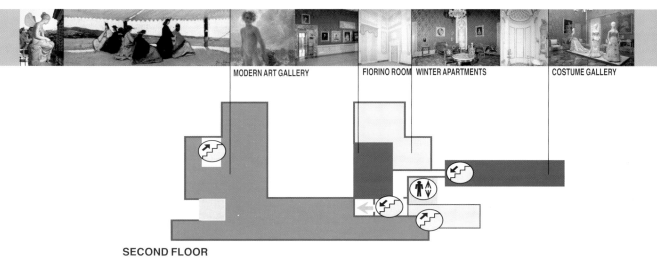

MODERN ART GALLERY    FIORINO ROOM   WINTER APARTMENTS    COSTUME GALLERY

**SECOND FLOOR**

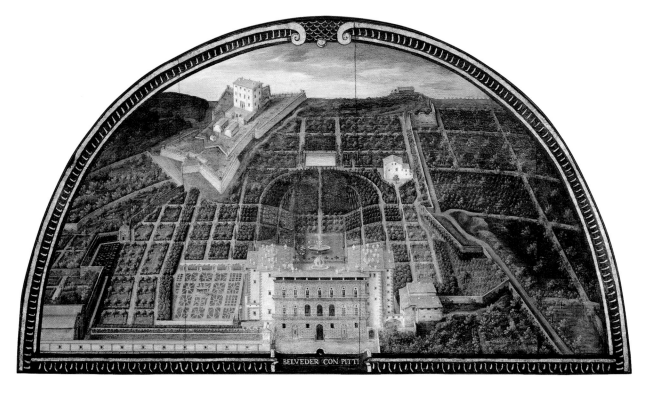

# The Pitti Palace
# Home of Three Dynasties

Laura Baldini Giusti

## The Origin

The origin of the Pitti Palace is still one of the most debated questions in the history of Renaissance architecture. Unlike other important Florentine palaces, neither the Pitti's builder nor its date of construction is known for sure.

Vasari is responsible for the traditional identification of Brunelleschi as the building's original architect. In his *Lives*, Vasari also identifies Luca Fancelli as the builder who carried out the work. No direct documentary confirmation of this attribution has so far been found, however, although it remains the one most accredited by the majority of scholars.

The palace was already in existence in 1461, the year in which it is mentioned for the first time in an archival document. It had been built by Luca Pitti, a rich Florentine merchant whose property extended along the Boboli hills to the walls of the city. He wanted his new house to be adjacent to, and to connect with, the house in which his family had been living for some time.

The fifteenth-century building consisted of a square,

three-storied block. The façade, which had seven axes, had three main doors on the ground floor, alternating with four high windows. The building's depth was less than that of the current structure, since the open arcade, with its two upper floors, had not yet been built.

Luca died in 1473, leaving the building unfinished. It remain in the hands of the Pitti family until 1550, when it was sold, along with the rest of the property (houses, land and the square in front) for 9,000 scudi to Eleonora di Toledo, wife of Cosimo I and Duchess of Florence.

## The Medici Period

Two branches of the Medici family, that of Cosimo the Elder and that of Lorenzo the Elder, converged in Cosimo I. His mother, Maria Salviati, was the niece of Cosimo the Magnificent through her mother Lucrezia, while his father, Giovanni dalle Bande Nere, was the son of Caterina Sforza and Giovanni il Popolano, who was a descendant of the younger branch of the family.

Cosimo became Duke of Florence in 1537, at the

young age of eighteen, and married Eleonora di Toledo, daughter of the Viceroy of Naples, two years later.

After living for some time on Via Larga in the family palace (later known as the Medici-Riccardi Palace), the couple moved to the Palazzo Vecchio (the Old Palace), enlarged and renovated for the occasion by Vasari. But only a residence like the Pitti could fully satisfy Cosimo's ambition. Here he could create his own "palace", symbol of his princely power, rather than occupy the traditional seat of the Florentine republic.

The first work was done principally in the gardens, the dimensions of which were approximately equivalent to those which can be seen in Utens' *Lunetta*, painted some decades later. Various kinds of plants were started (grapevines, laurels, holm-oaks, wild plants, citrus trees, etc.), the Nursery was built by Vasari (later, Buontalenti would build the Large Grotto on this site), and, between 1553 and 1555, the Grotto of Madame was constructed, with plastic decoration by Giovanni Fancelli and pictorial decorations by Bachiacca.

In 1561, the first major extension of the palace was begun. Bartolomeo Ammannati, entrusted with the design and execution of the work, left the dimensions of the façade unchanged, altering only the ground floor by closing the two lateral doors and replacing them with windows (the design of which was invented by Michelangelo). On the internal façade, however, he doubled the building's depth and added two perpendicular wings, thus creating the monumental courtyard – the largest courtyard in any Florentine palace – characterised by its "rustic" quality, which the architect had

observed in the work of Sansovino and Sammicheli during his stays in Venice. The fourth side, on the other hand, was made only one floor higher, leaving the space above open to the gardens. A gradual, uninterrupted transition, from constructed to natural space, was thus created.

The left wing was completed by 1556. More time was required, however, for the right wing, begun only after the complete demolition of the old Pitti house. Two large staircases were built: the main staircase, still used today to reach the palace's upper floors, and the secondary, spiral, staircase, which was located in the left wing and demolished in the nineteenth century.

Duchess Eleonora, who had initiated the work, lived barely long enough to see it begun, since she died in 1562 of an attack of malaria, only a few days after the deaths of two of her eight children, Giovanni and Garzia.

A special papal bull granted Cosimo the title of Grand Duke of Tuscany, and from 1570 on, Cosimo gradually left the task of governing to his eldest son, Francesco. Tormented by gout and other ailments, he died in Castello in April 1574, at the age of fifty-five.

In 1576, Francesco I was thus invested as the next Grand Duke by Emperor Maximilian, whose sister, Giovanna of Austria, he had married. After the death of Giovanna, Francesco married Bianca Cappello, a Venetian noblewoman. He died in 1587, without any legitimate male sons. His brother Ferdinando, who had been chosen by his father for an ecclesiastical career, gave up his cardinalate and succeeded to the throne of Tuscany, in order to ensure the continuation of the dynasty.

It should be pointed out here that under Cosimo I and Francesco I. the Pitti Palace, undergoing major renovations, was not yet the main Medici residence. The family did maintain private apartments in the Pit-

Alessandro Allori, Predella, Florence, the Santo Spirito Church, *detail of the original façade of the fifteenth-century palace.*

Anonymous, Florence, Pitti Palace, Silverworks Museum, Portrait of a Noblewoman, *detail of the palace façade after the work done by Bartolomeo Ammannati.*

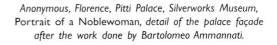

ti but only made occasional use of them, on special occasions. The Pitti had a mainly diplomatic function during this period, serving as a kind of sumptuous hotel in which the family's most important guests could be conveniently accommodated. It was used to lodge sovereigns and diplomatic missions and to hold celebrations and performances, for which purpose the large courtyard served as a magnificent setting. It was thus all the worldly aspects of court life that took place in the Pitti, but official audiences were still always held in the "Duke's Palace", that is, the Palazzo Vecchio (the Old Palace).

In fact, in 1564, in order directly to connect the two residences, official and private, Cosimo had commissioned Vasari (who at the time was directing the work on the new Uffizi building) to construct a link between the two palaces. The Duke wanted a kind of raised passageway that would allow him to move quickly and in complete safety between the seat of government and his new property. The result was the Vasari Corridor, a singular arcade from which there is an unusual and fascinating view of part of the city centre along the Arno.

With Ferdinando I, the Pitti Palace ceased being an occasional residence and became the definitive Medici palace. Very soon thereafter, however, it became clear that it was necessary to build a series of service rooms, including enormous new kitchens. In addition to making a new and more decorous organisation of the rooms on the courtyard possible, the service rooms were also

*View of Ammannati's courtyard, looking towards the Boboli Gardens. Photograph and engraving.*

a better solution to the demands of a permanent and very numerous court. This new building, constructed out of pre-existing buildings, is clearly visible in Utens' *Lunetta,* on the right side of the palace, to which it is connected by an open bridge, aptly called the "kitchen bridge".

In 1589, Ferdinando I married Cristina of Lorraine, the favourite niece of Caterina de' Medici, and by doing so he married into the court of France and continued the matrimonial policy by means of which his family had already linked itself to the royal houses of Spain and Austria. The most spectacular of the many celebrations organised for the occasion was undoubtedly a *Naumachia* performed in the courtyard which, covered and transformed into a water basin, became the theatre for a realistic miniature naval battle.

Archival documents make it possible for us to know with considerable exactness the nature of the organisation of the Grand Duke's residence at the end of the sixteenth century. We know, for example, that Ferdinando and Cristina had their apartments on the first floor, in the left wing; that the second floor was, on the other hand, given over for the most part to their numerous children and to their niece Maria, the eldest daughter of Francesco I and the future queen of France; and that the second floor was also the location of the Drama Room, where, in 1600, Rinuccini's *Euridice* was performed for the first time, to music by Jacopo Peri.

On the death of Ferdinando (1609), his eldest son

*G. Zocchi, View of the Royal Pitti Palace, Residence of the Reigning Sovereigns, Florence, 1744. The façade dimensions are those attained after the Parigi's seventeenth-century expansion.*

took the throne, with the name Cosimo II. His marriage to the Austrian archduchess, Maria Magdalena, sister of Emperor Ferdinand II and of the queen of Spain, increased the prestige of the Medici considerably.

The Pitti Palace, even given the additions made to it during the sixteenth century, was by now too small to contain a court that had become very large indeed (Cosimo was the first of nine children and had eight of his own). Moreover, the family, connected by marriage to the most important reigning houses, was obliged to maintain a high level of grandness and magnificence.

Cosimo therefore commissioned Giulio Parigi, Ammannati's grandson, to design a new expansion, as a result of which the palace reached its actual size (excluding the two Rondos) (a round area typical of Italian garden architecture) and an appearance that was still evident, approximately a century later, in an engraving by Zocchi.

*Remigio Cantagallina, The Pitti Palace During the Expansion Work, 1632, Sansepolcro, private collection.*

The expansion project began in 1618, on the Santa Felicità side of the building, but the Grand Duke, only thirty-one years old, died shortly thereafter, in 1621. The work was continued under the regency of Cristina of Lorraine and Maria Magdalena of Austria, respectively the grandmother and mother of the new Grand Duke, Ferdinando II, who was only eleven.

By 1631, the first wing had been finished and work began on the second wing, towards the Roman Gate, continuing until around 1640. Twenty or so years later, a new section was added to the building, alongside the secondary staircase.

The criteria that had determined the nature of the work done in the past were now replaced by new objectives. As opposed to Ammannati, who had prioritised expansion towards the hill, leaving the proportions of the fifteenth-century façade unchanged, the Parigis (Giulio, and then later, his son Alfonso) extended the building onto the square, increasing the number of windows from seven to twenty-three and creating a long façade which totally altered the original proportions. The horizontal plane now prevailed completely, barely affected by the variations in height of the building's stories, which remain three in proportion to the first three windows and are reduced to two in proportion to the other five. The palace's grandiosity, representative of the importance of the dynasty and of the court, must have been immediately perceptible, itself a tangible sign of power.

The state of the palace during the expansion work is partially visible in a famous drawing by Remigio Cantagallina, showing the back of the building, with the new wing on the north side.

During the same years, the stone amphitheatre was built in the Boboli Gardens, replacing the amphitheatre of greenery visible in the *Lunetta*. The "palace-courtyard-amphitheatre" relationship thus created a very suggestive scenographic sequence. The gardens were further enlarged with the acquisition of other properties towards the Roman Gate, until they assumed approximately their current size.

In 1637, Ferdinando II, who had by now become Grand Duke, married his cousin Vittoria Della Rovere, heir of the Dukes of Urbino.

During Ferdinando and Vittoria's long reign (the former died in 1670, his wife survived him by twenty-three years), the Grand Duke's court grew to unprecedented size, and the princes' renewed patronage

*Jacopo Chiavistelli, Crown Room vault, Juno Room vault, Vittoria della Rovere's ground-floor bedroom and detail of the painted Gallery.*

resulted in the palace being enriched with refined decorative cycles and prestigious collections.

On the ground floor, the rooms that today contain the Medici Treasures were frescoed by painters from Florence and Bologna, while the Lombard artist Jacopo Chiavistelli worked in the two wings in the courtyard, where he decorated the rooms destined for Prince Cosimo (later Cosimo III) and his young wife Marguérite-Louise d'Orléans, as well as some rooms in Vittoria Della Rovere's apartment. Chiavistelli also worked in Prince Cosimo's large library (later, in the Lorraine period, made over and subdivided) on the second floor, and in other rooms later radically renovated. But the most significant changes were made on the ground floor, where Ferdinando I had already commissioned the most important Florentine painters of the period to decorate the Foreigners' Apartment.

Under Ferdinando II – who, after his marriage to Vittoria, commissioned Volterrano to decorate the vault of the Grand Duchesses' bedroom with a celebration of the events of della Rovere's life – the most significant presence in the Pitti was that of Pietro da Cortona. This artist created the fresco, *The Four Ages of Man,* in the Stove Room, and decorated, along with Salvator Rosa, the Little Mule Mezzanine. With Ciro Ferri (who completed the work after da Cortona's definitive return to Rome), he realised the five major rooms, called the Planets, in the public apartment on the first floor. When Ferdinando II died in 1670, he was succeeded by his son, Cosimo III, during whose long reign no events significant to the history of the palace took place, apart from certain projects commissioned by Grand Prince Ferdinando. Ferdinando, the Grand Duke's eldest son, was responsible for the creation of a bedroom with an alcove, decorated with stuccowork and grotesqueries and facing a small, internal garden called the Camellia Garden. This garden is one of the many small, and little known, marvels of the Pitti: as spring approaches, the two rows of plants along the length of the garden (actual trees, which meet and enclose the space over the visitor's head) become covered with camellias, whose colour turns from the purest white to pink to an intense red, thus forming a flowering corridor that leads from the palace to the Boboli amphitheatre.

In 1707, again for Ferdinando, Sebastiano Ricci frescoed the vault of a room in the ground-floor apartment with the loves of *Venus and Adonis.* This was the last major project of the Medici period. After the death of

*D. M. Marmi,* View from Cosimo III's Library.
*Pietro da Cortona,* The "Little Mule" Mezzanine *(detail)*
*and* Venus Room vault, Palatine Gallery.
*Sebastiano Ricci,* Venus and Adonis, *decoration.*

*The Stuccowork Room (later called the White Room).*

the Grand Prince (1713), neither the aged Cosimo III, who survived the former by ten years, nor his brother Gian Gastone, the last Grand Duke, undertook to work on the palace in any way and it remained in a state of almost total abandonment. The death of Gian Gastone marked the end of Medici rule and the transition to Tuscany under the Lorraines. His sister, Anna Maria Luisa, Palatine Electress and the dynasty's last descendant, had the "Family Pact" drawn up, whereby she ceded the Medici inheritance to the new princes, but with the condition that "all that which serves as State ornamentation, as public utility, and as an attraction to the curiosity of foreigners, shall not be transported and removed outside the capital nor outside the State of the Grand Duchy". Thus the great heritage of works of art and culture collected by the Medici for over three centuries was not dispersed, saved by the last member of the family with a gesture that to a certain extent redeems the faults of her closest relatives, who were responsible for the definitive decline of the dynasty.

*Camellia Garden.*

## The Lorraine Period

The new Grand Duke, Francis Stephen of Lorraine, arrived in Florence in January 1739, with his young wife, Maria Theresa of Austria. The couple, destined for the imperial throne, remained in Florence for only a few months, leaving in the following April and entrusting the Government to a Regency Council.

After a long period of stasis, major work was begun on the Pitti in 1760. The architect Giuseppe Ruggieri built the Rondò near the Roman Gate; between 1763 and 1765, Ignazio Pellegrini, a brilliant amateur from Verona, created two splendid rooms on the ground floor, the Formal Room (better known as the Oval Drawing Room) and the Dressing Room, thus completing the series of room towards the Roman Gate. The first of these two rooms has an elliptical shape and an extraordinary elegance, accentuated by the colours and by the refined gilded stuccowork on the splendid ceiling; the other room is a small but exquisite rococo drawing room destined for the Grand

*The Niches Room, in a photo from the period.*

Duchess's *toilette*.

On September 13, 1765, Peter Leopold, with his consort Maria Luisa, the Infanta of Spain, finally arrived in Florence.

Having decided to put an end to waste and excessive expense, the new Grand Duke suspended the work for a grandiose chapel that Pellegrini had planned for the entrance to the Boboli Gardens. He also gave instructions that the Apollo Room in the ground floor apartment of Marguérite-Louise d'Orléans be allocated for worship. He commissioned the painter Vincenzo Meucci to convert the mythological scenes, painted in the seventeenth century by Chiavistelli, into sacred representations more appropriate to the room's new role.

Peter Leopold, departing from the choice made by the Medici, established the Grand Ducal residence in the right wing of the palace and reserved for himself the most internal rooms on the ground floor, leaving the quarters facing the square to the Grand Duchess. Under the direction of Niccolò Gaspero Paoletti, the decorations in all the rooms set aside for the Grand Dukes were renewed and the "carriage ceiling" vault was reconstructed. Finally, the Round Drawing Room, above the Rondo, was created, adjacent to the Oval Drawing Room, and was decorated with stuccowork and wall paintings.

Between 1774 and 1776, Grato and Giocondo Albertolli, plasterers from Lugano, transformed the Foreigners' Room into the Stuccowork Room, which became known, inaccurately, as the White Room after an unfortunate overall repainting had covered the original colours, recently rediscovered during careful restoration.

The second floor also underwent major changes. In the rooms facing the square, set aside for the Grand Duchess, new ceilings were made, giving rise to a mezzanine floor, called "the Eyes" floor because of the round windows, from which there is an incomparable view.

Peter Leopold left the Grand Duchy in 1790 for the imperial throne. His son Ferdinando, who took the name Ferdinando III in order to emphasise the continuity between the Medici and Lorraine dynasties, succeeded him in Tuscany.

The first work ordered by the new Grand Duke concerned the second floor. Ferdinando wanted "Winter Quarters" to be created in the right wing and entrusted the project, once again, to Paoletti, who began by dividing the old Drama Room, making out of it the Music Room, decorated by Giuseppe Terreni.

Terreni was also responsible for the changes made to the Niches Room, which, according to sixteenth-century descriptions, was papered in red and decorated with ten black marble niches. Terreni modified the colours into the paler shades we can see still today.

In 1783, Paoletti designed and supervised the construction of the second Rondo (later called the Bacchus Rondo), which replaced the original "Firewood Room", and began the construction of the Meridian Building, which replaced the old Medici "Spice Room".

*Palatine Chapel vault and view towards the organ.*

This latter project was continued by Giuseppe Cacialli in the nineteenth century and completed by Pasquale Poccianti. There were, on the other hand, few decorative changes in this period, with the exception of the work done in the Palatine Chapel, given its definitive appearance by the painter Luigi Ademollo.

In the Grand Duchess' quarters, Luigi Catani decorated the three "Withdrawing Rooms" and the two new bathrooms, one of which was round. He frescoed the cylindrical walls of the round bathroom with six scenes with classical themes.

Ferdinando was obliged to leave for Vienna in March of 1799 and shortly after, in 1801, he had to turn Tuscany over to the French conquerors, who made it into the Kingdom of Etruria, under the governance of Lodovico and Maria Luisa di Borbone Parma.

During this period, most of the work on the palace was done on the second floor. The left wing was rebuilt, making it symmetrical to the Winter Quarters, and work was done in the rooms occupied by the Palatine Library.

In 1807, Maria Luisa, regent for her son after the death of her husband, left Florence for Portugal. Elisa Bonaparte took possession in her place, and in 1809 Napoleon reinstituted the Grand Duchy for her in Tuscany.

Drawn by the patronage of the new sovereign, sculptors, painters, and musicians converged on Florence. In the Villa Bellosguardo, Ugo Foscolo created *The Graces*, perhaps inspired by the atmosphere in the Florentine palace, where the cult of beauty that had characterised the refined Renaissance courts flourished once more.

The new imperial taste, based on neo-classicism, became manifest above all in the changes made to the ground floor's left wing, where the former quarters of the Medici Grand Dukes were made over to accommodate their Imperial Majesties. Only the rooms done by Pietro da Cortona (including the Stove Room), the so-called Poccetti Gallery and the Volteranno Room remained unaltered. The decorative aspects of the other rooms were completely changed, under the direction of Giuseppe Cacialli, giving the rooms a completely new appearance. Some of these rooms, such as the Bathroom and the small boudoir adjacent to it, were exquisitely refined. These latter two rooms were created for the Empress, who never lived in the quarters that had been made over especially for her.

Elisa's reign was also very short. After the fall of Napoleon, the Vienna Congress returned Tuscany to the Lorraines, and, in 1814, Ferdinando III moved back into the Pitti.

One of the first projects undertaken in the second Lorraine period was the creation of a passageway between the central courtyard and a second, adjacent courtyard, called the Columns Courtyard or the Unfinished Courtyard. To make the passageway, Pasquale Poccianti demolished the secondary, sixteenth-century staircase, which began with a ramp perpendicular to the arcade, and constructed, in its place, a new, monumental staircase. At the same time, he set up the vestibule in the main entrance.

Poccianti also intervened on the second floor, where he finished the Winter Quarters and, on the other side of the courtyard, worked on the "New Quarters", arranged around the new staircase, changing the existing rooms in accordance with neo-classical canons.

Ferdinando III died in 1824 and was succeeded by his son Leopoldo II, nicknamed "Canapone" by the Florentines.

Leopoldo's diaries provide a surprising portrayal of Grand Ducal life, similar to the life of any bourgeois family. The diaries help us understand the Grand Duke's decision to leave the ground-floor apartments in favour of the new Meridian Building, which seemed to correspond better to his taste.

By now, however, the Lorraine period was also coming to an end. On April 27th, 1859, with the peaceful departure of "Canapone" and his family, sent on their way with the respectful farewell greetings of the people – perhaps a unique case in the history of revolutions – the Grand Duchy ceased to exist. Two years later, Tuscany was annexed by the newborn Kingdom of Italy.

### The Savoy Period

On February 3rd, 1865, Vittorio Emanuele II of Savoy arrived in Florence, the kingdom's new capital, bringing with him the Piedmont court.

He, too, decided to live in the Meridian, where the brighter and more "domestic" rooms, even if duly ornamented and decorated, permitted a style of life that today we might call more "people friendly", organised according to the regular rhythms of daily activities and political commitments.

Even later, when Florence as no longer the capital, the sovereign presence in the Pitti continued. In July of 1871, a small apartment was prepared above the Winter Quarters for the Prince of Naples, the eldest son of Umberto I and Margherita of Savoy. No major architectural projects were undertaken in this period, however, except for the building of a staircase leading to the Palatine Gallery from the Boboli Gardens, realised at the end of the nineteenth century by Luigi Del Moro and inspired by the revival of Renaissance art.

Changes were made instead to the carpeting and furnishings, giving the palace its definitive appearance and reflecting a taste very different from that of the Lorraines. Recent work has made it possible to set up the rooms as they are described in the last inventory of the palace, made in 1911. The Savoy apartments on the ground floor as well as those of the Aosta (Duchess Anna Elena of France, wife of Amedeo d'Aosta, and Prince Luigi, Duke of the Abruzzi) have therefore been rearranged. The Aosta lived in the Winter Quarters and in the mezzanine above, even after the palace became the premises of State Administration offices. They, along with Emanuele Filiberto, the Count of Turin, who had his residence in the Meridian Building, were the last to leave the Pitti Palace, which had by then been chosen for other uses after having been, for approximately four centuries, the home of three dynasties.

*The Royal Apartments, the King's Studio.*

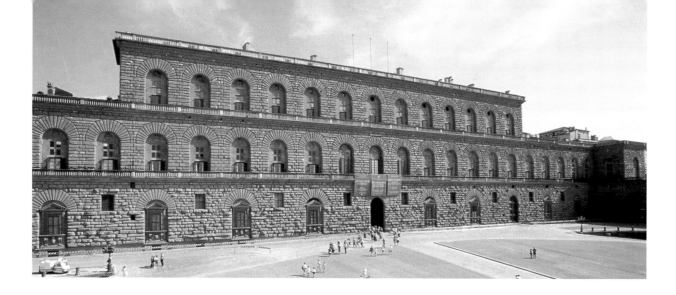

# The Collections

MARCO CHIARINI

The Pitti Palace's enormous façade of Florentine ashlar, which owes its present size to architectural changes that went on for over four centuries, is emblematic of the imposing mass of the Pitti Palace on the slopes of the Boboli hills, on the left bank of the Arno. It is also symbolic not only of the events in the lives of the three families who lived in the palace – the Medici, the Lorraines and the Savoys – but also of the location of the three prestigious museums that were established in the Palace during the eighteenth and nineteenth centuries, in parallel with the changes that the complex underwent as it evolved over the centuries.

Ferdinando I and his wife, Cristina of Lorraine – the favourite niece of Catherine de' Medici, the queen of France – were the first to use the building as a palace, and as a repository for works of art, thus beginning the tradition that has made the Pitti famous today.

Ferdinando's son, Cosimo II, the brevity of his reign notwithstanding, gave the building and its collections an impetus that was to determine its development over the following centuries. He initiated the art collections, decided upon the arrangement of the Grand Ducal apartments and commissioned the building of the chapel that was to contain the collection of the family's treasures (later displayed in the wing today known as the Volterrano wing, in the apartment of Grand Duchess Maria Magdalena of Austria). He organised the works brought by his wife as part of her dowry, as well as those works that he commissioned and systematically purchased in the Rome art market. At the time, the Roman market was the country's most active art market. It was there that Cosimo acquired paintings by Gherardo delle Notti, Manfred, and other realistic painters in the wake of Caravaggio, as well as paintings by Artemisia Gentileschi and Battistello Caracciolo, painters of the first-generation Caravaggio school who worked in Florence for the Grand Duke. Cosimo's acquisitions were thus a fundamental stimulus to the family's habit of collecting, which, throughout the following generations, became more of a passion than a habit. The Grand Duke's love of northern painting, stimulated by the tastes of his Austrian consort, set a trend that, subsequent estrangements notwithstanding, gave the Pitti collections the international character for which it is known today.

Ferdinando II, son of Cosimo II, following in his father's footsteps, continued the extension of the palace towards the west and, most significantly, commissioned the cycles of frescoes and stuccowork that still today are reflective of the change in taste, to a baroque sensibility, in the decoration of the interiors. The Summer Apartment on the first floor – today the home of the Medici Treasures – was frescoed by the Florentine painters Giovanni da San Giovanni, Francesco Furini, Cecco Bravo and Ottavio Vannini, and later by the Bolognese painters Agostino Mitelli

*The Pitti Palace's main façade.*

On the following page:
*Pietro da Cortona, detail of the Mars Room vault, with depiction of the Medici coat of arms, 1644-1646, Palatine Gallery.*

and Angelo Maria Colonna, specialists in mock architecture. The decoration of the rooms in the Grand Duke's official apartment on the first floor (later known as the "Planets") were entrusted to one of the originators of the baroque style, Pietro da Cortona. Decorated with stuccowork and frescoes according to a complex planetary allegory that alluded both to the reigning Grand Duke and to Galileo's discovery of the planets, these rooms became the stupendous setting for the Palatine Gallery at the end of the eighteenth century.

Ferdinando concerned himself mainly with the layout of the palace. Not to be forgotten, of course, are the artistic treasures that were part of the dowry brought by his wife, his cousin Vittoria della Rovere, the last heir of the Dukes of Urbino, and which are still an essential part of the Florentine collections, as well as the masterpieces he acquired during his reign, such as Rubens' *The Four Philosophers* and Paolo Veronese's *The Baptism of Christ.* It was his brothers, however, Giancarlo and Leopoldo, both cardinals, who were the more passionate collectors. This was especially true of Leopoldo, who occupied the palace's second floor, and who assembled paintings that

became one of the most important core collections of the Florentine galleries. His love for sixteenth-century Venetian painting brought to Florence some of the masterworks of that school, today exhibited in the Palatine Gallery, such as Titian's *Concert* and *Portrait of Tommaso Mosti*, Paolo Veronese's *Portrait of a Man in Furs* and *Goldsmith*, Tintoretto's *Immaculate Conception* and *Christ's Entrance into Jerusalem*, Paris Bordone's *Lady in Red*, Schiavone's *Adoration of the Shepherds* and *Cain and Abel*. Other masterpieces from his collection, however, ended up in the Palatine gallery, such as Raphael's *Portrait of Tommaso Inghirami*, Caravaggio's *Sleeping Cupid*, Guido Reni's *Charity* and *Cleopatra*, and Ruben's *The Three Graces*, as well as other works by Bolognese, Ferrarese, Flemish and Dutch artists.

As we will see, his brother Giancarlo also contributed, if to a lesser degree, to the core of the future Palatine Gallery, but the most significant impulse to the future gallery was given by Prince Ferdinando, son of Grand Duke Cosimo III and grandson of Ferdinando II.

Ferdinando, heir to the Grand Duchy of Tuscany, never came to the throne, since he pre-deceased his father. He lived on the palace's ground floor in the wing that in the nineteenth century was made over into the Royal Apartments. There he assembled a collection consisting of approximately one thousand paintings, some of which he chose from the ancestral collections, and some of which he purchased.

When Ferdinando, child of his century, gained possession of paintings with which he

*Pietro da Cortona,* The Golden Age, *detail of the Stove Room decoration, Palatine Gallery.*

had become infatuated, he had new frames made for them, regardless of where they came from or of the period to which they belonged. This reframing also had a decorative role, with respect to the dimensions of the new frames and their placement on the walls chosen for them. The new frames were also often made in relation to the subject matter of the paintings. This was the origin of the magnificent, carved and gilded baroque frames that today enclose the paintings in the Palatine Gallery. Ferdinando thus established the criteria adopted for the arrangement of the gallery in the nineteenth century. The large altarpieces in the centre of the walls were completely surrounded by a dense array of smaller paintings that reached up to the mouldings. The paintings were also hung above the doors, a common practice in seventeenth-century picture galleries.

In love with great sixteenth- and seventeenth-century Italian and foreign painting, Ferdinando had no scruples about removing pictorial treasures from important locations – such as churches and convents in Tuscany, as well as in Emilia and in the area around Venice. It was in this way the altarpieces by Andrea del Sarto, Fra' Bartolemeo, Rosso Fiorentino, Ludovico Cigoli, Parmigianino (the famous *Long-necked Madonna* later taken to the Uffizi), Veronese, Lanfranco, Orazio Riminaldi and Guercino, found their way to the Pitti. Raphael's *Mother and Child and Saints*, a long-coveted treasure even though unfinished, stands out from among them all.

Ferdinando, like his great-uncle Leopoldo,

*Palatine Gallery, view of the Saturn Room.*

Peter Paul Rubens, The Consequences of War, 1637-1638, detail, Palatine Gallery, Mars Room.

was also an admirer of sixteenth- and seventeenth-century portraiture, which thus became another distinctive element of the future Palatine Gallery. Fifteenth-century Italian masterpieces such as Titian's *Portrait of Pietro Aretino* (inherited from Cosimo I) and *The Grey-eyed Nobleman*, Tintoretto's *Portrait of Alvise Cornaro* and *Portrait of Vincenzo Zeno*, and seventeenth-century Flemish works such as Van Dyck's *Cardinal Bentivoglio* and Rembrandt's so-called *Rabbi* (later taken to the Uffizi), thus became part of his collection, as well as paintings of events in history, among which Rubens' great canvas *The Consequences of War* is foremost.

This extraordinary collection of paintings was re-organised for the first time by Grand Duke Cosimo III who, on the death of his son in 1713, re-arranged it, eliminating lesser works and adding masterpieces from the collections of his father Ferdinando, his mother Vittoria della Rovere and his uncles Giancarlo and Leopoldo. He also exchanged paintings with the Uffizi Gallery. It was in this way that Raphael's renowned masterpiece *Mother and Child with St John the Baptist*, until then housed in the Law Courts and today one of the works most symbolic of the Palatine Gallery, arrived at the Pitti. Other works acquired in this way include Raphael's so-called *Portrait of a Woman*, one of the masterpieces of portraiture from the

Raphael, Madonna and Child with Saints ("Madonna del baldacchino"), detail, ca 1508, Palatine Gallery, Saturn Room.

painter's Florentine period, and a group of famous paintings from the sixteenth and seventeenth centuries, such as Titian's *The Concert, Portrait of a Young Woman, Portrait of Ippolito de' Medici*, and *Madgalen,* Cristofano Allori's *Judith Holding the Head of Holofernes*, the group of works by Salvator Rosa, and Luca Giordano's *Riberae*, all of which are still kept in the Gallery.

The group of paintings kept in the Palatine was definitively established by the Lorraines, who succeeded to the Grand Ducal throne, after the Medici, in 1736. It was Peter Leopold and Ferdinand III of Lorraine, son and nephew, respectively, of Empress Maria Theresa of Austria, who decided to create the palace gallery in what had been the Medici Grand Ducal apartment (also called the "Pietro da Cortona" apartment, after its decorator).

The Palatine Gallery assumed its definitive character from the end of the eighteenth century until after the Restoration, during which period the masterpieces taken from Napoleon were brought to Florence.

Between the end of the eighteenth century and 1828 – the year in which the palace was opened to the public - Ferdinand III and his son Leopoldo chose approximately five hundred paintings, mostly from Prince Ferdinando de' Medici's apartment, adding to them certain important acquisitions assembled in the wake of the Medici choices. Thus it was that Perugino's masterpiece, *Lamentation*, and Andrea del Sarto's *Lamentation Over the Dead Christ* (added to the painter's other fifteen works already in the collection) were brought to the Pitti. The already considerable number of works by Raphael, collected in accordance with a classical canon that heavily influenced sixteenth-century pictorial choices, was increased

*Grand Ducal Workshops, table, inlaid with precious stones, XVII century, Silverworks Museum.*

with two important acquisitions, the *Mother and Child*, and the *Portrait of Maddalena Doni*. Sensitive to trends in European taste, they also acquired for the gallery ten paintings from the Gerini Gallery, including Rembrandt's *Self-portrait as a Young Man* (taken to the Uffizi in this century), Anton van Dyck's *Rest During the Flight into Egypt*, and famous paintings by Carlo Dolci *(St Andrew Before the Cross)*, Furini and Batoni (today in the Pitti Modern Art Gallery). Gaspard Dughet's four *Landscapes* and works by a group of Dutch painters (Ruisdael, Huysum, Ruysch, and Backhuysen) were added in order to give the collection a larger modern component. In order to satisfy the public's interest in fifteenth-century Florentine painting, attention was focussed on Filippo Lippi's great *Life of St Anne* in the Prometheus Room, which was largely dedicated to works from the Florentine Renaissance.

The Lorraine Grand Dukes wanted the gallery to

reflect the magnificence that had been characteristic of the palace's seventeenth-century furnishings during the time of the Medici and therefore embellished the rooms set aside for the paintings. They not only completed the ceiling decorations with a series of frescoes that gave the ceilings a modern appearance but they also assembled in the rooms a series of tables and furnishings. Some of these objects were taken from the palace's store-rooms and some were made specifically for this purpose by the "Opificio delle Pietre Dure" (the "Semi-precious Stones Workshop"), which underwent a renaissance of its own in the Lorraine period, at least until the middle of the nineteenth century. A number of famous statues, such as Antonio Canova's *Venus* and Luigi Bartolini's *Charity,* were placed in the centre of some of the rooms. The impression of richness and splendour was further augmented by large Sèvres porcelain vases mounted on bronze pedestals, a table with a Russian malachite top mounted on a gilded bronze pedestal made in Paris by J.Ph.Thomire, consoles with plaster tops, bronze candelabra, and crystal chandeliers. Ancient statues, most of which were brought from the Villa Medici in Rome, were placed in the gallery entrance in order to emphasise the regal solemnity of the rooms.

When the Palatine Gallery officially opened its

*Valerio Belli, small chest, rock crystal intaglio, mounted in gilded and enamelled silver, 1532, Silverworks Museum.*

*Milan manufacture, two-handled bowl (with two-faced mask), rock crystal intaglio, enamelled and chased gold, middle of the XVI century, Silverworks Museum.*

*Manufacture of Doccia, L. Ginori Lisci, Cup, 1865, Porcelain Museum.*

doors in 1828, it immediately attracted the attention of visitors and tourists, who found in it a reflection of the magnificence that had once been characteristic of the palace and of the collections that had once belonged to the Medici.

In the nineteenth century, the Lorraines had intended to extend the palace towards the east, in order to create space for the many precious objects that had accumulated in the palace, as well as in other locations, dating back to the time when Lorenzo the Magnificent had begun to assemble his "treasure". Historical events, however, caused their plans to be changed, and it wasn't until after the First World War, when Vittorio Emanuele III of Savoy ceded the Palace to the State, that the current Medici Treasures exhibition was arranged where the Summer Apartment of the Medici Grand Dukes had once been. In order to rationalise the various collections, the pieces that had been part of the personal collections of precious objects gathered by generations of Medici family members were brought together. These ranged from Lorenzo the Magnificent's antique vases to the crystals and enamelled objects brought by Cristina of Lorraine as part of her dowry, from vases inlaid with lapis lazuli and semi-precious stones (incomparable objects made by the "Opificio di Pietre Dure), to ambers belonging to Mary Magdalene of Austria, to German ivories from the Mattias collection, to cabinets made for Cosimo III in the Grand Ducal workshops, to jewels belonging to Anna Maria Luisa de' Medici, Palatine Electress. The treasure belonging to the bishops of Salzburg was also added and included vases, water pitchers, gilded silver cups and gold statuettes made in Germany in the sixteenth and seventeenth centuries. This treasure, brought to Florence by Ferdinand III of Lorraine in 1814, was an unparalleled display of objects of extremely high quality. The collec-

tion of neo-classical cameos was added to the overall collection as well. To all of this was added, at the end of the nineteenth century, the porcelain collection already in the palace and today displayed in the Knight's Garden in the Boboli Gardens, and which contained extraordinary examples of European porcelain from the seventeenth and nineteenth centuries.

The Pitti collections have still other surprises in store, on the second floor, in the wing once occupied by the young Medici and Lorraine princes and the Palatine Library. The more modern paintings in the collections were gathered here, as well as works acquired during the reigns of the Lorraines and the Savoys, and to which was later added the Macchiaioli collection, most of which came from the City of Florence. And, finally, statues, furniture and other furnishings from the Lorraine and Savoy periods were added, creating an overall collection homogeneous with the collection on the first floor, in the Royal Apartments.

The Pitti today offers a cross-section of various eras that does not have the modern museographic organisation characteristic of some of the eighteenth-century museums (the Louvre in Paris, the Kunsthistorisches Museum in Vienna, the Metropolitan Museum in New York) but has its own decorative and architectonic framework, a context that draws attention to the significance of those eras and their successive historical phases. The building that was a residence for the three dynasties that governed Tuscany from the fifteenth to the nineteenth centuries – the Medici, the Lorraines and the Savoys – has slowly become, without any preordained plan, the location of one of the most prestigious museographic complexes in the world. The works of art exhibited here, beneath frescoed ceilings and crystal chandeliers, have found an incomparable setting.

*Luigi Ademollo, detail of the Music Room vault, ca 1815, Palatine Gallery.*

## First Floor

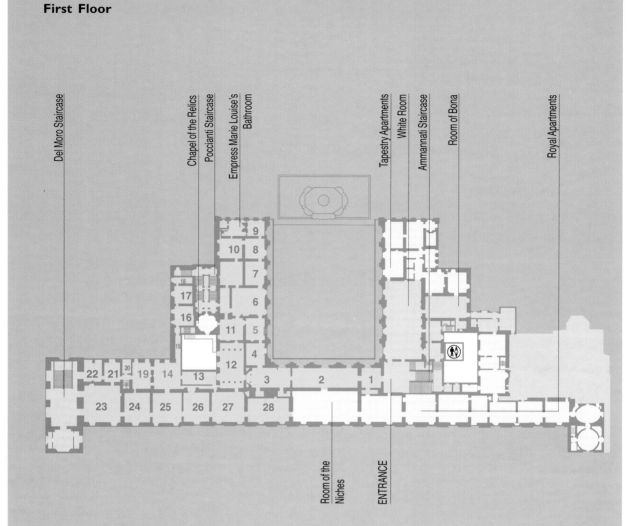

Del Moro Staircase

Chapel of the Relics
Poccianti Staircase
Empress Marie Louise's Bathroom

Tapestry Apartments
White Room
Ammannati Staircase
Room of Bona

Royal Apartments

Room of the Niches

ENTRANCE

# Palatine Gallery

*Marco Chiarini*

A monumental stairway in the right-hand corner of the courtyard leads to the entrance of the Palatine Gallery. It was called "Palatina", signifying that the gallery was "of the palace" of the ruling family, when first opened to the public by Leopold II of Lorraine in 1828. The Gallery occupies the most important rooms on the piano nobile, or first floor: six rooms overlooking the piazza and those in the north wing at the rear of the building, previously the winter apartments of the Medici Grand Dukes. When the ruling family vacated these rooms for those on the floor above they were used, from the end of the eighteenth century, for the permanent display of the finest paintings in the Pitti Palace, originally some five hundred works, collected for the most part by the Medici. It is difficult to imagine a more ideal setting than these rooms on the façade, magnificently decorated with frescoes and stucco by Pietro da Cortona and Ciro Ferri between 1641 and 1647. These housed the nu-

cleus of the collection, notable for the number of large altarpieces and monumental works, and a tour of the collection would originally have begun in the first room, the Venus Room. For practical reasons vistors now enter from the Statue Gallery, with antique sculpture taken from the Villa Medici in Rome, and from the Castagnoli Room, in which stands the Table of the Muses, a supreme technical achievement produced by the Opificio delle Pietre Dure in 1853, and mounted on a bronze base by Giovanni Dupré.

The Castagnoli Room leads, on the right, into the Volterrano wing (sometimes closed). These were the private apartments of the Grand Duchesses from the time of Cosimo II de' Medici until the death here of the last of the family, Anna Maria Luisa, in 1743. At her death she bequeathed all the treasures of the Medici collections to the people of Florence to the perpetual enrichment of her city. The sequence of the rooms was altered following their restoration and redecoration, begun in 1815.

*Iliad Room.*

*Rosso Fiorentino,* Madonna and Child enthroned with Saints ("Pala Dei"), *1522, oil on panel, 350 × 259 cm.*

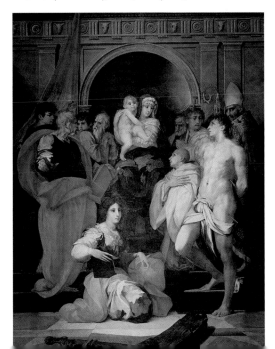

## Allegories Room (Sala delle Allegorie)

*Ceiling decorated with fresco and stucco work by Volterrano, for the Grand Duchess Vittoria della Rovere, the wife of Ferdi-*

*nando II, in the middle of the seventeenth century.*

### VOLTERRANO
### The Joke played on the Priest Arlotto
ca 1640
Tempera on canvas,
107 × 150 cm

Volterrano was the most Baroque of all the Florentine decorative painters in the seventeenth century. There are nevertheless traces of his early training with the late-Mannerist painter Giovanni da San Giovanni in his early works, also evident in this lively episode. It is one of many illustrating scenes from the life of Arlotto Mainardi, the parish priest of S. Cresci a Maciuoli, who was famous for his pranks. Here Volterrano, treating the figures with expressive energy, gives us a spirited interpretation of a party in the courtyard of a villa outside Florence.

### EMILIO ZOCCHI
### Michelangelo as a child
1861
Marble 60 cm

This romantic depiction of Michelangelo as a child sculpting the head of a faun in the San Marco gardens, reflects popular local mythology surrounding the life of the great Florentine artist, recorded in the *Lives of the Artists* by Vasari.

## GIOVANNI DA SAN GIOVANNI
### *Venus Combing Cupid's Hair*
ca 1630
Oil on canvas, 229 × 173 cm

A curious subject, chosen by the most lively of seventeenth-century Florentine painters. San Giovanni loved allegorical representations in which he could give free rein to his imagination, inventing and creating novelties, such as in the frescoes in the large ground-floor drawing room of the Pitti Palace, where the Medici Treasures are displayed. Three other of the artist's works in this room are evidence of his narrative energy, especially the great painting called *The First Night of Marriage*. Volterrano, whose painting, *The Joke Played on the Priest Arlotto*, another "playful" work, is exhibited in this room, was one of San Giovanni's disciples.

## Room of the Fine Arts
## (Sala delle Belle Arti)

*Fresco depicting* Jupiter sending Minerva to enkindle an interest in the Arts on earth *by Domenico Podestà (1817).*

### CIGOLI
### *The Martyrdom of St Stephen*
1597
Oil on canvas, 480 × 287 cm

This altarpiece, painted in 1597 for the convent of Montedomini in Florence, became part of the Florentine galleries collection at the beginning of the nineteenth century and has been in the Pitti since 1928. Cigoli, then the leading painter of the Florentine school, shows remarkable success in creating an alternative to the dominant late Mannerist style in Italy. While Caravaggio revolutionised painting with his unprecedented realism, Cigoli turned to Venetian painting, notably Tintoretto, to instil his works with a pictorial vitality usually associated with Baroque painters, earning this painting the particualr admiration of both Rubens and Pietro da Cortona.

### Hercules Room (Sala d'Ercole)

*Decorated by Pietro Benvenuti in 1828 with the* Labours of Hercules. *In the centre of the room stands a large Sèvres porcelain and gilt-bronze vase by Pierre Philippe Thomire.*

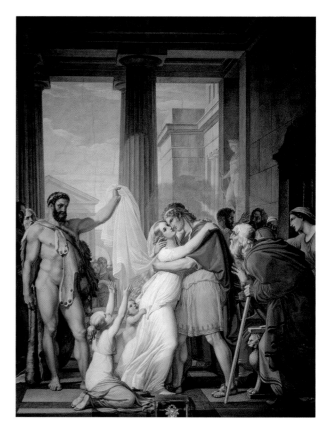

PIETRO BENVENUTI
*The Story of Hercules*
1828
Fresco

The neo-classical architect Giuseppe Cacialli, who restored several of the rooms in the Pitti after the Restoration (1814), renovated this room, which was the Guardroom during the time of the Medici. The decoration – which alludes, by means of Hercules, to the re-institution of Lorraine rule in Tuscany after the Napoleonic period – was done by Benvenuti in 1828. Events from Hercules' life are depicted on the vaults and on the coloured and monochrome frescoed walls, in a somewhat heavy, magniloquent style that is not without, however, a certain "academic" bravura.

### Dawn Room (Sala dell'Aurora)

*Gaspare Martelli painted the fresco of Dawn between 1815-17.*

### Berenice Room (Sala di Berenice)

*Frescoed by Giuseppe Bezzuoli with* Titus abandoning Berenice *and figures of the* Cardinal Virtues *in the lunettes.*

### Psyche Room (Sala di Psiche)

*Frescoed by Giuseppe Collignon this room brings together the greatest collection of paintings by the Neapolitan, Salvator Rosa, dating from his Florentine period.*

SALVATOR ROSA
*Battle*
ca 1640
Oil on canvas, 234 × 350 cm

This painting for Ferdinando II, Grand Duke of Tuscany, by the lively and genial Neapolitan Salvator Rosa, was executed at the beginning of his sojourn in Florence which lasted some ten years (c.1640-49). He painted almost exclusively for the Medici and his additional involvement in literary and theatrical activities secured him a preminent position in Florentine culture of the period. His paintings in the Palatine Gallery started a vogue in European painting for battle scenes and this canvas is a superb example of the genre.

## Music Room (Sala della Musica)

*The private musical gatherings held in this room have influenced the style of the furniture and the decorative* appliques. *The Neo-Classical room has columns in Sienese yellow and frescoes on the ceiling painted by Luigi Ademollo (ca 1815) illustrating episodes from the Seige of Vienna of 1683 when the Imperial army defeated the Turk together with a remarkable monochrome trompe l'oeil frieze imitating sculpture in low-relief. The gilt-bronze and malachite table was made by Pierre Philippe Thomire in 1819.*

## Poccetti Corridor (Corridoio del Poccetti)

*The frescoes on the ceiling by Matteo Rosselli and assistants, were once attributed to Bernardo Barbatelli, known as Poccetti.*

FRANCESCO FURINI

*Hylas and the Nymphs*
ca 1635
Oil on canvas, 230 × 261 cm

Francesco Furini gained considerable renown both for his revival of the *sfumato* technique, or shading, introduced by Leonardo, no longer used in the seventeenth century, and for his ability to render the female body in all its seductive charm. This painting, his masterpiece, was painted for Agnolo Galli and purchased for the Florentine galleries at the beginning of this century. Furini has invented a pictorial dream in which the intertwining nymphs create an impression of overwhelming sensuality.

GASPARD DUGHET

*Landscape with
a dancing faun*
ca 1667-68
Oil on canvas, 51 × 87 cm

Dughet is the least well known of the three French painters who revolutionised landscape painting in the seventeenth and eighteenth centuries. Brother-in-law to Nicholas Poussin, he was initially influenced by Poussin's classical treatment of landscape but later became susceptible to Claude Lorraine's greater naturalism. The painting is one of four.

## Prometheus Room (Sala di Prometeo)

*The fine fresco decoration by Giuseppe Collignon (ca 1830-40) shows the* Chariot of the Sun *and* Prometheus *bringing fire to man. The room houses the oldest paintings in the collections including fifteenth-century Florentine tondos.*

*The fine vase decorated with brightly coloured bunches of flowers and gilt-bronze mounts was produced by the Sevres factory in 1844 after a design by L. Schilt.*

### BOTTICELLI
*Portrait of a young man wearing a "mazzocchio"*
ca 1470
Oil on panel, 51 × 34 cm

This small and little known portrait of a young man wearing the typical Florentine head-dress of the period is a fine example of a genre which first appeared in Florence in the early fifteenth century and was developed in a distinctive way by Botticelli. Clearly derived from the work of Paolo Uccello and Andrea del Castagno, the portrait with its slightly turned, three-quarter pose is here given an unprecedented individuality. The surface of the painting has suffered from over enthusiastic cleaning in the past.

### LUCA SIGNORELLI
*Holy Family with St Catherine*
Oil on canvas, diam. 99 cm

Signorelli was particularly famous in central Italy, and his masterpiece is the cycle of frescoes in the San Brizio chapel in the Orvieto cathedral. Very active as a painter of altarpieces for churches, Signorelli nevertheless also adopted the Florentine "tondo" form for more private and intimate works, such as this beautiful painting done in his mature years. The monumentality of the figures is underlined by the strong plasticity of the forms and by the intense local colour, as well as by the luminous, nearly metallic, reflections.

## PONTORMO
### *Adoration of the Magi*
1520
Oil on canvas, 85 × 191 cm

Recent restoration has revealed the painting's dazzling colours and superb draughtsmanship (see the detail above), reflecting the influence of Northern painting, on the twenty-seven year old Pontormo, the same influence apparent in his frescoes in the Certosa monastery at Galluzzo. In this detailed composition a debt to Michelangelo is also discernible combined with a narrative strain well suited to the private nature of the commission. Together with other panels by Granacci, Franciabigio and Andrea del Sarto it was intended to decorate a room in the palazzo of Giovanni Maria Benintendi. The figure looking out of the painting is a self-portrait of Pontormo.

## FILIPPO LIPPI

### Virgin and Child with Scenes from the Life of St Anne ("Tondo Bartolini")

1450
Oil on panel, diam. 135 cm

Little is known either of the patron or of the intended destination of this large tondo "da stanza" of the early fifteenth century, first mentioned in the Pitti in the seventeenth century. There is a large autograph drawing on the back of the painting of a coat of arms very like that of the Martelli family for whom Lippi worked so the painting may well have been a Martelli commission. In this tondo, the only one produced by Lippi and one of the largest painted in the Quattrocento, he still relies on the medieval tradition of bringing together various episodes in a single painting. The Virgin is enthroned with the Christ Child on her knee, holding up a seed from an opened pomegranite, a symbol of His Passion and Death. Behind the Virgin to the right, her parents Anne and Joachim meet at the Golden Gate; to the left St Anne gives birth to Mary while in the middle distance on the right female figures are shown bearing gifts to St Anne. The composition is unified by the skilful use of perspective, creating well-defined chromatic areas which also serve as an effective foil to the figures in movement. The linear elegance of the painting is a prelude to the achievements of Filippo Lippi's most celebrated pupil, Sandro Botticelli.

### Corridor of the Columns (Corridoio delle Colonne)

*This corridor takes its name from two alabaster columns standing at one end and has walls covered with a series of small Dutch and Flemish paintings.*

**Justice Room
(Sala della Giustizia)**

*Fresco by Antonio Fedi
(after 1815).*

## TITIAN

### *Portrait of Tommaso Mosti (?)*

ca 1520-30
Oil on canvas, 85 × 66 cm

This fine portrait was bought for the collection of Cardinal Leopoldo de' Medici as a portrait of Tommaso Mosti, a courtier in Urbino. It was only after restoration this century that it was unanimously accepted as the work of Titian, and recognised as a masterpiece of the early years of his maturity. The degree of psychological penetration in the depiction of the young man's face and the incomparable skill in the rendering of the fur-lined jacket and the other details of his costume in tones of black grey and white are typical of Titian's best work.

**Flora Room
(Sala di Flora)**

*Ceiling fresco of an allegory of Flora painted by Antonio Marini (after 1815).*

## PERUGINO

### *Mary Magdalen*

ca 1496-1500
Oil on panel, 47 × 34 cm
The gold letters on her bodice read: S. MARIA MADALENA.

This work epitomises the alluring serenity which made Perugino, and hence the Umbrian school, so popular. Here he combines the use of *chiaroscuro* or shading, in the manner of Leonardo, with the attention to minute detail of the Flemish school in a distinctly personal synthesis.

PALATINE GALLERY

35

**ANTON VAN DYCK**

*Rest During the Flight into Egypt*
ca 1630
Oil on canvas, 133 x 195 cm

The painting was acquired for the Palatine Gallery, along with others, from the Gerini Gallery in 1818.

Generally considered to be a workshop piece from the artist's English period, and a minor version of an analogous composition now found in the Hermitage Museum in St Petersburg. A recent restoration has dispelled former doubts concerning the identity of the painter, since the painting has been shown to be almost completely by the great Flemish artist (the small angels in the top right corner perhaps made the identification easier). Famous as a portraitist, Van Dyck – who was Peter Paul Rubens' most brilliant student – also dealt with religious and mythological themes, although more rarely. In this painting, the pictorial and chromatic delicacy that the artist achieved after his move to England, where he was a painter in the court of Charles I, is clearly evident.

**ALESSANDRO ALLORI**

*Madonna and Child*
ca 1590
Oil on canvas, 133 × 94 cm

This delightful picture, painted after the Council of Trent, clearly reflects the spirit of court art in its elegance and formal perfection. Alessandro Allori trained in the workshop of his uncle, Bronzino, to whom he was strongly indebted, reinterpreting his models in the sweeter style prevalent in the courts of Europe at the end of the sixteenth century.

### RACHEL RUYSCH
#### *Still-life*
1716
Oil on canvas, 89 × 79 cm

This work, dated 1716 was painted as the *pendant*, or companion piece, to an exuberant *Vase of flowers* and was acquired by Ferdinand III of Lorraine for the Gallery in the Pitti Palace at the beginning of the nineteenth century. Ruysch, the daughter of a botanist and the pupil of Willem van Aelst, here displays her unrivalled technical virtuosity as one of the last exponents of this genre which flourished in Holland in the seventeenth century.

### WILLEM VAN AELST
#### *Still-life*
1652
Oil on canvas, 77 × 102 cm

Van Aelst enjoyed great popularity in Rome and more especially in Florence where he was for a long time employed by the Medici, creating many works still in the Florentine collections. He was trained in the great tradition of Dutch seventeenth century still-life painting, combining sumptuous colour and detail with acute realism, as in this still-life depicting precious pieces from the Medici collections, still in the Pitti (Museo degli Argenti). A *Still-life with fruit* painted as a *pendant* is also in the Gallery.

## PETER PAUL RUBENS
### The Three Graces
ca 1620-23
Oil on canvas, 47 × 34 cm

Cardinal Leopoldo de' Medici was a great admirer of Flemish painting and he added this *grisaille* to his collection which also included a large number of sketches. This small painting was designed as the subject for an ivory vase, a decorative technique extremely popular in Northern Europe in the sixteenth and seventeenth centuries.

## Ulysses Room (Sala di Ulisse)

*Gaspare Martelli frescoed the ceiling with the* Return of Ulysses, *alluding to the return to Florence of the Grand Duke Ferdinand III of Lorraine in 1815.*

## FILIPPINO LIPPI
### The death of Lucretia
ca 1470
Oil on panel, 42 × 126 cm

This painting is the length of a wedding chest, a typical piece of Florentine furniture in the 15th Century. A companion work depicting the *Death of the Virgin* is in the Louvre. Filippino, the son of Fra' Filippo Lippi, trained with Sandro Botticelli and his work aspires to the same linear beauty which here animates the various episodes to create a lively narrative against the architectural unity of the background.

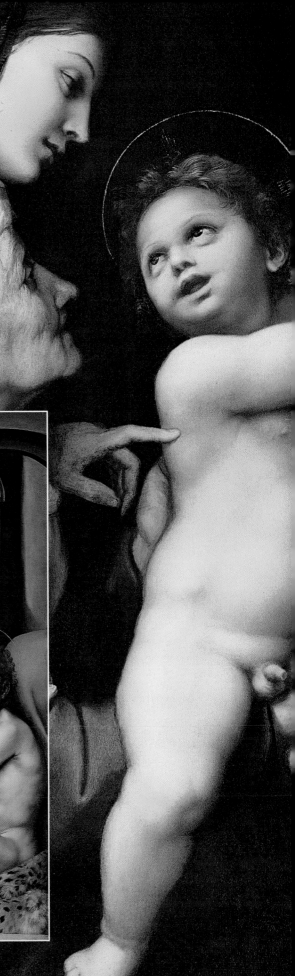

## Madonna and Child, St John the Baptist and Saints ("Madonna dell'impannata")

ca 1514
Oil on canvas, 160 × 127 cm

This Virgin and Child commissioned for Bindi Altoviti, a banker for the Papal curia, has an interesting history. X-ray treatment has revealed St Joseph holding the Baptist in his arms underneath the existing figure of the infant John, now looking straight out of the picture. The composition was simplified in order to keep the group enclosed around the central figure of the Christ Child. The painting, called the Madonna of the "impannata" because of the cloth covering the window in the background to the right, was added to the Medici collections at the time of Cosimo I.

## ANDREA DEL SARTO

### Madonna and Child with Saints ("Pala di Gambassi")
1525-26
Oil on canvas, 215 × 175 cm

This altarpiece, commissioned by a friend of the painter, "Becuccio bicchieraio", or Becuccio the glass-maker, from Gambassi ca 1525-26, echoes motifs already used by del Sarto (*Trinity*, Saturn Room) in an extraordinarily graceful composition, enhanced by the soft tones and sophisticated colouring. Portraits of Becuccio and his wife were painted in two tondi (now in the Art Institute of Chicago) and inserted in a predella panel which has since been lost.

## CIGOLI

### Ecce Homo
ca 1604-6
Oil on canvas, 175 × 135 cm

Cigoli's most famous work was painted at the same time as an *Ecce Homo* by Caravaggio, and was judged superior. Cigoli gives the theme a highly dramatic but intensely religious interpretation and the composition is emblematic of religious art in the counter-reformation. The passages of thicker brushwork and the references to Venetian painting were imitated, not least by Cigoli most successful pupils, Domenico Fetti and Cristofano Allori.

### Napoleon's Bathroom (Bagno di Napoleone)

*This Neo-Classical bathroom built for Napoleon Bonaparte by his sister, Elisa Baciocchi, Grand Duchess of Tuscany, between 1808 and 1813 was designed by Giuseppe Cacialli.*

## Education of Jupiter Room
**(Sala dell'Educazione di Giove)**

*Frescoes by Luigi Catani commissioned as decoration for the bedroom intended for Napoleon Bonaparte (ca 1811-15).*

### CARLO DOLCI
*St Andrew before the Cross*
1646
Oil on canvas, 122 × 99 cm

This version of the subject, and there are several others, was painted for Carlo Gerini. In 1818 it was acquired for the Palatine Gallery together with other pictures from the same collection. Despite the large number of paintings in the gallery by Dolci, who enjoyed the patronage of the Grand Duchess Vittoria della Rovere (her portrait by Dolci is in the Saturn Room) this highly accomplished work was a significant addition to the Gallery.

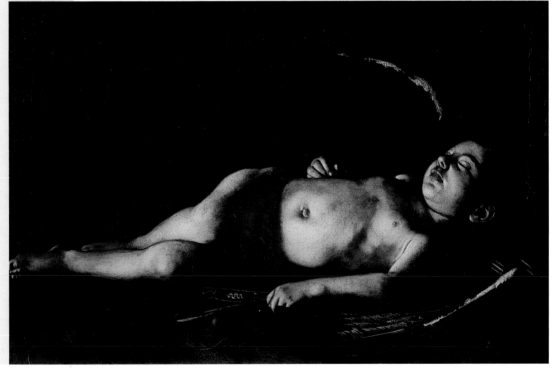

### CARAVAGGIO
*Sleeping Cupid*
1608
Oil on canvas, 71 × 105 cm

Caravaggio, born near Milan, introduced a startling new realism into European painting. This *Sleeping Cupid* was produced in 1608 during his stay in Malta for a member of the Order of Malta, the Florentine Niccolò dell'Antella. Recent research has shown that Caravaggio's model was a dead child as the body bears signs of a fatal infantile infection. By supplying the sleeping corpse with wings and an arrow Caravaggio deconsecrated the traditional interpretation of sweet and ethereal Love to create a powerful, dramatic and contemporary image.

## CRISTOFANO ALLORI

### Judith holding the head of Holofernes

ca 1620
Oil on canvas, 139 × 116 cm

This painting by Cristofano Allori, allegedly the son of the late Mannerist follower of Bronzino, Alessandro Allori, although unfinished (Judith's cloak, for example, has no clasp or cord) is a masterpiece of the new realism of the early decades of the seventeenth century. Allori, in his treatment of the subject was strongly influenced by the intense realism of Caravaggio, and was also conscious of the interpretation by Artemisia Gentileschi (*Judith*, Iliad Room). Holofernes's head is a self-portrait of the artist while his mistress Mazzafirra is depicted as Judith holding his head by the hair. This picture made a powerful impact when first created and was understandably much admired by Romantic painters.

### Stove Room (Sala della Stufa)

*The adjacent room, the Stove Room, which once housed the heating pipes to warm the neighbouring bedrooms, was decorated, between 1638 and 1641, for Ferdinando III by Pietro da Cortona with a cycle showing the* Four Ages of Man.

### Iliad Room (Sala dell'Iliade)

*Frescoes on the ceiling depict scenes from Mount Olympus while the lunettes are decorated with episodes from Homer's* Iliad *(1819-25), painted by Luigi Sabatelli.*

## ARTEMISIA GENTILESCHI

### Judith

ca 1614-20
Oil on canvas, 117 × 93 cm

A powerful and dramatic picture with the mirror positioning of the two turned, or *contrapposto*, figures and a chromatic range derived from Caravaggio and from the painter's father, Orazio. This work, together with the *Magdalen*, also painted during Artemisia Gentileschi's stay at the court of Tuscany from 1613-20, had a profound influence on Florentine painting at the time (see Cristofano Allori, *Judith*, Education of Jupiter Room).

RAPHAEL

*Portrait of a woman ("La Gravida")*
ca 1507
Oil on panel, 66.8 × 52.7 cm

This dignified portrait of a pregnant woman is one of the finest portraits painted by the young Raphael during his last stay in Florence. The bold colouring of the woman's garment against the dense, dark background and the painting's formal complexity distinguish this work from those executed during Raphael's first Roman period.

RIDOLFO DEL GHIRLANDAIO

*Portrait of a Woman*
1508
Oil on panel, 61 × 47 cm

This portrait, the work of the gifted son of the more famous Domenico Ghirlandaio, is clearly indebted to Raphael's portrait painting of his Florentine period.

JUSTUS SUSTERMANS

*Portrait of Prince Mattias de' Medici*
ca 1660
Oil on canvas, 76 × 60 cm

Sustermans, who arrived at the Florentine court in 1619-20, then served as the official painter of the Medici until his death some sixty years later. His spirited style developed after his early training with Pourbus, whose influence is apparent in another portrait by Sustermans of *Waldemar Christian, Prince of Denmark*, also in this room. He was a friend of Rubens and was influenced by both Van Dyck and Velazquez. Sustermans's absorption of the Baroque conception of painting are fully evident in the chromatic range and internal dynamics in this lively depiction of Prince Mattias de' Medici, governor of Siena.

## ANDREA DEL SARTO
### Assumption of the Virgin ("Assunta Panciatichi")

1522-23
Oil on panel, 362 × 209 cm

This enormous altarpiece, commissioned by Bartolomeo Panciatichi for the altar of his chapel in the church of Notre-Dame du Confort in Lyons, never reached its destination but was purchased for the Medici collections in the middle of the seventeenth century.

The monumental and revolutionary composition with the dramatic division of the episode on two levels and Andrea del Sarto's use of shot and strongly contrasting colours had a lasting impact on sixteenth and seventeenth century painting and gained this picture admiration from Rubens. Andrea del Sarto adopted the same composition in 1526 in his altarpiece of the same subject for the Passerini family in Cortona, also acquired by the Medici at the end of the seventeenth century. The altarpiece is still positioned opposite the earlier painting according to the dictates of nineteenth-century taste which favoured the aethetics of display based on a harmony of shape, size and colour.

## VERONESE
### The Baptism of Christ
ca 1575
Oil on canvas, 196 × 133 cm

A work from Veronese's mature period it is stylistically reminiscent of the *Preaching of the Baptist* (Rome, Villa Borghese) while the colours suffused in a warm, golden light are typical of Veronese's late works.

## ANNIBALE CARRACCI
### Christ in glory with Saints
ca 1597-98
Oil on canvas, 194 × 142 cm

Annibale Carracci is the Bolognese painter whose work clearly marks the transition from the late sixteenth to the new century and the beginnings of the Baroque style. He united the Tuscan-Roman approach to drawing with Venetian colouring to create a novel synthesis reflected in this composition painted for Cardinal Odoardo Farnese, portrayed in the lower left of the painting. The painting was acquired by Ferdinando de' Medici at the end of the seventeenth century.

## Saturn Room (Sala di Saturno)

*Frescoes and stucco by Ciro Ferri, the pupil of Pietro da Cortona, who here worked following the designs of his master between 1663-65. Here the prince, in the guise of Hercules, ascends Mount Olympus to be greeted by the gods while the four lunettes depict scenes from the lives of Scipio, Lycurgus, Sylla and Syrus.*

RAPHAEL

*Madonna and Child*
*("Madonna del Granduca")*
ca 1506
Oil on panel, 84.5 × 55.9 cm

This Virgin and Child is known as the "Madonna del Granduca" because it was acquired by the Grand Duke Ferdinand III of Lorraine when in exile during the Napoleon period in Tuscany. It is one of several "Belle Madonne" painted during Raphael's visits to Florence before 1507, but this is not only the simplest but also the most moving portrayal of the Holy Mother and Child. Inspired by Leonardo's use of *chiaroscuro* in the soft modelling of the figures emerging from the dark ground, Raphael also reveals his precise drawing and "geometrical" conception of form, acquired in the workshop of Perugino. The painting is unusual in comparison with other treatments of the same theme in that a landscape background is here eliminated in favour of a dense, dark ground, focusing attention fully on the Madonna and Child.

## ANDREA DEL SARTO

### *Dispute on the Trinity*
1517
Oil on panel, 232 × 193 cm

This solemn assembly of saints with St Augustine, St
Lawrence, St Dominic and St Francis standing and
the Magdalen and St John the Baptist kneeling in the
foreground, echoes Raphael's magnificent fresco in
the Vatican and must have created a powerful impact
when placed above the altar in the Augustinian church
of San Gallo. Painted in 1517, the quality of the work
lies in the beauty of the colouring combined with soft
shading derived from Leonardo together with the
strength of Michelangelo's modelling of form.

## RAPHAEL

### *Portrait of Tommaso Inghirami ("Fedra")*
ca 1510
Oil on panel, 89.5 × 62.3 cm

Inghirami, a nobleman from Volterra and friend of
Leo X de' Medici, who created him librarian at the
Vatican, is here depicted in the more powerful of the
two portraits attributed to Raphael (the other is in the
Isabella Stewart Gardner Collection, Boston).
Raphael's portrait of Tommaso Inghirami (nick-named
Fedra in allusion to his part in the play by Seneca)
probably dates to 1510, the year he was nominated
cardinal. The portrait reflects a new monumentality in
the treatment of the half figure, with his head turned
to conceal a squint, and marks the beginning of
Raphael's Roman period.

RAPHAEL
*Portrait of Agnolo Doni*
1505-6
Oil on panel, 65 × 45.7 cm

This fine portrait was painted as the companion to one of Agnolo's wife, Maddalena Strozzi, perhaps forming a diptych in the style of Piero della Francesca's portrayal of the Duke and Duchess of Urbino. The couple were married in 1503 but the portrait of Agnolo is later than that of Maddalena as the landscape background does not conceal an interior view, initially applied to his wife's portrait. The Doni were great art collectors (Donatello) and commissioned the *Holy Family* from Michelangelo which still bears their name (*Tondo Doni,* Uffizi).

RAPHAEL
*Portrait of Maddalena Doni*
ca 1505-6
Oil on panel, 65 × 45.7 cm

The portrait is clearly influenced by Leonardo's painting of the *Mona Lisa* (Louvre). X-ray research has revealed that Raphael originally draughted the figure seated in a room, later substituted for the enchanting spring landscape which serves as the transculent link uniting the two Doni portraits. Both paintings reveal a close attention to minute detail, especially of dress and jewellery, so characteristic of Flemish painting (Memling).

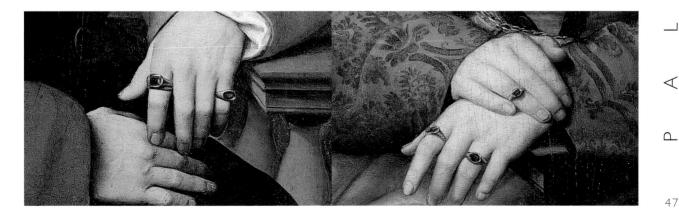

### RAPHAEL

*Madonna del Baldacchino*
ca 1508
Oil on panel, 279 × 217 cm

This painting was unfinished when Raphael left Florence for the last time to work at the Papal court in Rome. It was commissioned by Benedetto Dei for the altar of the family chapel in the church of Santo Spirito, but was never put in place. A large altarpiece by Rosso Fiorentino, now also in the Pitti in the Apollo Room, was hung there instead. Although the painting is unfinished, most noticeably in the two angels in the foreground, the composition shows an unprecedented architectural grandeur and complexity: the throne is set in a semi-circular chapel with columns in imitation of those designed by Brunelleschi for Santo Spirito, breaking with the tradition of the fifteenth-century Florentine "Sacra Conversazione".

### PERUGINO

*Lamentation*
1495
Oil on panel, 214 × 195 cm

Perugino, influenced at an early age by Piero della Francesca, introduced the Umbrian style to Florence when he continued his training in Verrocchio's workshop. Perugino's importance lies in the serene classicism of his pictures with large areas devoted to the depiction of landscape, a trait apparent in the work of his most gifted pupil, Raphael. This *Lamentation*, painted for the convent of the Poor Clares in Florence, is typical of the controlled lyricism of Perugino's composition set in a dreamy landscape, later echoed by Raphael in his panel of the *Entombment* painted for Atalanta Baglioni in 1507 (Rome, Villa Borghese).

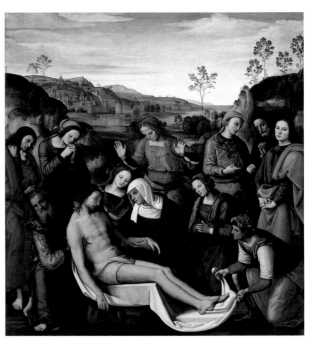

### RAPHAEL

*The Vision of Ezechiel*
ca 1518
Oil on panel, 47.7 × 29.5 cm

This small painting, painted in 1518 for a member of the Hercolani family, was later bought by Francesco I de' Medici. It concentrates all the formal strength evident in Raphael's work during his last years in Rome, culminating in the Vatican *Transfiguration*.
Both works reflect the same concentration of energy and the sublime imagination which Raphael deployed in the creation of a naturalistic cosmic vision based on a complex balance of form, light and colour.

RAPHAEL

*Madonna and Child with St John the Baptist ("Madonna della Seggiola")*
ca 1516
Oil on panel, diam. 71 cm

The most famous of Raphael's Madonnas, it belongs to the artist's highly productive late period in Rome, and although it is uncertain who commissioned the work it may well have been Pope Leo X de' Medici. Raphael made a number of paintings of the Virgin and Child but this is the only tondo, reviving the circular composition popular in Florence, used once by Michelangelo in his painting of the *Tondo Doni* (Uffizi) and twice in his sculpture (*Tondo Taddei*, Royal Academy, London; *Tondo Pitti,* Bargello Museum, Florence). It was not these however that provided Raphael's inspiration but the more distant works of Donatello, showing Mother and Child in close embrace which had already attracted him during his Florentine period (*Madonna Tempi*, Alte Pinakothek, Munich). In this composition the intertwined forms create a more complex rhythm, more monumental and underscored by full, glowing, almost Venetian colouring.

49

## SEBASTIANO DEL PIOMBO
### Martyrdom of St Agatha
1520
Oil on canvas, 127 x 178 cm

The painting is dated 1520 and was done in Rome for Cardinal Rangoni, deacon of the Church of St Agatha. It became part of Cardinal Leopoldo di' Medici's collection in the Pitti Palace in the seventeenth century and has remained there ever since.

A work much admired and discussed by Vasari, it shows the artist's Venetian training (Giorgione) although del Piombo, once arrived in Rome, was heavily influenced by Michelangelo's drawing principles, evidenced by the solid plasticism of the figures and by the torsion in the saint's body

## Jupiter Room (Sala di Giove)

*Once the throne room of the Grand Ducal apartments, it was decorated with stucco and frescoes by Pietro da Cortona, between 1642 and 1644.*

## ANDREA DEL SARTO
### St John the Baptist
ca 1523
Oil on panel, 94 x 68 cm

Although commissioned as a private devotional painting the decisive bearing and forthright stance of the young John the Baptist suggest a public work and have gained it great popularity. The sculptural quality of the figure enhanced by the soft shading or *sfumato* derived from Leonardo, together with the classical pose in the manner of Raphael, are seen to full advantage swathed in the red mantle, foreshadowing the dramatic contrasts favoured by Caravaggio.

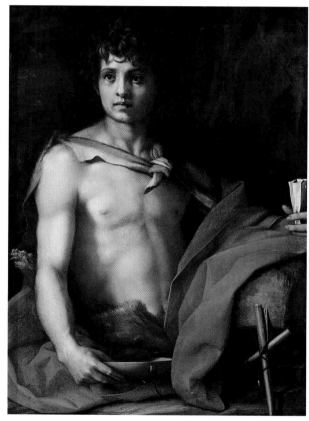

## GIOVANNI LANFRANCO
### The Ecstasy of Saint Margherita of Cortona
1622
Oil on canvas, 230 x 185 cm

Painted in 1622 by the Emilian Lanfranco for the altar of the Venuti in Santa Maria Nuova in Cortona it was obtained directly from Cortona for the collection of Ferdinando de' Medici.

Lanfranco was one of the earliest exponents of the Baroque manner, exemplified in this composition full of movement and suffused with transcendental light.

## FRA' BARTOLOMEO
### *Pietà*
ca 1511-12
Oil on panel, 158 × 199 cm

Despite the loss of the top section of this painting, originally an altarpiece for the church of San Gallo, it remains one
of the most influential works of the early sixteenth century
in Florence. It shows a powerful debt to Raphael's classicism which Fra' Bartolomeo combines with a purity and
fluidity of design and an intense chromatic range, reminiscent of Venetian painting.

## RAPHAEL
### *Portrait of a Young Woman ("La Velata")*
ca 1516
Oil on canvas, 82 × 60.5 cm

With this portrait of an unknown, veiled woman (modern
scholarship has exploded the romantic tale linking her of
Raphael's mythical lover, "La Fornarina") the artist's creative journey comes to an entirely original and unmistak-
able conclusion, having passed through the Florentine experiences (Leonardo) whose influence is noticeable in other female portraits in the Pitti (*Maddalena Doni*, *La Gravida*). From the sculptural feeling of those pictures we come
to a diffused luminosity and a freedom of technique that
can only be explained as the result of Raphael's new pictorial mastery acquired while working on the frescoes in the
Vatican *Stanze*. The loveliness of the face framed by the veil,
recalling Antonello da Messina's *Virgin Annunciate*, is
matched by the bravura "set piece" of the ruched silken
sleeve, an inimitable pictorial *tour de force*. The intensity of
the sitter's gaze and the beauty of her face (she is possibly
the same model as that used for the *Sistine Madonna* now in
Dresden) linger in the memory, as summits of formal perfection never to be reached again.

## GIORGIONE
### *The Three Ages of Man*
ca 1500
Oil on panel, 62 × 77 cm

The allegorical significance of this painting is now rejected
and it is seen rather as a singing lesson or "concert of voic-
es", typical of the musical Venetian culture to which Giorgione belonged. The attribution to Giorgione is fairly recent; other Venetian artists, including Bellini and Lotto having at various times been linked to the painting. The modern consensus is that this is a youthful work, strongly reminiscent of both Bellini and Leonardo, but already rich in
motifs that the artist would develop in later years.

*On the ceiling an allegory of War and Peace surrounds a triumphal vision of the Medici coat of arms, painted by Pietro da Cortona between 1644 and 1646.*

PETER PAUL RUBENS

*The Consequences of War*
1637-38
Oil on canvas, 206 × 345 cm

The allegorical title obscures the painting's true subject: on the left Europe, dressed in black, casts her eyes and her hands upwards before the open-doored temple of Janus, while in the centre naked Venus endeavours to restrain Mars, who grasps a shield and a drawn sword as he strides into battle, dragged by the Furies. In his march he tramples on books and overturns the Arts, as well as a young woman with a baby at her breast. Sending this painting in 1638 to his colleague Justus Sustermans, court painter to the Medici, Rubens explained its meaning in relation to the Thirty Years' War which was raging in his homeland. A late masterpiece of the great Flemish painter, the picture is also an open homage to Italian art of the full Renaissance, from Titian onwards.

PETER PAUL RUBENS

*The four Philosophers*

1611-12
Oil on panel, 164 × 139 cm

Rubens painted this large quadruple portrait around 1611-12, in memory of his brother Philip, a pupil of the philosopher Justus Lipsius, who is also shown. Both men had recently died. The artist portrayed himself in upper left, and in the lower right he added Jan van de Wouvere, a fellow student of Philip's. The four tulips beside the bust of Seneca (which Rubens acquired in Rome) symbolise the lives of the four sitters (two have already opened out). The books lying on the carpet-covered table, the view of the Palatine hill in the background, the gestures and the intensity of the glances make this group portrait a masterpiece of seventeenth-century art.

## ANDREA DEL SARTO

### Stories from the Life of Joseph
1515-16
Oil on panel, 98 × 135 cm

These two panels, painted in 1515-16 for the bridal chamber of Pierfrancesco Borgherini and Margherita Acciaioli (together with works by Pontormo, Granacci and Bachiacca, now dispersed in various museums in Europe) soon became so celebrated that they were sought by Francis I of France. It was however Francesco I de' Medici who acquired them in 1584 and exhibited them in the Tribuna of the Uffizi Gallery from where they were brought to the Pitti a century later. The Florentine painter arranges the complex narrative of the episodes from the life of Joseph into clearly defined groups, unified in their translucent vision of an Egyptian landscape dominated by Renaissance architectural splendours and dazzling fifteenth-century costumes.

## BARTOLOMÉ ESTEBAN MURILLO

### Madonna and Child
ca 1650
Oil on canvas, 157 × 107 cm

The example of Raphael is very clearly present in this sweet *Madonna and Child*. Instead of the *chiaroscuro* contrasts typical of Murillo's more youthful productions, such as the *Madonna of the Rosary* in the same room, there is here soft modelling with transparent and almost pastel colours that pervade the figures with interior light. The picture may have been acquired by Ferdinando II de' Medici.

## VERONESE

### Portrait of a man in furs
ca 1550-60
Oil on canvas, 140 × 107 cm

Paolo Veronese, the third great Venetian painter of the full Renaissance, is especially famous for his sacred and mythological scenes which decorate the churches and palazzi of Venice and the Veneto. However he also, if rarely, attempted portraits, and managed to achieve a personal manner in a genre at which both Titian and Tintoretto excelled.

This is certainly true of the monumental portrait of a gentleman in the Pitti Gallery, which although influenced by Titian's portraits attains a highly individual style most evident in the superb painterly treatment of the furs.

## TINTORETTO

### Portrait of Alvise Cornaro
ca 1560-65
Oil on canvas, 113 × 85 cm

Alvise Cornaro (1475-1566), an aristocratic man of letters, spent his life in Padua, the centre of university studies, where he protected scientists and scholars, and wrote a number of treatises (including *Della vita sobria*, On the sober life). Rather than emphasise his sitter's versatility, Tintoretto concentrates on his very human aspect, through a sombre harmony of greys and blacks. The portrait was acquired by Cardinal Leopoldo de' Medici.

ANTHONY VAN DYCK

*Portrait of Cardinal Bentivoglio*
ca 1625
Oil on canvas, 195 × 147 cm

This extraordinary symphony of red – the colour of
the cardinalate – was meant to celebrate the elevation
to the Sacred College of Guido Bentivoglio. His portrait is the concluding masterpiece of the Italian period of the greatest genius among Rubens's pupils. The
full-length, life-sized figure dominates its surround-
ings with the nobility of its lineaments, the elegance of
the hands, the refinement of the clothing. The cardinal emerges from the background with a majestic presence, subtly controlled by acute psychological insight.
Guido Bentivoglio was Papal Legate to the Low Countries, and wrote a history of the wars there.

TITIAN

*Portrait of Ippolito de' Medici*
1533
Oil on canvas, 139 × 107 cm

Ippolito de' Medici, son of Giuliano Duke of Nemours,
was created cardinal at the age of eighteen by Clement
VII. More interested in war than a career in the Church,
he had himself painted by Titian when he was in
Bologna in 1533, dressed in the Hungarian style in
memory of his role in the siege of Vienna by the Turks.
The harmony of violet and magenta emphasise the mar-
tial bearing and somewhat cruel expression of the
youthful warrior.

## Apollo Room
## (Sala di Apollo)

*The decoration was begun by Pietro da Cortona in 1646, and completed by his pupil Ciro Ferri (1659-61), following the master's design.*

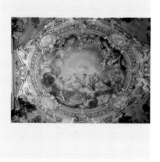

### TITIAN
### *The Magdalen*
ca 1535
Oil on panel, 84 × 69 cm

Signed "TITIANUS", this picture, copied by the artist himself and by his workshop in numerous versions, was painted for the court of Urbino in about 1535. The voluptuous physical beauty of the model is barely concealed by the rippling mass of auburn hair, of the colour indeed that we call "Titian". The work is characterized by the masterly harmony of chromatic tones and a technique in which painterly freedom outweighs concerns of draughtsmanship.

### ANDREA DEL SARTO
### *Lamentation over the dead Christ*
### *("Pietà di Luco")*
1523-24
Oil on panel, 238 × 198 cm

This is the third Pietà (the other two being those of Perugino and of Fra' Bartolomeo) in the Pitti Gallery. Andrea del Sarto invests it with a formal monumentality derived from Michelangelo and Raphael. The colour harmonies of bright and transparent hues, with bold juxtapositions, foreshadow the achievements of the Mannerist painters, Pontormo and Rosso Fiorentino (both represented by remarkable works in the Gallery). The painting was intended for the high altar in the church of San Pietro a Luco, in the Mugello, where it was replaced by a copy (it came to the Pitti Palace in 1782).

**TITIAN**

*Portrait of a man ("The grey-eyed nobleman" or "Englishman")*
ca 1545
Oil on canvas, 111 × 96 cm

Romantic critics have identified the salient features of this portrait of a young man: the attentive, almost magnetic gaze of the pale grey eyes, and the *sprezzatura* or courtly nonchalance which earned it the titles noted above (and also the title *The Duke of Norfolk*). In point of fact we know nothing about the identity of the sitter, who must however have been of exalted station, as appears from the sober but elaborate dark suit, the heavy gold chain, the gloves held in the right hand, and the faintly haughty expression. The very dimensions of the portrait must be indicative of the patron's importance, as too must its pictorial quality. Here Titian has given us one of the masterpieces of his early maturity, a subtly introspective analysis of the sitter's personality, but also a colouristic harmony of tones depending on the interplay of greys and blacks to emphasise the authority in the youthful visage.

### Andrea del Sarto

*Madonna and Child with
St Elizabeth and St John the Baptist
("Sacra Famiglia Medici")*
1529
Oil on panel, 140 × 104 cm

This *Holy Family,* painted for Ottaviano de' Medici in 1529, is one of Andrea del Sarto's most important private devotional works. The composition pays tribute to the three most significant artists of the High Renaissance; Leonardo, Michelangelo and Raphael. The *sfumato* or shading effects are derived from the first, the clarity of the design and the sculptural quality of the figures from the second, and the felicitous composition from the third, clearly derived from the *Holy Families* of Raphael's Florentine period. The combination of these influences, fused with Andrea del Sarto's particular solemnity results in an individual and most appealing style.

### Guido Reni

*Cleopatra*
ca 1638-39
Oil on canvas, 122 × 96 cm

The pathetic pose derived from sculpture and the accentuated lighting on the silken brushwork are typical of the style of Guido Reni. He was one of the leading figures in European painting in the middle of the seventeenth century and it was works like this which gained him the epithet "divine". The picture was commissioned by Cardinal Leopoldo de' Medici.

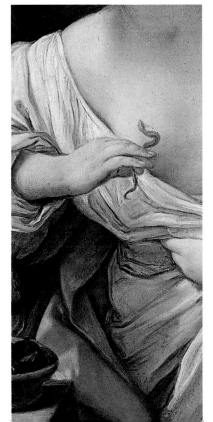

### Carlo Maratta

*The Madonna appearing
to St Philip Neri*
ca 1675
Oil on canvas, 343 × 197 cm

A masterpiece by the leading painter of the Roman school at the end of the seventeenth century this painting combines the achievements of the Roman Baroque with the stylistic innovations of Guido Reni. The diagonal emphasis of the composition and the pale colouring are clearly indebted to the *Vision of Andrea Corsini,* painted for the Barberini. This large altarpiece adorned the church of San Giovanni dei Fiorentini in Rome, before the Medici acquired it at the end of the seventeenth century.

## Venus Room (Sala di Venere)

*The fresco and plasterwork decoration of the ceiling was executed by Pietro da Cortona from 1641-42. The centre of the ceiling shows the young prince, Cosimo III, being dragged from the arms of Venus by Pallas Athene, the goddess of War, towards Hercules, or glory. The lunettes contain episodes from antiquity alluding to the power and magnanimity of the Medici princes, while the oval stucco frames contain portraits of the Medici popes and Grand Dukes.*

### ANTONIO CANOVA
### Venus ("Venere Italica")
1810-11
Carrara marble, h. 172 cm

This work by the greatest Neoclassical sculptor in Europe, active in the last years of the eighteenth century and the first two decades of the nineteenth, reflects Canova's "modern" interpretation of the classical *Venere callipigia*. The smooth surface finish of the marble body and the folds of the drapery reflect a supreme technical ability unparalleled since the work of Bernini some two hundred years earlier. Canova's *Venus* was commissioned as a replacement for the *Venus dei Medici* which Napoleon had taken as booty to Paris but which was returned in 1816 and now stands in the Tribuna of the Uffizi Gallery in Florence.

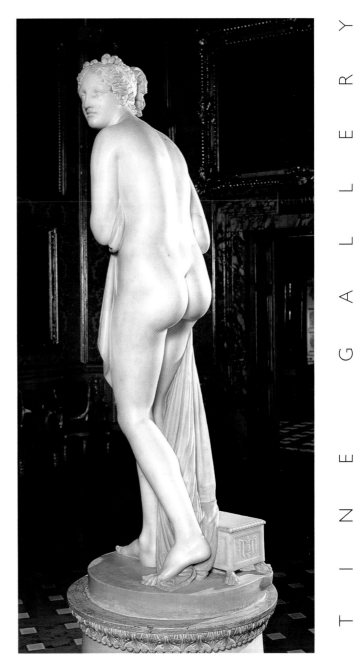

### PETER PAUL RUBENS
### Peasants returning from the fields
ca 1640
Oil on panel, 121 × 194 cm

This painting and the companion work showing *Ulysses on the island of the Phaeacians*, in the same room, are examples of landscape painting by the greatest of the Dutch Baroque painters. Rubens, who painted various views of the countryside around Malines, here creates a serene vision of the natural world with the peasants, animals and trees bathed in the warm glow of the setting sun. Both paintings originally belonged to the Duke of Richelieu and were then acquired by the Hapsburgs before being brought to Florence from Vienna by Peter Leopold of Lorraine who became Grand Duke in 1756.

### TITIAN
*The concert*
1510-12
Oil on canvas, 86.5 × 123.5 cm

Cardinal Leopoldo de' Medici, an enthusiastic collector of Venetian painting, bought this picture in Venice in 1654 as a work by Giorgione. The painting is now thought to be an early work by Giorgione's greatest pupil, Titian. In both style and poetical subject matter the painting is still strongly reminiscent of Giorgione's slightly unreal world (*Fête champetre*, Louvre, Paris) in which the figures appear spiritually remote, a prelude to the later interpretations of the Romantic painters

### SALVATOR ROSA
*Harbour at sunset*
ca 1645
Oil on canvas, 234 × 395 cm

This large canvas by the Neapolitan Salvator Rosa, together with the companion work depicting a *Harbour with a lighthouse*, was painted for Cardinal Giovan Carlo de' Medici during the artist's Florentine period, lasting almost ten years from 1640-49. In this grandiose yet serene view a sense of depth is created by the soft light of the setting sun, inspired by the work of Claude Lorraine. Rosa's landscapes, and there are several fine examples in the Gallery (Psyche Room), had a considerable impact on the development of the genre in the seventeenth and eighteenth centuries.

## TITIAN

### Portrait of a Young Woman ("La Bella")

ca 1536
Oil on canvas, 89 × 75.5 cm

The title of *La Bella,* describing Titian's subject, a beautiful woman with fine dark eyes commanding our attention, could hardly be disputed, although her identity is still open to debate. She is dressed in a fine blue gown embroidered in gold, with full slashed sleeves with touches of white, has a gold chain, pearl earrings and a heavy golden belt. Traditionally she is identified with Francesco Maria della Rovere, the Duke of Urbino's lover. In a letter sent by the Duke to Titian in 1536 he urges the painter to send him the work, referring to the subject as the "woman in the blue dress". She was probably Titian's model for the *Venus of Urbino* (Uffizi Gallery, Florence), also commissioned by the Duke. Whatever her identity, both paintings are masterpieces of Titian's early maturity and confirm his reputation as a superb portraitist and the leading painter of the Venetian school.

## TITIAN

### Portrait of Pietro Aretino

ca 1545
Oil on canvas, 96.7 × 76.6 cm

This portrait marks the friendship between Titian and Aretino, the celebrated man of letters and satirist, who launched attacks on the European political scene from his base in Venice, a friendship which failed to survive the painting's completion. Aretino disliked it and accused Titian of working in haste, having little understanding of Titian's painterly technique, which became increasingly impressionistic in his later years. The writer therefore sent it to the first Grand Duke, Cosimo I, asking for a substantial payment in return. Aretino's inability to appreciate this powerful portrait, with its debt to Michelangelo in the proud expression and bearing of the head, led to Florence acquiring one of the finest of Titian's portraits.

# First Floor

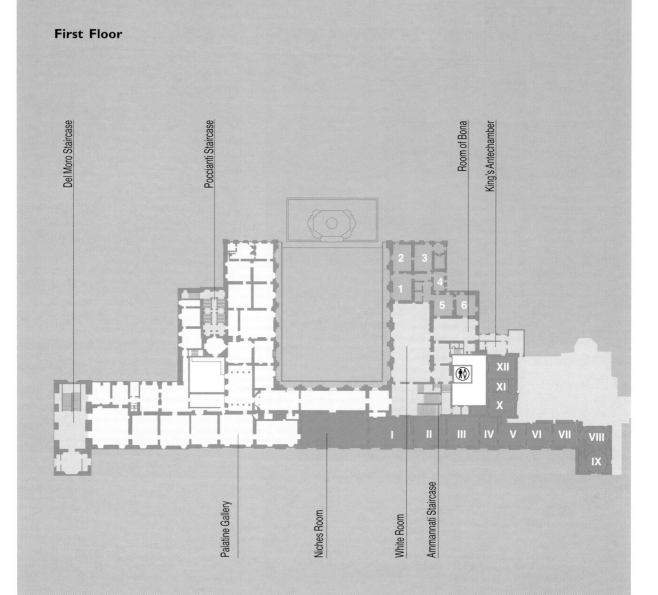

ROYAL APARTMENTS

I GREEN ROOM
II RED ROOM (THRONE ROOM)
III BLUE ROOM
IV CHAPEL
V PARROT ROOM
VI QUEEN'S DRAWING ROOM
VII QUEEN'S BEDROOM
VIII OVAL ROOM
IX ROUND ROOM
X KING'S BEDROOM
XI KING'S STUDIO
XII RED ROOM

TAPESTRY APARTMENTS

1 FAITH ROOM
2 CHARITY ROOM
3 JUSTICE ROOM
4 ALLORI'S LOGGETTA
5 PRUDENCE ROOM
6 TEMPERANCE ROOM

*The Green Room.*

# Royal Apartments

Fausta Navarro

The fourteen magnificent rooms that open out along the right side of the Pitti Palace façade are today known as the Royal Apartments.

From the seventeenth century on, these majestic rooms were the residence of the Grand Ducal Medici family, then of the Lorraines and finally, as of 1865, of the Savoys, when Florence became the second capital of unified Italy and Vittorio Emanuele chose to make the Pitti the royal residence.

There remain but few traces of the oldest, Medici period, and those that do remain are connected most of all with Grand Prince Ferdinando, the son of Cosimo III, who assembled in these rooms his impressive collection of Renaissance and baroque masterpieces from the Venetian, Florentine and Emilian schools, a collection which is still the core of the Palatine Gallery and Uffizi collections.

The prevailing appearance of the Royal Apartments as we see them today is that given them by the neo-classical taste of the Hapsburg-Lorraines in the fourth and fifth decades of the nineteenth century, an appearance given its definitive and final character by the strongly eclectic stamp of the Savoys. The work commissioned by the Savoys and carried out between the end of the eighteenth and the beginning of the nineteenth centuries, described in the 1911 Inventory of Pitti Palace paintings and furniture, has been chosen as the basis for the recent re-furbishing of the Apartments, completed

between 1987 and 1993. The major exhibition of Italian sixteenth-century painting, organised in these rooms shortly after the First World War, in 1922, as well as the exhibition of French tapestries from the Crocetta Palace, had resulted in a significant alteration in the placement of the furniture, changing an arrangement that had gradually evolved over centuries. In addition, following a general re-organisation of the Florentine galleries, a series of important paintings had been transferred from the Apartments to the Palatine Gallery or to the Uffizi, and the large Lorraine and Savoy mirrors, the furniture, furnishings and everything else that had created a homogeneous, decorative and historical whole had been moved to villas or simply placed in storage.

The last chapter in the story of the restoration of the Apartments ends with the re-arranging of the "Tapestry" or "Foreigners'" Apartment, of the five rooms, that is, which extend behind the White Room, distinguished by the presence of seventeenth- and eighteenth-century Florentine and French tapestries.

## The Niches Room

The grandiose stairway created by Bartolomeo Ammannati leads the visitor to the Statues Gallery, from which one passes to the Niches Room, the vast drawing room, in the centre of the palace's longitudinal axis and dividing the Palatine Gallery from the Royal

*View of the Green Room.*

*Caravaggio*, Portrait of Fra' Marcantonio Martelli, *oil on canvas, 115 × 95 cm, ca 1608-1609.*

Apartments. The Niches Room is part of the oldest core of the fifteenth-century building. It was built by Cosimo I, who wanted the six (originally ten) niches to be an *antiquarium* containing the most prestigious of the ancient statues in his collection. The decoration of the ceiling and walls with architectonic and plant motifs and panoplies of weapons, realised as a monochrome with gold highlights by Giuseppe Maria Terreni and Giuseppe Castagnoli at the end of eighteenth century, reflect the neo-classical taste of the time. The room's furnishings are also extremely refined. During the Medici period, the Niches Room was used as an antechamber for receiving guests, while the first Lorraines used it for receptions and performances. It was only in the later Lorraine period that this room began to be reserved for meals, becoming a dining room. This was a function that up until that time was not filled by any particular room (meals were previously served wherever they were required). The concept of a room reserved for dining began with the growing English middle class and spread throughout Europe during the nineteenth century. The Savoys used the room for this purpose as well, and in 1938 a banquet was held here in honour of Hitler.

*Jean Marc Nattier*, Portrait of Henrietta of France as Flora, *oil on canvas, 94,5 × 128,5 cm, 1742.*

## Green Room

The Green Room is the first of the three rooms that make up the "Fabric Quarter", given this name in the nineteenth century because of the damask silks in various colours that cover the walls. The first room thus has splendid green damask silk with large racemes; in the next room, the Red or Throne Room, the walls are covered with red silk lampas made in France; and the last room, the Blue Room, has the most

*View of the Throne Room.*

beautiful walls of any of the rooms, covered in blue silk with an exquisite design of amphora, vases and lyres inscribed with garlands of flowers. The Green Room, also called the "Guardroom", was the antechamber of Prince Ferdinando's apartment. All that remains from that period (1663–1713) is the canvas depicting the *Allegory of the Peace Between the Florentines and the Fiesolani* by Luca Giordano, set in the ceiling, which was decorated in 1823 by Giuseppe Castagnoli with monochrome grey, green and gold frescoes. The magnificent baroque appearance of this room is due not only to the elegant and refined furniture but also to the numerous paintings on the walls. These paintings, with elaborately carved frames, include the group of paintings of the French royal family that was brought from Parma in 1868, with works by Jean Marc Nattier, Jean François de Troy and Carl van Loo. *The Portrait of Fra' Marcantonio Martelli* by Caravaggio, one of the last works by great Lombard painter, datable to 1608–1609, is of particular interest. The small wooden table beside the canvas (in the centre of the room), veneered and with a top inlaid with an ornamental design of semi-precious stones, and the cabinet of ebony and semi-precious stones (which belonged to Grand Duchess Vittoria della Rovere and stands against the west wall), are, on the other hand, representative of the apex of very high quality reached by Florentine manufacture during the seventeenth century.

## Red Room

The next room, the Red Room, was named the Throne Room when, during the Savoy era, the throne, canopy and balustrade were placed here. Earlier, during the time of Prince Ferdinando, it was used as an Audience Room; the Lorraines later used it for similar purposes (called by them the Chamberlains' Room). The French wallcoverings of silk lampas with a crimson background are matched by the beautiful carpet with spiralling acanthus leaf motifs, made by the royal factory in Tournai in 1854, along with the other carpets in the Fabric Quarter, expressly for the decoration of these rooms. The furnishings in this room also date from this period, while the contemporary pair of candelabra with Japanese Imari vases is based on a seventeenth-century model found also in the adjoining Blue Room.

*View of the Blue Room.*

## Blue Room

The Blue Room, previously known as the Cymbal Room because of the concerts performed there for Grand Prince Ferdinando, contains only a few examples of the original furnishings, among which the beautiful wallcoverings, the blue French damask, and the Tournai carpet. The white and gold stuccoed ceiling and the delicate fireplace made in 1765 and called the "eagle" fireplace, are older, from the time of Peter Leopold of Lorraine. In order to fill the spaces

## Chapel

The next room is the Chapel, created by the Lorraines in the eighteenth century out of the original Alcove, that is, the "official" bedroom of Grand Prince Ferdinando. The changeover notwithstanding, the Chapel retains a large part of its original, late-baroque, Medici-era decoration. The white and gold stuccowork and the cartouches bearing symbols and sayings relating to Prince Ferdinando were designed by Giovan Battista Foggini, to whom is also attributed the design of the carved and gilded wooden grating that encloses the arch behind which the prince's bed was originally concealed. The altar, with its ivory *Crucifix* and the *boiseries* by G.B. Dolci (1765), added during the Lorraine period, can be still be seen, while the crimson damask that covers the walls, and the French carpet, were added during the following century. Between 1867 and 1868, a number of furnishings were brought from the residences of the Bourbons of Parma in order to soften the chapel's austerity. They include the large mirror (the original coat-of-arms was replaced with that of the Savoys), and the exquisite French table cover from the middle of the seventeenth century, made of velvet embroidered with silver threads, paillettes and silver tinsel.

*View of the Chapel.*

*Antonie van Dyck,* Portrait of a Noblewoman, *oil on paper, 34 × 27 cm, 1623.*

left by tapestries sent to Rome in 1922, ten full-figure Medici portraits, painted by Giusto di Sustermans between 1621 and 1645, and which hung in these same rooms during the time of Grand Prince Ferdinando, have been gathered here. The splendid wooden chandelier, carved and gilded in 1697 by the Dutch artist Vittorio Crosten for Cosimo III's country villa, "The Hovel", replaces the 1854 triton chandelier, sent to the Chamber of Deputies in Rome.

And, like Grand Prince Ferdinando, who arranged in this room some of the most valuable paintings in his collection (Titians, Rembrandts, Van Dycks), the Savoys hung here some of their best and most visually striking paintings from the sixteenth and seventeenth centuries, such as Carlo Dolci's *Mother with Child*. This painting had originally belonged to Vittoria della Rovere and was later enclosed in a very elaborate frame made in the Grand Ducal workshops on the basis of a design by Giovan Battista Foggini.

## The Parrot Room

The Parrot Room is named for the bird motif (the birds are actually imperial eagles) in the beautiful silk lampas wallcoverings, which have a green background and were made in France. The room divides the King's Apartment, extending along the internal courtyard, from the Queen's Apartment, which follows the southern axis. The Savoys' eclectic taste is particularly evident in these public and private and rooms, as described in the 1911 Inventory. Of particular note is the clock, with its chased and gilded bronze shelf and black marble base, made in 1812 by the famous Parisian bronze maker, Pierre Philippe Thomire. The clock is a not un-

*View of the Parrot Room.*

*Domenico Puligo,*
**The Magdalen**, *oil on panel, 61 × 51 cm, ca 1515.*

common case of the "recycling" of works of art typical of the Restoration: the original bust of Napoleon was replaced with the bust of Ferdinando III and the imperial eagle with the allegorical figure of Tuscany. The table cover of silk and gilded silver, in Louis XV style, is in particularly good taste. Filippo Napoletano's *Impruneta Fair*, a depiction of the famous fair held near Florence every October 18th, is, on the other hand, more consistent with popular themes and sensibility.

*Yellow Room, Queen's Apartment.*

### *The Queen's Apartment*
### **The Queen's Drawing Room, or Yellow Room**

The next room was originally Ferdinando de' Medici's "real" bedroom, and then that of the Grand Duchesses of the House of Lorraine. It became the Queen's Drawing Room in the Savoy period and was also referred to as the Yellow room because of the yellow silk lampas wallcoverings, made in France around 1805. The carpet was purchased in France in 1815, at the Piat-Lefèvre factory in Tournai and repeats the type of decoration – the sixteen *Cohorts* of the Legion of Honour – that had already been used for the carpet in Napoleon's Grand Chamber in the Saint-Cloud castle. The cabinet of ebony, ivory, alabaster and gilded bronze comes from the Medici-period furnishings. It is a successful re-adaptation of some of the oldest pieces that belonged to Cardinal Leopold (the small ivory sculptures and the frontal relief), done by the Grand Ducal workshops, under the direction of Giovan Battista Foggini, in 1704. Vittorio Emanuele II of Savoy commissioned the impressive nineteenth-century romantic Tuscan paintings on the walls.

## The Queen's Bedroom

First known as Ferdinando di' Medici's Games Room, the Queen's Bedroom was decorated for Margherita of Savoy with furniture from various periods. The room contains an incredible mixture of objects and furnishings that we may find a little excessive but that are fully reflective of late nineteenth-century neo-baroque and neo-classical taste. Thus the yellow and blue silk brocatelle wallcoverings, made in France, harmonise with the large canopied bed, the chaise longue and the small armchair covered in blue silk made in Italy at the end of the nineteenth century. Beside the bed, the ebony prie-dieu and the gilded bronzes, decorated with inlaid semi-precious stones, were made by the Grand Ducal workshops, under the direction of Leonard van der Vine (1687). The stoup placed above the bed was made by the same Grand Ducal workshops on the basis of drawings made by Giovan Battista Foggini, while the chairs, armchairs and the divan are in the neo-classical style and were made in 1806. There is also a touch of chinoiserie alongside all the other furnishings of varying origins: the carved and lacquered screen was made in China in the nineteenth century, and the four seventieth-eighteenth century Chinese vases, is from the Qing Dynasty.

*View of the Queen's Bedroom and the Oval Drawing Room, Queen's Apartment.*

## Oval Room

The last two rooms in the Queen's Apartment were added between 1763 and 1765 for Grand Duchess Maria Luisa, wife of Peter Leopold of Lorraine. The room, created by Ignazio Pellegrini, is covered with beautiful wallcoverings and curtains of embroidered silk with a white background and a Chinese design, made in Florence between 1780 and 1783. The room's refined appearance is accentuated by the ceiling's coloured stuccowork by F. Visetti and by the rococo fireplace in Spanish brocatelle.

## The Round Room

The Round Room, the second room designed by Pellegrini, was first decorated ten years later by Domenico Ruschi with white and gold stuccowork on the walls, and by Giuliano Traballesi with the fresco in the centre of the ceiling representing *The Three Graces*, a favourite neo-classical theme. The original, simple, Lorraine-period furnishings, which consisted of a series of six divans, made by Lorenzo Dolci (1775) and placed along the walls, were supplemented with numerous Italian and French armchairs, chairs and small tables, used by Margherita of Savoy and her ladies for their conversation, reading, and inevitable "lady's tasks".

*View of the King's Bedroom, King's Apartment.*

## The King's Apartment
### The King's Bedroom

The rooms comprising the King's Apartment are more austerely furnished, although amidst an abundance of the oldest handmade articles inherited from the Medici and the Lorraines. The first room, the King's Bedroom, contains beautiful furniture in the imperial style and a number of masterpieces from the seventeenth-century, Medici Grand Ducal workshops, such as the stoup and the prie-dieu, commissioned by Cosimo II for his daughter Anna Maria Luisa and designed by Giovan Battista Foggini. The refined silk lampas wallcoverings with a yellow background were acquired by Ferdinando III of Lorraine during his exile in France and brought to the Pitti when he was repatriated in 1814. The canopy bed, on the other hand, was originally made for the Lorraines by Florentine artisans at the end of eighteenth century and the King of the House of Savoy added the Savoy coat-of-arms as a sign of new ownership.

*View of the King's Studio, King's Apartment.*

## The King's Studio

Here, as well, the oldest furnishings were kept, such as the superbly carved consoles by Giovan Battista Dolci (1765) and the refined rococo mirrors, while the writing desk with its "bois de violette" veneer, rosewood and chased and gilded bronze, an exquisite piece made by Pierre Migeon (ca. 1750), had belonged to the Duchess of Parma, who had acquired it in Paris. The Savoys, evidently impressed with the piece's workmanship, brought it to Florence from Parma in 1868, along with the rare and exquisite ebony and ivory cabinet in "Beidermeier" style, taken from Bologna.

## The Red Room

The Red Room, on the other hand, bears the stamp of neo-baroque taste, in the more modern furnishings acquired by Vittorio Emanuele at the 1861 Italian World's Fair, with the intention of maintaining and confirming the evident continuity of style already manifest in the rooms of the Pitti Palace. The pair of French-made chairs, covered in red damask, are older (1750) and are attributed to the Parisian "carpenters" Tilliard and Foliot. Older still is the chased and gilded bronze clock by Galle e Thomas (1812?), inherited from the brief but intense reign of Elisa Baciocchi, Grand Duchess of Tuscany.

# Tapestry Apartments

Fausta Navarro

The room that leads to the Tapestry Apartment was originally used as an antechamber to the King's Apartment. Vittorio Emanuele had this room re-decorated as well, making some very particular choices. For example, he acquired Francesco Saverio Altamura's *The Good Old Days* at the 1861 World's Fair. The painting is an amiable and ironic reflection on the traditionalism of previous generations, and yet another sign of the sovereign's faith in progress and in the future.

After having passed through the large Bona Room – frescoed by Bernardino Poccetti between 1608 and 1609 with *Stories of the War Against the Turks*, one of which, *The Conquest of the City of Bona*, gives its name to the room – one enters the Tapestry Apartment.

Ferdinando I de' Medici, who had the apartment built, intended it for the women of the Medici family. It was later also used to host high-ranking guests, as a result of which it became known as the "Cardinals' and Foreigner Princes' Quarters".

The rooms' ceiling decorations are among the oldest in the palace. They were commissioned by Ferdinando I de' Medici, to whom is owed the choice of the refined iconographic design. The most important mannerist painters of the early years of the seventeenth century worked on the project, including Ludovico Cigoli, Domenico Passignano, Cristofano Allori and Bernardino Poccetti. They depicted the allegorical figure of one of the Virtues in the centre of each ceiling, surrounding the image with a decoration of polychrome stuccowork and grotesqueries. On the ceiling of the first room, Cristofano Allori created *Hope*, while the *Charity* in the second room was entrusted to Cigoli. It is not known with certainty which artist is responsible for *Justice*, in the Pope's Bedroom. Passignano did the frescoes of the *Prudence* figures in the *Garden Maidens'* Room, as well as *Temperance* in the Bona antechamber. As was done in other parts of the palace, the rooms in this apartment have been set up so as to look the way the Savoys had arranged them during the nineteenth and at the beginning of the twentieth centuries. A number of pieces that are evidence of the Savoys' particular and very eclectic taste have been added, such as the veneered table inlaid with tortoiseshell and mother of pearl and decorated with chinoiseries, or the Mexican vases, now among the Medici Treasures, that were in the first room. On the other hand, the tapestries hung by the Medici on the walls of each room, and left there by the Lorraines, have been kept as they were, such as the seventeenth-century tapestries from the Royal Gobelins Factory in the *Hope* Room, which were based on cartoons by Charles Le Brun and depict *Earth*, *Water* and *Fire*. The next room, the *Charity* room, is also decorated with three Gobelins tapestries, showing *Stories from the Iliad*, based on cartoons by J.B. Deshais (1729 – 1765), as well as with eighteenth-century Florentine tapestries with allegorical figures of *Neptune (Water)* and *Juno (Air),* based on cartoons by G.C. Sagrestani. In the room given to Pope Pius IX in 1854 during his visit to the Tuscan sovereigns, and hence known as the Pope's Bedroom, the decoration is more rich and magnificent, partly due to the presence of the monumen-

On the previous page:
*View of the Charity Room.*

*View of the Pope's Bedroom.*

tal carved and gilded bed, with four female half-figures on the sides and a canopy, the latter a nineteenth-century reconstruction done by court artisans using older pieces. Here, too, the wall tapestries have a dominating presence, such as the *Madonna with Cat* from a painting by Federico Barocci and woven by the French artist Pierre Févère (1664), and the *Death of Cleopatra*, made in Brussels in the seventeenth century, and, beside the bed, in the beautiful frame by Petitot, the *Crucifix*, based on cartoons by J.B. Van Loo, from the Royal Gobelins Factory, dated 1751.

The next room is one of the most suggestive in the palace. It originally consisted of an arcade, open to the Pages' Courtyard and facing the exquisite camellia garden. It was frescoed by Alessandro Allori and his workshop in 1588, as part of the work ordered by Ferdinando I for the Medici ladies' apartments. The three walls of the arcade, enclosed in the nineteenth century with three large windows, are decorated with river landscapes, animals and small figures within sceno-

*Alessandro Allori, overall view and details of the Arcade vault.*

graphic, architectonic perspectives. The ceiling vault, on the other hand, is frescoed with six female figures engaged in domestic tasks and in making their toilet. In the centre, the Medici coat-of-arms surmounted with a cardinal's hat, is a reference to the commissioning of the work by Ferdinando I in 1588, the year before his marriage to Christine of Lorraine, when he was still a cardinal.

The next room takes its name from its series of three eighteenth-century tapestries from the Royal Gobelins Factory, with the famous theme of the *Garden Maidens*. The mood of refined country life given to the room by the tapestries is complemented by the beautiful chandelier of blown Murano glass, decorated with tulips

*View of the Garden Maiden's Room.*

and other flowers, motifs that also appear in the veneered and inlaid wooden bureau, made by the Grand Ducal workshops in the first quarter of the eighteenth century, currently in the Porcelain Museum. The last room, the *Temperance* Room, is decorated with tapestries portraying *Stories of St John the Baptist*, based on frescoes by Andrea del Sarto in the Scalzo Cloister and woven by Pierre Févère in the seventeenth century. Savoyard taste is recognisable in the touch of neo-baroque magnificence in the beautiful carved and gilded consoles and in the divan, upholstered with red damask, with its elegantly curving back and arms, inspired by divans carved by Thomas Chippendale in the middle of the eighteenth century.

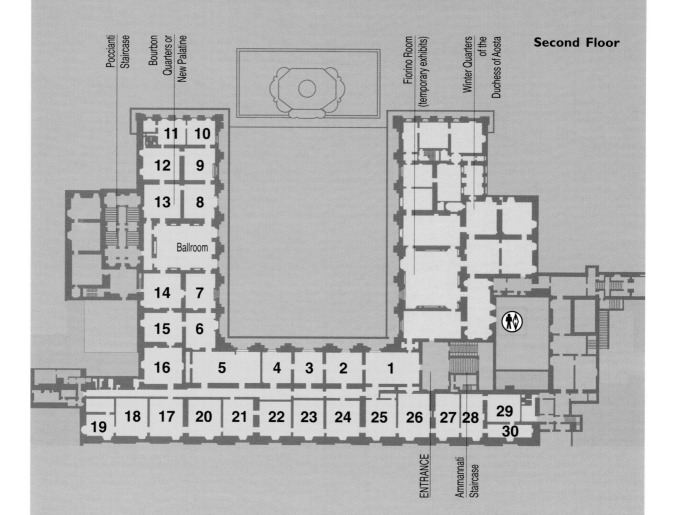

**Second Floor**

Poccianti Staircase

Bourbon Quarters or New Palatine

Fiorino Room (temporary exhibits)

Winter Quarters of the Duchess of Aosta

| 11 | 10 |
| 12 | 9 |
| 13 | 8 |

Ballroom

| 14 | 7 |
| 15 | 6 |

16 5 4 3 2 1

19 18 17 20 21 22 23 24 25 26 27 28 29 30

ENTRANCE

Ammannati Staircase

# Modern Art Gallery

Carlo Sisi

## The birth of a museum

The history of the Gallery begins in about 1748, when the grand duke Pietro Leopoldo of Lorraine began the remodelling of the Florentine Academy, establishing a Modern Art Gallery in its interior (next to the classical art collection made up of works once suppressed by ecclesiastical bans). The gallery was to contain the paintings and sculptures that received awards in academic competitions, as well as entries in the *pensionato artistico* contests. In those same years, due to the need to decorate Pitti Palace, works of art were being collecting by order of the grand duke. By the middle of the 19th century, they were already so numerous that was necessary to transfer many of them to the Crocetta Palace (which today houses the Archaeological Museum), which was thus destined, in these early years, to become the new Modern Art Museum. The project was interrupted due to the expulsion of the Lorraine in 1850, but the unification government hastened to provide an official home for the major Florentine collections of modern art. A debate was in fact underway at the time regarding the position of the Academy of Fine Arts as a scholastic institution and the possibility of establishing a museum there. In con-

comitance with the reform of 1867, all the works of the Lorraine collections were thus brought together in the Modern Gallery of the Academy, as the new institute came to be called, while those more linked to pedagogy were destined for the school.

As had already occurred during the Lorraine era, the House of Savoy also became interested in acquiring modern works of art for the apartments of Pitti Palace. This was especially true of Vittorio Emanuele II, who enlarged the collections with paintings, sculptures and decorations that had inspired admiration during the exhibits of the time, beginning with the 1861 World Fair in Florence celebrating the Unification of Italy. To supplement the major collections of the Academy and the Savoys, towards the century's end, a policy of acquisitions was begun by the Florence City Council, which in 1867 took possession of a collection of *macchiaioli* paintings that had belonged to Diego Martelli. It was then that the idea was advanced of uniting the city's modern art collections. The aim was to historically consolidate the art of the recent past with the important contributions of the *macchiaioli* and works of national contemporary art, whose acquisition had been under the guidance of an active municipal commission between 1901 and 1910. Thus, in 1914 the Italian State and the Florence City Council reached an agreement on the administration of the nascent Modern Art Gallery, in which the various collections would be brought together, irrespective of their ownership (state or municipal). The convention moreover set up a specific Commission of experts to oversee acquisitions. With regards to physical site, the hypothesis emerged of locating the Gallery in Pitti Palace, an idea that was realised in 1922, when the royal family vacated the second-floor apartments.

The first lay-out was inaugurated in 1924 and, as described by Jahn Rusconi in his *Guida* to the museum published in 1934, the artistic itinerary favoured the most recent aspects of art, beginning with the *macchiaioli,* thereby foregoing the figurative documents of neo-classicism and romanticism. From then up to the 1970s, the Gallery would experience a broad expansion, mainly through addition of 20th-century collections. The art housed in the Gallery today is the result of the regular purchases of the Commission in the period between the two world wars, the continuous stream of works destined by statute to the Gallery, as well as those having received the contemporary art awards of the annual Fiorino exhibit. However its resources are far from static. Still today, the incessant flow of loans and donations is testament to the vital presence of the Modern Art Gallery within Florence's museum system.

*Luigi Catani,* A classroom of the University of Science, Room 11

*Luigi Catani,* Presentation of the discovery of the telescope in Venice, Room 11.

## The visit

The current museum collection comprises thirty rooms that trace a wide chronological arc: from the time of Pietro Leopoldo up to the First World War. The tour, organised in chronological order and by historical-topical category, attempts to furnish the visitor with a clear view of the histories of the various core collections and enable a correct reading of the diverse atmospheres, marked as they are by the personal tastes of the royal families alternating in their reigns. These comprise the second-floor rooms of Pitti Palace which have been passed on to us in their original Lorraine arrangement, attributed mainly to Pasquale Poccianti, except for rooms 14, 15 and 16, in which the roofs decorated in the time of Ferdinando II de' Medici are still conserved. The *suite* on the facade side (rooms 17-25) was called the "District of the Archduchesses", while the rooms that give on to the patio up to the Ballroom constituted the "New District" (rooms 1-7), which led to the apartment called the "Bourbon or New Palatine" (rooms 8-13). The roofs of some of these rooms were decorated during the Restoration by some of Tuscany's major artists: Giorgio Berti, *Cincinnatus receiving the Roman Senate* (room 7); Niccola Monti, *The Victory of the True Cross* (room 8); Gaspare Martellini, *Tu Marcellus eris* (room 9); Luigi Catani, *Facts and personages of Philosophy and Science* (rooms 10-11); Giuseppe Bezzuoli, *Alessandro in Apelle's study* (room 12); Antonio Luzzi, *Achilles brought by Tetis to Chiron the Centaur* (room 13).

## Room 1
### Aspects of neo-classicism in Tuscany

*With the remodelling of the Fine Arts Academy initiated by Pietro Leopoldo in 1784, Florence was endowed with an institute of artistic instruction modernised according to the standards of international neo-classicism and as renowned as those of Vienna or Milan, likewise of Habsburg origin. It is in this environment, that late Baroque aesthetics are to be transcended in Tuscany, thanks to the teachings, amongst others, of Santi Pacini and Pietro Pedroni; to the presence of Pompeo Batoni; to the 'classicising' tastes of Francesco Carradori and Stefano Ricci; and to the renewed figurative culture underlying the grand duke's acquisition of Gaspare Landi's paintings and some foresighted commissions, such as the famous statue,* Abandoned Psyche *that Medici Lenzoni charged to Pietro Tenerani, magisterially ratifying the neo-classical primacy of ideal beauty and a style that was to find success throughout all spheres of art even during the years of the Restoration.*

PIETRO TENERANI
*Abandoned Psyche*
Marble, h. 118 cm

This is the first marble version made from the mould, today in the "Museo di Roma", carried out between 1816 and 1817 and later reproduced with some variation by Tenerani himself on commission for Italian and foreign collectors. The Florentine version belonged to the house of Medici Lenzoni, where it earned the admiration of Niccolini, Leopardi and Lorenzo Bartolini, that is to say, the *élite* of classical romanticism, who probably saw the work as the highest translation of those concepts that, in literature as well as art, were undermining the rigid canons of neo-classicism. Already from the second decade of the century, we begin to see the integration of more flexible observations on nature and its multiple manifestations, along the lines of the incipient aesthetics of Purism.

79

## POMPEO GIROLAMO BATONI
### Hercules at the crossroads
Oil on canvas, 93.5 × 73 cm

This painting, together with its companion piece, *The child Hercules choking a serpent,* was acquired specifically for Pitti Palace by grand duke Ferdinando III in 1818. Commissioned by the Gerini family in 1740 and carried out in 1742, it represents a elegant example of the ongoing shift from the rococo style to the formal order of neo-classicism, confirming Batoni as the Tuscan founder of the classicist trends that characterise, even in Florence, the figurative culture of the first decades of the 19th Century. In fact, it was by consciousness of this modernity, that the grand duke reserved the works of this Luccan painter for the Palace decorations, rather than for the rooms of the Royal Gallery, thus acknowledging Batoni's eminent role in the ongoing evolution of art in its passage from 18th-century style and grace to the recovery of classical methodology.

## PIETRO BENVENUTI
### The oath of the Saxons to Napoleon
Oil on canvas, 380 × 480 cm

The painting was commissioned by order of the Napoleonic Civil List probably after a journey by Benvenuti to Paris in 1809. It was destined for the Palace of Versailles along with other paintings that Napoleon had charged to major European artists in celebration of his own military feats. In 1812 it was exhibited in the Gallery of the Academy of Fine Arts in Florence before being sent to France. Without a doubt the sensational aspect of the painting is the night-lighting effect that Benvenuti choose to impart dramatic elements to the scene which could temper the encomiastic theme and, at the same time, testify to the artist's command of the pre-romantic aspects of contemporary figurative culture. In 1815 the grand duke Ferdinando III would send Benvenuti to Paris as emissary to reclaim the works of Tuscan art that the French had requisitioned. It was on this occasion that the painting was returned and, after changing hands a number of times, was acquired by the Italian state in 1914.

### Room 2
### Primacy of French Art between the Revolution and the Empire

*The occupation of Florence by Napoleon's troops in 1807, and the advent of the Grand Duchy of Elisa Baciocchi were political episodes of great moment, affecting the development of the arts in Tuscany, as well. The French court that had settled in Pitti Palace immediately revealed their sensitivity and propensity to promoting taste, assigning commissions in all branches of the arts. The indisputable leaders of this brief but prolific period were Pietro Benvenuti, who Elisa named director of the Academy of Fine Arts, the French painters – Boguet, Gauffier, Fabre and Gagneraux – who emigrated from Rome at the end of the 18th Century, and Antonio Canova, pride of the court, whose contributions to the Palace collection included the bust of* Calliope *and the* Italian Venus, *sculpted in order to compensate the Florentines for the loss of the de' Medici collection transferred to France. In order to celebrate this 'Athens of Italy', the selfsame Benvenuti executed the large painting of* Elisa amongst the artists, *destined for Versailles and thanks to which we can document, not only the presence of these illustrious personages, but also the elegance of the interior decoration which the French had remodelled, introducing to Pitti Palace notable examples of Empire furniture.*

## ANTONIO CANOVA
*Calliope*
Marble, h. 46 cm

This idealised head was sculpted in 1812, commissioned by Giovanni Rosini who, as testified to by Isabella Teotochi Albrizzi, kept it on display in his house in Pisa in a small temple consecrated to the fine arts, an emblem of classicist idealism to which the man of letters had dedicated his life's work. The sculpture was acquired in 1855 by the director of the Royal Gallery of Florence, who exchanged it with the bust of Rosini that Tenerani had sculpted at the express request of his son, and sent to the Modern Gallery of the Academy, whence it would later be transferred to Pitti Palace. The refined execution of the head, with the pliant tenderness and elegant varieties in the rendering of the hair and ribbon crossing the forehead is proof of Canova's authorship and a valid argument in allowing identification of the work as the "Muse" often referred to in the sculptor's correspondence with Rosini and others.

## LOUIS GAUFFIER
*Self-portrait with his wife and two children*
Oil on canvas, 72.5 × 54.5 cm

The artist resolved the theme as a group of whole figures within a landscape of evident classicist suggestion continuing in the style of the valued *conversation pièce* in demand with the bourgeois commissions of those years. The background, with the temple and high marble base on which leans Gauffier's wife, Paolina Chatillon – also his pupil and, according to records at Pitti, author of artist's figure that appears to the right – confirms the painter's adhesion to neoclassical canons. Gauffier, well-known mainly for his compositions of the historical and mythological genre, had lived in Villa Medici and was forced to flee to Florence during the anti-French uprisings.

## Room 3

### Iconography of pre-unification Tuscan dynasties: the Habsburg-Lorraine, the Bourbons of Lucca, Maria Beatrice d'Este, Duchess of Massa

*The paintings, sculptures and objects that have remained in the decorations and the storeroom of Pitti Palace allow us today to journey through the early 19th-century succession of dynasties up to the government of Tuscany. We can thus trace the evolution of trends in taste and the principles of art determined by the various commissions carried out for the Palace, as the rooms were modernised with prestigious European furniture and decorations. The portraits of the sovereigns, from Pietro Leopoldo to Ferdinando III, from Napoleon to the queen of Etruria, from Elisa Baciocchi to Leopoldo II, all recall the various phases of Florentine history between the French Revolution and the Unification of Italy, while the decorations of priceless execution testify to the attention that those taking over the city's government had devoted to progress.*

### FRANÇOIS-XAVIER FABRE

#### Portrait of Maria Luisa of Bourbon, Queen of Etruria
Oil on canvas, 58 × 45.5 cm

Regent of the Grand Duchy of Tuscany on behalf of her son from 1803 to 1807, the 'infanta' Maria Luisa of Bourbon is depicted by Fabre with the insignias and jewels for which the queen is said to have nurtured an maniacal passion. The painting demonstrates the artist's observance of neo-classical cannons and was executed as a study for the official portrait of the Bourbon family carried out between 1801 and 1804. A refugee with other French citizens in Florence in 1793 after the Roman rebellions, here the painter became acquainted with the countess d'Albany and eventually court artist for Elisa Baciocchi. Fabre distinguished himself mainly as a portrait artist, though Lord Bristol provided him with the occasion to try his hand at the historical genre, charging him, in 1800, with *Filottete* and the *Judgement of Salomon*.

### GALLERY OF WORKS

AFTER DESIGN OF CARLO CARLIERI

#### Table centrepiece
1807-16
Lapislazuli with chalcedony mosaics, pearls and gilded bronze ornamentation, 298 × 73 cm

It was Maria Luisa of Bourbon who in 1807 initiated the creation of this magnificent ornament, entrusting its execution to the extraordinary skills of artisans then active at the Grand Duchy's Gallery of Works. The exquisite materials, such as the lapislazuli, were set in an original decoration containing more than a thousand inlaid pearls. At its inception, the work was destined for Napoleon, whose initials were inscribed in a crown of laurel in the central area of the piece, as appears in a first draft of the work by Carlo Carlieri. After being sent to France by Elisa Baciocchi, this so-called *dessert* was returned to Ferdinando III who, in 1816 had the work completed, ordering all signs of Napoleon to be eliminated and adding the chiselled bronze work by Andrea Fondelli.

## Room 4

### The Demidoff in Florence and the art of the Restoration

*In the years of the Restoration, the presence of the Demidoff family in Florence had profound influences on the cultural balance of the city. The lifestyle that the Russian princes led in the spectacular residence of San Donato was almost a challenge to the Tuscan aristocrats and the court of the Grand Duchy itself. The mindfulness that they demonstrated to all genres of art was unrivalled, a fact attested to by the extraordinary breadth of their collections. Theirs is also the merit of having fostered in Tuscany awareness of French historical painting – Ingres, Delacroix, Delaroche – and providing impetus to the development of the applied arts, especially the historicist furnishings of Falcini and Frullini. Perhaps their most important contributions are the many works they commissioned to Lorenzo Bartolini and Giuseppe Bezzuoli, who in those years represented the acme of the new poetics of romanticism.*

### ARY SCHEFFER
#### *Portrait of the princess Matilde Bonaparte Demidoff*
Oil on canvas, 176 × 89.5 cm

From the collection of the Demidoff princes that was kept on display in the villa of San Donato and later in Pratolino, the painting was donated by Paolo Karageorgevich to the Florentine Galleries in 1969. Princess Matilde (1820-1904), who was educated in Rome and Florence, married Anatolio Demidoff in 1840 and left him in 1846 in order to go and live in Paris, where during the time of Napoleon III she would kept the most frequented drawing-room in the capital. Scheffer painted this portrait in 1844, keeping well in mind, in both its design and composition, the famous models of Ingres. It was framed only later by the Pacetti brothers in Florence, who demonstrated great skill in engraving the frame's ornamental motif in the form of laurels.

### LORENZO BARTOLINI
#### *Model of the monument to Nicola Demidoff*
Marble, h. 200 cm

This is the model of the monument that Anatolio and his brother Paolo wished to erect to their Father, Nicola along the Lungarno alle Grazie, near the public institutes sponsored by the family – an act of philanthropy very much appreciated by the moderate Tuscans and the Vieusseux Cabinet. Exhibited in Paris in 1840, it was subsequently sent to the villa of San Donato, and finally to the Villa Pratolino when the property was acquired by the Demidoff in 1872. The allegory of the monument, alluding to the moral qualities of Nicola and his civic and cultural generosity, is represented by the statues of the pedestal, sculpted with the natural grace that characterises the stage of transition from neo-classical abstraction to the uneasy truths of Purism.

## GIUSEPPE BEZZUOLI

### Christ borne to the Sepulchre
Oil on canvas, 99 × 122 cm

A very suggestive example of how Bezzuoli translated his own knowledge of 16th and 17th-century painting into a modern style. The painting makes reference to the heroic landscape of the classicist tradition of Lorrain and Poussin, but accentuates the contrasting effects of light and shadow as required by the canons of the sublime romantic. Executed in about 1843, the work was admired for the harmonious consonance between the natural spectacle and the funereal epilogue to Christ's life, which was a way of recognising Bezzuoli's ability to merge the new naturalist poetics with his background as a pre-eminent historical painter.

## Room 5

### Romantic painting of historical genre

*"Finally the Venuses, Adonises, Cupids, Minervas, Psyches and Ganymides, the venerable and frightening beards of Jupiter and Pluto, all the mad and obscene adventures of mythology have been banished from sensible 19th-century painting." Thus wrote Defendente Sacchi in 1830 in celebration of the painting of Hayez representing the generous feats of medieval and renaissance heroes, facts of the fatherland's history that could foster new passions and new fancies in romantic man. This is precisely the idea of the progress of art that was embodied in the historical genre painting practised at the Academy for artists, such as the Sabatelli or Giuseppe Bezzuoli – artists who had in fact been formed during the crisis of neo-classicism. They were convinced that, in order to overcome the canons imposed by antiquated models, it was necessary, not only to invoke the themes of modern history, but to make them more attractive by reclaiming the grand pictorial examples of 16th and 17th-century Italian art, considered the most appropriate for expression of sublime concepts and 'natural' passions.*

## GIUSEPPE BEZZUOLI

### Carlo VIII entering Florence
Oil on canvas, 290 × 356 cm

Commissioned by the grand duke in 1827, the painting was finished in 1829. The composition was inspired by the passage recounting the entrance of Carlo VIII into Florence to be found in the *Histories of the city of Florence* by Jacopo Nardi (1535). The painter however stoops to some rather pathetic suggestions – for example, in concealing the distress and anger of some of its personages – as well as to some rather cautious nationalist allusions – by placing at the painting's right the highest representatives of the opposition to imperial aims (Capponi, Savonarola, Baccio Valori and Macchiavelli). Received as the most beautiful creation "of the modern Italians", the painting would constitute the fundamental point of reference for the nascent painting of historical genre, demonstrating how a careful study of 17th-century naturalism could contribute to rendering the principle of truth more flexible, and the expression of feelings, more touching.

### *The two Foscari*
Oil on canvas, 121 × 167.5 cm

The painting was carried out in Milan around 1852 and acquired in 1854 by Andrea Maffei who donated it to the Royal Galleries of Florence in 1886. Its 'political' subject was taken from Daru's edition of the *History of the Venetian Republic* (1826). However, the figurative transposition of the subject, rich in tragic and pathetic elements, is due Byron's famous drama *The two Foscari,* which Hayez illustrates through recourse to scenographic expedients providing a spectacular result and an equally captivating painting style, with its noble references to the great Venetian tradition of the 16th Century.

AMOS CASSIOLI
### *The battle of Legnano*
Oil on canvas, 370 × 640 cm

Cassioli entered this painting in the Ricasoli Competition decreed by the Provisional Government of Tuscany on September 23, 1859 under the section "historical paintings", which called for the execution of paintings depicting glorious episodes of ancient and modern Italian history. The painting was finished only at the end of 1870, receiving nevertheless great acclaim, even during its execution, from the panel of judges, who appreciated both the excellence of the historical documentation and the novelty of the style, modernised in the grand manner of contemporary French painting without however omitting the 'truths' introduced into historical painting by the examples of the Neapolitan, Domenico Morelli, who was very highly esteemed in Tuscany.

## Room 6

### Inquiry into 'the real' between Florence and Naples

*Just after mid-century, the romantic canons linked to the composition of historical painting were overcome and began to give way to impassioned inquiry, both cognitive and emotional, into the diverse aspects of Nature and the events of contemporary history – the first fertile domain of the debate conducted by the generation of* macchiaioli *painters. In fact, around 1856 new ideas on the principle of truth and reality converged upon Florence, brought mainly by Domenico Morelli and Saverio Altamura, who just back from Paris, proclaimed the urgent need for experimentation outside the constricting limits of artistic genres. The works of Cabianca and Borrani serve as good examples of the transition from constrained art to the representation of reality through well–matched luminous contrasts: a compositional method which in these years was also common to the academic, Stefano Ussi, who uses it mainly in sketches and highly intimate portraits, as well as Giovanni Fattori, who in tackling the then fashionable themes of history, avoids commemorative tones thanks to an atmospheric painting, in poetic harmony with the anti-heroic mundanity of the topics dealt with.*

GIUSEPPE ABBATI
*Cloister*
Oil on cardboard, 19.3 × 25.2 cm

It is one of the works that Abbati, who arrived in Florence in late 1860, painted while directly involved with the artistic atmosphere of Caffè Michelangelo, especially the works of D'Ancona and Sernesi, aimed at the study of volume and light. In this regard, Diego Martelli wrote that the painter who practised in the cloisters of Santa Croce "where, as the monument was being restored at the time, many multi-coloured marble masses were produced, offering the observant student the advantages of finding himself before masses of very well-defined shapes, definite contrasts and almost elementary colours and chiaroscuro".

VINCENZO CABIANCA
*The Florentine storytellers*
Oil on canvas, 76 × 100 cm

Displayed at the Italian Fair of 1861, where it was acquired by Vittorio Emanuele II, the painting, romantic only in part, evokes the most nostalgic and lyrical aspects of medieval civilisation. Although approximating the canons of historical genre in the choice of topic and some of its formal aspects, this work by Cabianca, dated 1861, in fact reveals clear evidence of his experimentation with colour and light that demonstrates a direct knowledge of the results simultaneously attained by the Neapolitans (mainly Morelli and Altamura) in the study and rendering of truth, thus acquiring representational autonomy from the ethical and didactic values of the art of romanticism.

## ODOARDO BORRANI
*Middle Age*
Oil on canvas, 145 × 121 cm

This painting, dated 1864, is a nostalgic return to Medieval Tuscany concentrated in an episode of a city feud with the sunlit hills of San Miniato in the background. Trained at the school of Gaetano Bianchi and, therefore, in the cult of fresco painting of the 14th and 15th Centuries, here Borrani evokes a scene of the past – which in those years could find analogies in the pre-Raphaelite revivals – with figurative devices modernised according to the new vision of the 'macchia'. The work demonstrates how it was possible to bring about the union of avant-garde poetics with the noble academic tradition still represented by the historical painting of Giuseppe Bezzuoli.

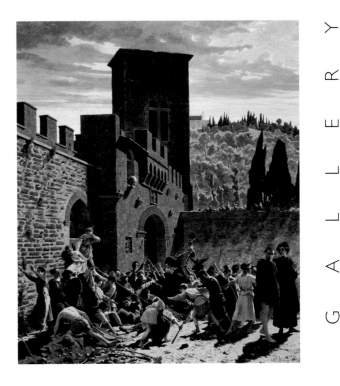

### ROOM 7
Antonio Ciseri and the commemorative portrait

*When Antonio Ciseri organised a exhibit of the portraits from his study on Via delle Belle Donne in 1871, the number of visitors was such that entrance to the show had to be temporarily suspended in order to avoid dangerous overcrowding – an obvious indication of the fame enjoyed by the artist, especially in official cultural circles. Ciseri championed the primacy of design and form, that while excluding spontaneous naturalism, adhered to reality, appealing, like the French after Ingres, to the rigorous devices of analogy. Renowned for his ability to fix physiognomy in drawing, Ciseri's portraits instead resort to rendition through synthetic structures and the slow and meticulous study of form and figure, which is normally made to stand out from an abstract background – a true plane of pose – thus avoiding distraction from the focus on the physiology and temperament of the personage depicted. These qualities of style and introspection earned the artist important commissions and made him the unquestioned master of the official or commemorative portrait, in antithesis to the naturalistic studies of the latter half of the 19th Century.*

ANTONIO CISERI
*Portrait of Giovanni Dupré*
Oil on canvas, 67 × 54 cm

The Florentine Galleries commissioned the painting, completed in 1885, to Ciseri for the portrait collection of the Uffizi shortly after the death of the famous sculptor (1882). A copy of the portrait carried out for the Dupré family in 1868, the painting reveals Ciseri's exceptional abilities in portraiture, able to unify as a whole the observation of the real – often filtered through the use of new 'photographic' techniques – with coherent control of form, sustained by the imposing drawing that had its origins in the models of Ingres and his French pupils.

## Raffaello Sorbi

### Portrait of the sculptor Emilio Zocchi
Oil on canvas, 51.5 × 39 cm

Dedicated to his sculptor friend, in 1868 Sorbi signed this portrait demonstrating the influence that the teachings of Ciseri still had on the young painter. It also illustrates his going beyond the maestro's formal abstraction in favour of a more direct expression of feelings. These are the years when Florence sees animated discussion of the topics of truth and the need to overcome academic canons through experimentation of new techniques of vision. These are the years that mark the first important stages of Sorbi's career, directed mainly toward historical genre painting, but also able to depict fresh 'snapshots', which were to be admired by Telemaco Signorini, amongst others.

## Ballroom

*Part of the quarters called the "Bourbon" or the "New Palatine" the Ballroom was designed by Pasquale Poccianti around 1825, though never fully brought to completion, as can be surmised by observing the incomplete ornamental particulars of the roof. Today it contains a group of statues by Aristodemo Costoli, Giovanni Dupré, Odoardo Fantacchiotti and Pio Fedi, forming a sculptural coterie of the first half of the 19th Century in Tuscany.*

## Pio Fedi

### Saint Sebastian
Plaster, h. 163 cm

Sent from Rome as an entry in the contest for the *pensionato artistico*, it was exhibited in the Academy of Florence in 1844, where it commanded a certain amount of attention on the part of critics for the unexpected synthesis of classical and renaissance references and the modern sensibility of its depiction of reality. The favourable reception of the work, fostered by contemporary attention to the naturalistic trends in art determining the surpassing of the purist culture in which the same Fedi had been formed, occasioned several commissions for the sculptor, amongst which the important duty of realising the statues of Nicola Pisano and Andrea Cesalpino for the loggia of the Uffizi.

## Giovanni Dupré

### Bacchus of the cryptogam
Marble, h. 115 cm

Acquired by the State in 1974, along with the *Feasting Bacchus* – both from the Mylius palace, later The Rochefoucault of Genova – this marble work is dated 1859 and shows the interest of the Sienese sculptor in the theories which, in France and in the wake of Théophile Gautier, advocated the use of past figurative traditions to carry out evocative and sensual functions. On the other hand, the idea of the work itself had matured through contact with the ancient treasures of Herculano and Pompeii, admired by Dupré during his stay in Naples, financed by the Tuscan grand duke, and reinterpreted here as an elegant formal means for representing a modern allegory.

## Room 8
### Portraits of the era of Florence the capital

*The graceful posture of many of the portraits painted after the second half of the 19th Century points out how, beginning in the 60s, even portraiture responded to the appeal of the renewing influences coming mainly from France. The refined formal balance that purist art had established in order to portray the moderation and civility of the main characters of the bourgeois restoration is shaken by the emergence of more direct feelings that infuse the portrait with the attributes of a 'snapshot'. The artist now captures and fixes as absolutes the gestures and expressions of a particularly charming biography. Thus, in the post-unification years, the formal austerity of Antonio Ciseri's commemorative portraits coexists with the sensitive sprightliness of the noblewoman Morrocchi di Puccinelli, with Cassioli's allusions to the portraiture of Degas, and with the solemn humanity of Giovanni Fattori's portraits – all indications of the experience of similar aesthetic adventures, in a manner of speaking, outside the* atelier.

### ANTONIO PUCCINELLI
**Portrait of the noblewoman Morrocchi**
Oil on canvas, 104 × 86 cm

This portrait, from between 1855 and 1860, is the maximum expression of the 'Ingres School', initiated by Luigi Mussini in mid-century and then carried on by Luigi Pollastrini and Antonio Ciseri, converting it into the most modern trend of Tuscan painting just prior to the advent of the *macchiaioli*. The portrait reveals in both its execution and accomplished form, what Ingres had adopted to idealise the main personages of France in the time of Napoleon III – the way to arrive at a renewal of academic canons, affording unexpected perspectives even to the portraits of aristocrats and high bourgeois.

### GIOVANNI FATTORI
**Self-portrait**
Oil on canvas, 59 × 47 cm

Executed in 1854, the painting was acquired in 1951 for the Uffizi collection of self-portraits. It represents an important stage in Fattori's early artistic formation, still marked by the style of his teacher, Giuseppe Bezzuoli, and by the years spent in the Academy of Florence studying both ancient and modern art. He was however already on the road to chromatic and formal experimentation that is to anticipate the imminent exercises of the *macchiaioli* on reality and how character and particularities of physiognomy are captured in painting without mediation, all with the purpose of seizing the truest identity.

## Room 9

### The landscape schools of the mid-19th Century: traditional aspects and the Barbizon influence

*During the first months of 1856, one of the most heatedly debated topics in the meetings at Caffè Michelangelo was that of landscape painting, a topic brought to the forefront by the enthusiastic narrations of Stefano De Tivoli and Altamura who, fresh from their Paris visit, mysteriously alluded to the* ton gris *adopted by French landscapers and the use of the black mirror which, by eliminating intermediates colours, allowed the artist to capture light and shadow, that is to say, the* chiaroscuro, *in its entirety, through the* macchia. *The immediate adherence of these painters to the poetics of Barbizon came to influence the first exercises* en plein air *of the so-called school of Staggia, that is, the same environment in which De Tivoli, Carlo and Andrea Markò had overcome the excitement of romantic landscape – still living on in the paintings of Fontanesi – for the sake of a more analytical naturalism, definitively freed from 17th-century models and other characteristic conventions of the genre.*

ANTONIO FONTANESI
*After the rain*
Oil on canvas, 128 × 192 cm

The painting, which won the medal of the Royal Commission at the 1861 Italian World Fair, was acquired by the king for two thousand six-hundred liras, thus becoming part of the dynastic collections of Pitti Palace and thereafter, the Modern Art Gallery. Together with the *Countryside with grazing flock*, also part of the royal collection, this large panorama represents, in contrast with the more lucid and abstract Tuscan vision, an example of landscape painting still strongly permeated by romantic feeling. It is nonetheless quite interesting because of the variety of atmospheric effects whose study was at the core of the ongoing reform of landscape painting in those years.

SERAFINO DE TIVOLI
*A pasture*
Oil on canvas, 102 × 73 cm

Exhibited in the Florentine Promotrice of 1859, it is one of the few paintings from this period remaining to us. It is the period that best documents De Tivoli's efforts to integrate his Parisian experiences with the Tuscan landscape tradition, which received much of its initial impetus from De Tivoli, together with the Markò brothers, Gelati and Ademollo. What impresses even more is the atmospheric effect and the simplicity of the topic, interpreted as a "piece of reality seen from the window" that is to say, described in same way that Martelli would read the paintings of the impressionists.

## Room 10
### The Cristiano Banti collection

*The collection has been in the possession of the Gallery since 1958, after having been bequeathed to Adriana Banti Ghiglia in 1955. It reflects the double personality of its original owner, a painter at first caught up by the French messages of Altamura, Morelli and De Tivoli, but also amateur and patron of unconventional tastes. The painter's works show preferences for the creations of the Roman, Nino Costa, as well as Fontanesi and, more generally, the naturalism of Corot and painters of Barbizon, re-read in light of a more cultured and formally mediated painting, able to introduce rural-life painting to those genres most often commissioned at the request of the bourgeois. The collector's paintings, however, recall to us the grand and cosmopolitanism home of Banti where, amongst others, Boldini would work, comfortably responding to the dictates of the atmosphere with the chic elegance of his portraits.*

**CRISTIANO BANTI**
*The wood-gathering women (The plunderers)*
Oil on canvas, 62.5 × 135.5 cm

The painting can be dated to around 1881 on the basis of a written testimony by Cecioni that surfaced in 1884 and describes the singular topic represented here. These asocial women were frequent in the fields of the Maremma, where they would go, dressed in colourful rags for clothing, to pilfer and poach, thus the epithets, 'plunderer' or 'wrong-doer'. Several sketches by Banti exist on the subject, all designed with the same diagonal arrangement of the scene and furious painting style – almost as an analogy to the theme – that mark this artist's stylistic and conceptual distance from Fattori and his vision of the Maremma swampland, more formally austere and less prone to narrative suggestion.

**GIOVANNI BOLDINI**
*Portrait of Alaide Banti*
Oil on wood-plate, 42.5 × 23 cm

This is one of the numerous portraits of Alaide (here at about the age of twelve) which Boldini painted in Tuscany, feeling the attraction of the elegant climate of Banti's home where he stayed as a guest during his years in Florence (1862-1869). There was even a romance between the painter, already mature and established in Paris, and Banti's daughter. However, the marriage plans were unexpectedly interrupted, leaving the young girl heart-broken. Of all of Boldini's portraits present in the collection, this is without a doubt the most famous and most suitable to documenting the style that he shared with the *macchiaioli*.

## FRANCESCO SAVERIO ALTAMURA
### Profile of a woman
Oil on canvas, 39 × 29 cm

Carried out four years after the painter's arrival in Florence, that is to say in 1852, this portrait likely represents his first wife, Elena, a painter of Greek origin, who he first met in the revolutionary atmosphere of Naples before 1848 and then again in Florence in 1852. In fact, the style of the work coincides with Altamura's Florentine paintings, in which the prevailing a naturalism is still contained within the rigorous execution.

## Room 11
### The Diego Martelli collection

*The painting collection of Diego Martelli, bequeathed to the city council of Florence in 1897, is tangible testimony to the aesthetic trends of the* macchiaioli'*s most attentive interpreter and was born of the affectionate intermingling of friendship, enthusiasm and polemics. The wood-plates of Abbati and Sernesi, the collector-critic's favourites, are along the lines of the works of the 'allied' southerners, Grita and Tedesco, and the sketches of Fattori and Lega, painted for the most part in Castiglioncello, where the hospitality of the Martelli family provided these artists with a tranquil and protracted relationship with nature and the opportunity to share their experiences. The echoes of the discussions in Caffè Michelangelo can be sensed in their preference for outdoor painting from life and the information on French art, to which refer the paintings of Camille Pissarro, acquired by Martelli at the time when the impressionists were subjected to unfortunate critical drubbing, as well as in the evident naturalistic inclinations of the works of Zandomeneghi and Cecioni, that recall the patient pedagogy of Martelli, committed to explaining to his doubtful and reluctant friends that in the greyness of the expositions, impressionist painting represented 'the window', because it was here that the light dominated.*

## SALVATORE GRITA
### The vow against nature
Plaster, h. 65.5 cm

Executed in Florence between 1860 and 1870, this is one of the very few known works of the Sicilian sculptor Salvatore Grita, who arrived in Tuscany during the time of the Risorgimento and was a friend of Martelli and the *macchiaioli*, as well as co-editor with them of the "Gazzetino delle arti del disegno". Later Gritas progressively reduced his sculpting in order to follow his vocation as socialist-leaning polemicist, already implied in this work denouncing the drama of forced ordinations, in a crude, expressive style, comparable to certain pages of the nascent realistic literature.

## FEDERICO ZANDOMENEGHI

### In bed
Oil on canvas, 60.5 × 73.5 cm

The painting was probably made during the same years that Diego Martelli was in Paris (1878-1879), that is, when the Florentine polemicist began his friendly relationships with Monet, Degas, Pissarro and Zola, sending their articles to several Italian newspapers to inform of the novelties emerging from the impressionist school. A fundamental chronicle of the contribution of French naturalism to the ongoing controversy on truth, the painting introduces to the intimist genre practised by the *macchiaioli* a note of great expressive freedom, fed by the literary topics and open-mindedness that many Italians had learned, during their stays Paris, to translate into luminous and evocative painting.

## CAMILLE PISSARRO

### Landscape (The storm's approach)
Oil on canvas, 60 × 74 cm

Pissarro gave this painting, together with another present in the collection, to Martelli so that he would exhibit it in the Florentine Promotrice of 1878. Neither of the paintings was sold, and both were severely criticised by the public and Florentine artists, who could not conceive of painting without a recognisable pictorial and formal design. However, Diego Martelli defended the two paintings, which remained in his collection as manifestos of impressionist painting in Italy, of which the critic was one of the most adamant champions. In fact, he considered it to be absolutely necessary to overcome the reticence of the Academy by admitting French innovation in colour and atmosphere.

**SILVESTRO LEGA**
*A walk in the garden*
Oil on canvas, 35 × 22.5 cm

Possibly the same painting that Lega presented at the 1870 National Exhibition of Parma under the title *Walk*, this painting represents a high-level expression of the spirit and style that distinguishes the Piagentina years, when the observation of truth, reserved to the cultivated and consoling aspects of the countryside near Florence, was translated into clear and composed volumes caressed by a light that is at once natural and abstracting, aiming to accentuate the constructive values of the 'macchia' applied to subjects with strong emotional content.

**FEDERICO ZANDOMENEGHI**
*Honeymoon (Fishing on the Seine)*
Oil on wood-plate, 16 × 29 cm

Martelli sent this painting to Florence, together with two paintings by Pissarro, some dry points by Desboutin and another work of Zandomeneghi, *In bed*, in order to inform the Tuscan public of the most advanced innovations emerging from Paris. Exhibited in the Promotrice of 1878 under the title *Honeymoon*, it caused a sensation for its innovative compositional arrangement and colour, considered to be strident and unreal. However, it demonstrated the painter's knowledge of the aesthetic concepts of Impressionism and what Martelli hoped would be performed in order to renew art.

## Room 12

### The theme of genre from the end of the grand duchy to unification

*The fervent Florentine discussions of the 1850s on the new ways of conceptualising painting, especially that of landscape, did not compromise the public and private fortunes of the other genre subjects. Historical themes, for example, unfettered by their traditional duties of civil education, gave rise to free and airy compositions, in which the philology of history was subordinated to the studied proportions of light and colour. Fragments of contemporary life also survived, receiving numerous commissions in mid-century, including above all the tearful and edifying paintings of Domenico Induno and the conversational scenes represented here in the paintings of Silvestro Lega and Pietro Saltini. The works of Cecioni were counterpoised to these in several ways – these same soothing topics were rendered grotesque and tragic by his introducing the restlessness of the post-unification era into the affective conventions of the Restoration.*

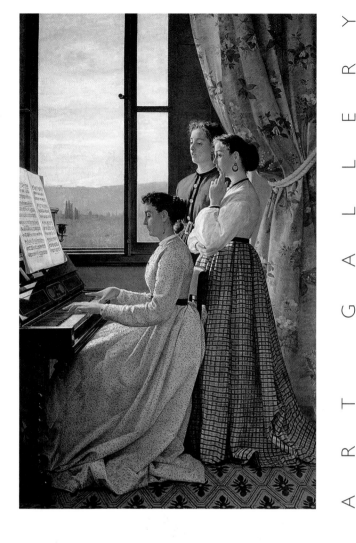

SILVESTRO LEGA
*The starling's song*
Oil on canvas, 158 × 98 cm

Exhibited for the first time in the Florentine Promotrice of 1867, from the outset the painting received notable acclaim from critics, who judged it one of the greatest achievements of the artist, who had reached his full creative maturity. The striking feature of the work is the description of the domestic episode which here is nearly transfigured by the sustained formal character, evidently inspired by 15th-century Tuscan painting, mainly that of Piero della Francesca. The painting dates back to the time of Piagentina, and the woman playing the piano is Virginia Batelli, sentimentally linked to the painter, in a moment of happy activity – in fact, one of the favourite pastimes of the woman and her hospitable family, whose villa was located in a picturesque locale in the immediate vicinity of Florence.

DOMENICO INDUNO
*The antique dealer*
Oil on canvas, 81 × 55 cm

The painting comes from the collections of the Academy, where it has been documented since 1888. It represents an interesting aspect of the genre painting practised in Lombardy, a genre dependent upon the educational and moral requirements consequent to public viewing – in antithesis to the abstract vocation of the Tuscans – and, therefore, prone to the illustration and study of emotions. Publicly acclaimed, Induno participates in numerous and important exhibitions, where he earns both awards and recognition, thanks precisely to his specialisation in the subject of the genre, very much to the tastes and demand of the current bourgeois.

## Room 13

### The patriotic theme with democratic overtones

*The need for a wide-spread, yet controlled dissemination of the facts occurring on the eve of Italian independence, suggested to the 1859 provisional Government the idea of holding a competition in several categories of art works. The entries were to commemorate the recomposing, under the protection of the Savoy monarchy, of a conflict that had occasioned new myths and new heroes for Italy to celebrate. So, the propaganda and hagiographic side of the undertaking saw the creation of exemplary and moving figurative episodes, while the democratic motives of some of the new generation of artists focused their attentions on minor episodes of the newly added chapters in Italy's history, those deemed the most touching in their revelations to oppressed and suffering mankind. A masterpiece of this poetic understanding of the fate of the 'vanquished' is* Magenta *by Fattori, around which are centred the military paintings by Lega and other artists that addressed patriotic issues with their minds on the actuality of the story and their willing hearts on resolving the drama and pain through the harmonious beauty of nature.*

GIOVANNI FATTORI

### The Italian camp after the battle of Magenta
Oil on canvas, 232 × 348 cm

Commissioned on the occasion of the Ricasoli competition of 1859 in the category of "battle paintings" (Curtatone, Palestro, Magenta and San Martino) commemorating the second war of independence, the painting was presented, still incomplete, at the 1861 Italian Fair in Florence, and later at the Florentine Promotrice of 1862. It is the first painting of the modern historical genre, in that it unifies attentive documentation of the attire and weapons through naturalistic observations translated in a controlled range of complementary colours – composed according to the canons of *macchiaioli* painting – and pathetic notations, by now participants in the imminent culture of Verismo.

## ALESSANDRO LANFREDINI

### *The Italian recruits of the Sigmund Regiment after the battle of Magenta.*
Oil on canvas, 173 × 232 cm

Like the painting by Fattori, this was entered in the Ricasoli competition of 1859 in the section "military episodes of the last war". It was presented incomplete at the 1861 Italian Fair in Florence, and nonetheless earned the artist a medal for the narrative efficacy of the composition and its brilliant execution in the purist tradition. The episode describes the moment in which, after the battle of Magenta, it was discovered that the cartridge holders of some Italian conscripts in the Austrian Regiment, found dead on the field of battle, had been emptied of their projectiles by the recruits themselves in order to not kill their countrymen of the Franco-Italian troops.

## Room 14

### Historical genres to the forefront of the exhibitions

*The experimental tensions that arose from the meetings in Caffè Michelangelo necessarily had to come to terms with the vital tradition of Tuscan academic art of the latter half of the century. The presentation at the exhibitions of many works of unquestionable quality based on recovering the techniques and form of past masters and French contemporaries, frequently caused young artists to doubt the much-debated suitability of reproducing truth while avoiding the exhausting practice of the atelier. The extraordinary capacity to merge observations of reality with the intellectual contributions of literary mediation, most evident in the works of Antonio Ciseri and, with the added aspects of a more captivating narration, those of Gabriele Castagnola and Rodolfo Morgari, constituted therefore a kind of formal counterpoint to the evolution of* macchiaioli *art, which placed experimentation of a renewed vision of nature before the frigid abstraction of academic subjects.*

### GABRIELE CASTAGNOLA

#### *The episode of Filippo Lippi and the Nun Buti*
Oil on canvas, 223 × 159 cm

The painting represents one of the most cordial aspects of the historical genre painting, illustrating the legendary episode in the life of Filippo Lippi within a narrative vein sustained by the masterful drawing and fanciful imagination that the painter exploits to evoke a fabulous and captivating renaissance, rather than the ethical and exemplary one preferred by the historical painting of romanticism. Castagnola moved from Genova to Florence in the crucial years of the Caffè Michelangelo, immediately affirming himself as a skilled narrator of historical episodes that were both picturesque and appropriate to transposing present-day customs and feelings onto an age-old story.

### ANTONIO CISERI

#### *Ecce Homo*
Oil on canvas, 292 × 380 cm

Exhibited for the first time in Ciseri's study shortly after his death, the large painting received overt acclaim even from the anti-academic Diego Martelli, who immediately praised its luminance and the transparency effects of the whites in the scene's background. The painting required from the artist a long period of work that would bear fruit in 1891, that is, when the formalist rigor of official painting had already begun to find profitable correspondence in similar trends in European art. It was then that Ciseri as well would be able to appropriate the literary elements of French painting – from the 'Romaness' of Gerôme to the positivist Christianity of Renan – and the aesthetic elements of the classicism of Alma Tadema.

## Room 15

### Stefano Ussi and the climate of the World Fairs

*The success attained with* The expulsion of the Duke of Athens *at the Italian Fair of 1861 demonstrated that the topic of ancient history continued to be a privileged field of formal experimentation – more appreciated, in fact, than the contemporary themes which some dissenting artists were trying to bring to the forefront in those years. Diego Martelli wrote openly of their divergence, criticising the official exhibition establishment which, opposed to the new, was celebrating the rhetoric of contents. Actually, Ussi's painting, as well as* Buonconte *by Smargiassi, represented the evolutionary summit of historical painting of the Romantic tradition of Domenico Morelli, committed as they were to strict narration of events arising from the definition of solid masses revealed and counterposed by the strong chiaroscuro, or to the prevalence of naturalist scenes painted as representations of the real.*

#### GABRIELE SMARGIASSI
#### *Buonconte di Montefeltro killed in battle*
Oil on canvas, 213 × 300 cm

The success of this work at the Italian Fair of 1861 convinced the king to buy it for his own collection, paying the highest price ever for a painting. As Salvatore di Giacomo wrote, underlining the prevalence of literary aspects in historical genre painting and, at the same time, the effect obtained by the broad atmosphere and paling colours of the scene: "Smargiassi wanted his characters to express something through a meditated, somewhat romantic and historical composition: he wanted them to nearly hover, as Dantesque spirits, the unearthly figures of saints or the heroic figures of Ariosto and Tasso".

#### STEFANO USSI
#### *The expulsion of the Duke of Athens*
Oil on canvas, 320 × 452 cm

Begun in Rome, where Ussi had been awarded a *pensionato artistico*, the painting was concluded in Florence in 1861 and presented at the national exhibition of that year, attaining notable success and the winning first prize. The topic of the painting comes from Machiavelli's *Istorie Florentine* and *The Duke of Athens* by Tommaseo, and represents Gualtieri di Brienne's indecision in signing his resignation from the *Signoria* of Florence. In spite of Martelli's protests, which accused the exhibition's jury of favouring the Academy, the painting marked the transcending of the historical romantic genre and demonstrated the painter's knowledge of the realism introduced in Florence by Domenico Morelli.

**The celebration of the post-unification Risorgimento: the rebirth of the applied arts**

*It was the opinion of Demetrio Carlo Finocchietti, enterprising administrator of the Savoy court at Pitti Palace, that in order to consolidate the bonds of fraternity forged on the battlefield, nothing else remained but to "measure oneself in the arena of industry", thus providing incentive to the tastes and creativity, not only of artists, but of the most disparate categories of artisans as well, who would find the national and international exhibitions to be the most appropriate forums for comparisons and emulation. It was certainly in keeping with these precepts that Vittorio Emanuele II proceeded to acquire paintings and decorations destined for the palace – which was thus transformed into the official gallery of the modern Italian style – though he also commissioned works that were to attest, in their content and formal conquests, to the creative vitality springing from the travails of the Risorgimento. The result was a weave of a multiplicity of aspirations and styles that, on behalf of the sought-for and accepted plurality, could enumerate the masterpieces of the avant-garde artists and works of the hagiographic Savoys – works admirable for the techniques employed, as well as their ability to achieve bold eclecticism.*

**VINCENZO GEMITO**
*Portrait of Giuseppe Verdi*
Bronze, h. 50 cm

We know that Giuseppe Verdi, giving in to the entreaties of Domenico Morelli, commissioned Gemito with his portrait when he was in Naples for the performances of *Don Carlos* and *Aida*. Verdi was a guest at the Crocelle Hotel, where the sculptor came to stay for the few days necessary to model the bust, experiencing not little indecision regarding the 'cut' to adopt in the portrait of the renowned musician. He would finish it in 1873, achieving noteworthy efficacy also in the impressionist rendering of the subsequent bronze cast of the plaster model. The original was placed in the Rest Home for musicians in Milan and later reproduced by the sculptor in many copies such as this one, which has been in the Gallery collection since 1927.

**ALESSANDRO MONTENERI, GUGLIELMO CIANI, DOMENICO BRUSCHI**
*Decorated cabinet for the Italian crown*
Mahogany marquetry with maple and mother-of-pearl, h. 327 cm

Begun in 1860 by the Perugian sculptor and marquetry master, Alessandro Monteneri, after the design of Bruschi and structural plan by Ciani, the cabinet was presented at the Italian Fair of 1861, as well as that in London in 1862. The Municipality of Perugia donated it to the king, who immediately placed it in Pitti Palace in order to demonstrate that the neo-renaissance style, accompanied by the refined readopting of ancient techniques, was valued and accorded the highest levels, also for its implicit social and politics values.

## Room 17
### Portraits from the era of Umberto I

*Italy's annexation of Rome (1870), and the transfer of the realm's capital there from Florence (1871) are the events that close, also in a symbolic sense, the period of the Risorgimento, thereby opening the long and arduous stage of building the unified state, a difficult undertaking, given the multitude of problems inherited from centuries of backwardness. The Progressivism of the Risorgimento, which had fostered the formal experiments of the* macchiaioli *in art, now gives way to a social conservatism, armed against the earliest insubordination of the subaltern classes, upheld by the aristocracy and bourgeoisie entrepreneurs. Celebration of the new protagonists, depicted in the luxury of officialdom or the comfortable peace of suburban villas, will be the task of artists such as Vittorio Corcos and Michele Gordigiani, who are careful to depict these men and women in a clear, very well-defined painting style, after the French example of the* salon *paintings – far indeed from the austere formalism that characterised the intimist preferences of the* macchiaioli.

| | |
|---|---|
| VITTORIO CORCOS | MICHELE GORDIGIANI |
| *The daughter of Jack la Bolina* | *Portrait of the painter's wife, Gabriella Coujère* |
| Oil on canvas, 139 × 105 cm | Oil on canvas, 72 × 58 cm |

Dated to around 1888, this portrait represents a example of the mundane style of Corcos, characterised by well-defined painting, after the example of French models from Carolus Duran to the impressionists, and aimed at exalting the new pomp of the high bourgeoisie entrepreneurs, often with strong literary implications. It is evident how the elegant nonchalance of the style is combined here with his ability to narrate almost the character's history, in its intimate sentimental mystery. It was such compositional aspects that earned Corcos extraordinary success at exhibitions, as well as the appellative: *peintre des jolies femmes.*

Towards the century's end, Gordigiani was considered one of Italy's most important portrait-artists for his ability to harmonise academic tradition with the innovation of European figurative culture, especially that of France. His mastery is evident in this elegant portrait of his wife, captured in the almost blinding reflection of the noonday light. The fame of the painter increased significantly in 1861, when he painted a portrait of Vittorio Emanuele II, and immediately thereafter one of the queen, as well as other royalty from France and England.

## Sala 18

### The municipal inventory of the years 1912-1925 (*macchiaioli* and other schools)

*The figurative journey that this room presents – bringing together works from the municipal store dating back to the years when the convention between the State and the Florence City Council was still in force – allows assessing the analogies and differences that link or distinguish the main personages of the time of the* macchiaioli. *It is a rich repertoire, whose highlights include some of the greatest achievements of Fattori and Signorini. The small studies of Vito D'Ancona, full of luminous matter, and the poetic analogies of form and colour studied directly on reality by Abbati, Sernesi and Borrani, constitute a visual and theoretical counterpoint to the independent evolution of the art of Fattori. It is a journey from the first* macchiaioli, *the pioneers of 1859, through the happy experiences in Leghorn and Castiglioncello, and up to the style of the last years when the most modern current within the movement, of which Signorini is the most international expression, dictates the dominance of sign over colour.*

### GIOVANNI FATTORI
**The Palmieri rotunda**
Oil on wood-plate, 12 × 35 cm

Painted in 1866, the plate represents some ladies resting at the rotunda of the well-known Leghorn bath houses, from which extends the luminous horizon, accented by the strong contrast of the shady area in the foreground, thus achieving the effect of a wide-open horizon, nonetheless contained within the reduced dimensions of the painting. This work is often cited as one of Fattori's greatest masterpieces, not only for its fresh immediacy and the attentive studiousness of its chromatic couplings, based on the principles of complementarity, but also for its compositional cut, attested to by his pictorial meditations during that summer of 1866, as well as a notebook full of preparatory drawings documenting the gradual steps leading from the study of reality to its rendering in the *atelier*.

### GIOVANNI FATTORI
**The stirrup**
Oil on canvas, 90 × 130 cm

When exhibited in Florence in 1880 it was interpreted as one of the apices of naturalistic aesthetics for the manner in which Fattori had succeeded in communicating the clear impression of the 'real', balancing parts defined by the drawing with others hardly outlined and thus amenable to rendering the tragic dynamism of the scene. It was Renato Fucini who suggested the theme to Fattori, while the artist was working on another subject, *The explosion of the chest*, equally set at an oblique view and the immediate rendering of a moving and spectacular event: images that well suited the sensibility of the artist in his old age.

### GIOVANNI FATTORI
*La libecciata*
*(The Southwesterly Gale)*
Oil on wood-plate, 28.5 × 68 cm

One of Fattori's most famous paintings, *La libecciata* expresses with great efficacy the poetics of the artist's last period, very different from that of the more idyllic and lyrical decade 1870-80. In fact, in describing the conflict of the elements of nature, Fattori paints a restless metaphor of his own existential condition, creating an image very akin to the symbolist naturalism of the contemporary poetry of Giovanni Pascoli and an idea of landscape seemingly abbreviated, but well suited to expressing a touching concept through almost sensory painting.

### TELEMACO SIGNORINI
*Roofs at Riomaggiore*
Oil on canvas, 79 × 55 cm

The painting depicts a view from above the town of Riomaggiore illuminated by blue-grey tones that highlight, in the absence of more decisive chromatic contrasts, the painting's drawing and perspective structure. Part of a series on the maritime village (1881-1897), it represents a visual counterpoint to the book *Riomaggiore*, written and illustrated by the selfsame Signorini.

### TELEMACO SIGNORINI
*Penitentiary of Portoferraio*
Oil on canvas, 56 × 80 cm

Carried out in 1894, it was presented the following year at the Florentine Promotrice and again in 1901 at the 8th Biennial of Venice. Together with the *Room of the anxious* and *The morning's awakening*, it represents the moment when Signorini began his adherence to those aspects of French naturalism which, in Italy, would unite in the literary and figurative poetics of social verismo. The idea of the painting came to Signorini after visiting the penitentiary during his first trip to Elba in 1888, and reveals in the artist an expressive charge clearly comparable with similar experiences in Mitteleurope.

### GIOVANNI FATTORI
*Portrait of his stepdaughter*
Oil on canvas, 71 × 55 cm

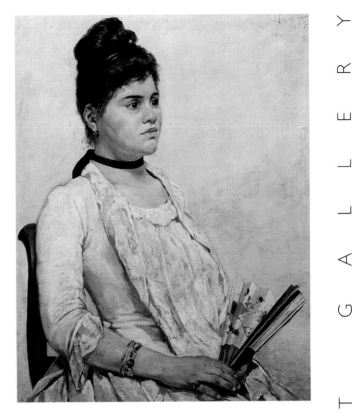

The youth depicted here is Giulia Marinelli, daughter of Marianna Bigazzi, who would wed Fattori as her second husband in 1891, the same year in which Giulia would also marry the Uruguayan, Domingo Laporte. It is commonly held that the painting represents an apex in the history of 19th-century portraiture, as much for its solid compositional idea, supported by the essentiality of the chromatic range and studied counterpoint of the tones, as for the psychological rendering of the youth, captured in the fixity of her pose, yet transmitting her physiological features, which the artist observes with lucid objectivity and subtle introspection.

### Sala 19

### The Ambron collection (*macchiaioli* and other schools)

*This room, like the preceding one, contains fundamental works of the* macchiaioli *and other particularly noteworthy Italian artists belonging to the schools of both the North and South, which thus provide a meaningful panorama of art in the latter half of the 19th Century. With paintings from the municipal inventory, this collection underscores the early recognition and consequent appreciation of the art of the* macchiaioli *in both the public and private spheres, each of which offers a fertile terrain for observations of the personalities within the movement, centred mainly in sketches and scribblings of the* macchia, *and the state of Art in post-unification Tuscany. It therefore provides the ideal occasion to visually summarise the time of the* macchiaioli – *parallel in its development to other important national experiences – from the years in Florence hosted a unitary and progressive movement caught up in the debate on 'truth', 'reality' and 'nature', on the heels of the discoveries of Piagentina and Castiglioncello, up to 1870, after which the personal styles of Fattori, Lega and Signorini emerge, outstanding, from the premises of the group.*

### GIOVANNI FATTORI
*Cousin Argia*
Oil on cardboard, 36.2 × 29 cm

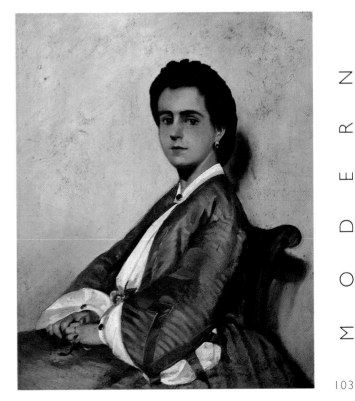

The portrait, chronologically the first of the artist's masterpieces in this genre, dates back to the early 1860s, when the painter spent long periods in Leghorn so that his wife, who suffered from tuberculosis, could benefit from the curative effects of the sea air. It is here, in fact, during the time spent with his family that Fattori develops an interest in portraiture, painting his cousin Argia with a fineness and introspection that recall the paintings of the Roman, Nino Costa and, through him, the enthralling vivacity of the portraits of Camille Corot.

## Adriano Cecioni

### Suicidal

Plaster, h. 217 cm

Modelled by Cecioni in Naples between 1865 and 1867 as the last work in his *pensionato artistico* from the Florentine Academy, the sculpture was acquired in 1891 by the Minister of Education, Pasquale Villari, for the Gallery of the Academy and transferred to Pitti Palace in 1924. The representation of the theme of suicide was judged to be immoral by the Florentine academe, which did not consider it worthy to be transferred to marble. On the other hand, it was very well received by defenders of verism in art, who extolled the innovation of the subject, the raw drama of the figure and, at the same time, the audacity of the allusion in the figure's pose to the ancient model of the orator.

## Antonio Mancini

### Self-portrait in his study

Oil on wood-plate, 21.5 × 31.5 cm

This intense self-portrait set in the artist's colourful study, full of moulds and models, was likely executed between 1875 and 1878, as evinced by the artist's youthful appearance and the analogies to another *self-portrait* dated 1878. The extremely original composition and strong pathos of the protagonist, indicate its having been made after Mancini's experiences in Paris, where the painter was involved with the artistic atmosphere surrounding the merchant Goupil; but they also foretell of the artist's growing hypochondria and the psychic alterations that henceforth would determine the introduction of eccentric formal solutions into his works.

## Telemaco Signorini

### Leith

Oil on canvas, 45 × 41.5 cm

This worked was probably painted around 1881 when Signorini was staying in Edinburgh and travelled to Leith several times, as testified to by a diary from those times. During his stay in Great Britain the painter develops a more synthetic and abstract, than impressionist style, as can be evinced from the painting's composition, concentrated wholly on the geometric and chromatic manifestations of the billboard and the curtailed dynamism with which the passers-by's figures are described.

## Room 20
### Campestral painting

*After 1870, a second generation of* macchiaioli *painters begins to affirm itself. Formed in direct contact with the movement's origins, they however took little time in separating themselves from the compositional measure of their maestri in order to follow the European aesthetics so wide-spread towards the end of the century. Amongst these artists, two major 'dynasties' emerge: that of the Gioli, linked to Fattori, and that of the Tommasi, influenced by Lega, who frequently spent time with them in the home of Bellariva. The occasion for their official debut was the 1886 exhibition in Leghorn, whose strongpoint was precisely this 'generation in between' composed of Ferroni, Francesco Gioli, Cannicci, Adolfo and Angiolo Tommasi, Cecconi and Panerai who in their studies from life in small format, common in these years also in the Roman and southern ambience, were already beginning to reveal their knowledge of the paintings of country-life presented in the Parisian* salons *by Jules Breton and Julien Bastien-Lepage.*

TELEMACO SIGNORINI
**September morning in Settignano**
Oil on canvas, 58.5 × 64 cm

The painting is probably *The Scheggi tavern in Settignano* exhibited at the Promotrice of Florence in 1891, which was acquired by Umberto I. Carried out between 1883 and 1890, the years in which Signorini works assiduously in the hills of Settignano, frequenting the tavern for two months in the summer of 1885, the painting is one of the most moving visions of the Tuscan painter's late work. The result obtained is one of a harmonious union of naturalism and delicate abstraction of form that allows for considerable heightening of detail and, at the same time, a suspended contemplative vision.

EGISTO FERRONI
**At the fountain**
Oil on canvas, 275 × 165 cm

Displayed in 1879 at the National Exhibition of Turin and the Florentine Promotrice the following year, the work was not appreciated by the juries, but was defended with great determination by the *macchiaioli* and Diego Martelli, who saw the large painting, formally ennobling topics that had until then been circumscribed within the domestic measure of genre painting, as Ferroni's keeping up with the monumental style of the paintings of campestral life being presented in contemporary Parisian *salons* by Jules Breton and Julien Bastien-Lepage.

## Room 21

### Manifestations of naturalism in Tuscany

*In the First Fine Arts Exhibition organised in Leghorn in 1886, apart from the due homage to the fathers of the* macchiaioli *(Signorini, Fattori, Lega), much space was devoted to the naturalistic painting of Cecconi, Cannicci, Ferroni and Francesco Gioli, while in the Paris World Fair of 1889, together with the same personages of the early* macchiaioli *school and painters from the generation of the 40s and 50s, younger painters made headway, such as Panerai, Nomellini, Edoardo Gordigiani and Ulvi Liegi, much appreciated by Signorini, who pointed out that their works represented "the conscientious and exact observation of the infinities of forms and characters" translated into roaming volumes and changing luminous effects. The victory attained over the realism of the distant Romantic foundations was also evident in the works of Ruggero Focardi, narrative yet noble and severe, and in those of Filadelfo Simi, veined by symbolist premonitions, not to mention the multiple manifestations of the modern principle of the 'real', which in the century's last years breached the remaining unity of Tuscan figurative culture.*

### ADOLFO TOMMASI

*Spring*
Oil on canvas, 150 × 200 cm

Acquired at the 1899 Exhibition of the Society of Fine Arts and donated by the king to the Modern Art Gallery, this enormous painting celebrates nature in almost epic forms, according to the sense of formal solemnity that, in the wake of Fattori's teachings, characterises Tuscan painting of the century's end. As occurs in other works by Tommasi, the topic, of evident realistic imprint, here consents expressing – as often happens in so–called 'campestral painting' – symbolist suggestions due to the mysterious solitude of the countryside and the animism, typical of Pascoli, of the vegetable fields.

### NICCOLÒ CANNICCI

*Thirst in the fields*
Oil on canvas, 54 × 45 cm

The topic of the painting, although linked to the campestral subjects typical of Cannicci and very much to the taste of the most learned bourgeois clientele, indicates, in its title, a precise will to adhere to the thematics of verismo. Its composition, on the other hand, represents a monumental form springing from knowledge of both French contemporary painting – which the artist acquired in Paris in 1875 in the company of Fattori, Banti and Ferroni – and the first instances of symbolism which, precisely through a new conception of the 'real', anticipated in art, as well as literature, the time of Decadentism.

## Room 22

Italian schools of the latter half of the 19th century

*In examining the most notable feats in the history of Tuscan art, which up to here has arrived at affirmation of the modern ideas surrounding the concepts of nature and 'truth', it is now necessary to compare all that was going on in the latter half of the century in other regions of Italy, where the same aesthetic debate often found reasons for appraisal or, through the artists, the occasion for fruitful meetings and exchanges. Southern Italy was specially interested, with its Palizzi, Morelli and Mancini, in the direct expression of a truth which was at times radiant, and at others charged with an existential restlessness reflected in works of great suggestiveness for the Tuscans as well. New light, more expressive than natural, colour the paintings of the Roman painters having arisen in the climate of D'Annunzio, depicting a countryside transfigured by barbaric myths; while some would chose the phenomena of nature itself for their turbid majesty, such as for example, the eruptions painted by Netti and De Nittis with spectacular results unknown amongst the measured Tuscan narration.*

### DOMENICO MORELLI

#### Meeting in a Constantinople cemetery
Oil on canvas, 46.2 × 71.5 cm

The painting, from 1894, appeared under the title *Memory of youthful readings* at the Festa di Arte e dei Fiori of 1896 – an imposing review of the most significant experiences of international art of the century's end. It is an document of those evocations of the East, coloured by sensuality and nostalgia, that Morelli gave precedence to over the interpretations of a reality otherwise observed through positivist inclemency and inflexible morality of the social 'poets', and which at the century's end was tinged with symbolist inflections.

### GIUSEPPE DE NITTIS

#### Rain of ashes
Oil on wood-plate, 45 × 30 cm

Carried out in 1872, this painting, typical of Neapolitan iconography, achieved great success, as did other studies of Mount Vesuvius, which De Nittis used as a means for trying out innovations on the countryside and varying atmospheric situations. The painting suggested analogies with the hundreds of views of Mt. Fujiama by Okusai, testament to the artist's vast culture that, in the cosmopolitan atmosphere of Paris, would continue the aesthetic experience of the impressionists, introducing notes of elegant mundanity into the representation of domestic life.

## Room 23
### Models and influences of Mitteleuropean culture

*The last two decades of the century are characterised by the significant influences of European art on Italian culture: from the neo-renaissance aesthetics of the pre-Raphaelite English, to the romantic Hellenism and Mediterranean myths of the German school. These new elements, either assimilated directly by the Italian artists or sparked by foreigners present in Rome and Florence, contributed to inducing a definitive crisis in the principles and forms of Risorgimento realism, displacing aesthetic study toward the obscurest and most disquieting areas of man and the world surrounding him. In the attempt to transfer the artistic cultural problems of the moment ever more towards a mystical and irrational plane, painters and poets discover the mythical origins of contemporary reality, thus populating the Roman countryside and reedbeds of the Arno's mouth with Centaurs, or seeking justification for a risky and alternative existence in the sunny silences of the East.*

### Otto Vermehren
### *Paolo and Francesca*
Oil on canvas, 152.5 × 97 cm

The work belongs to the mature years of the artist, formed in Weimar and then at the Art Academy of Munich, that is to say, in the ambience of the historicist and symbolist trends of the century's end. This painting is an example of Vermehren's Mitteleuropean style that approached the painting of Feuerbach, the late works of Henner and especially those of Böcklin, who was the artist's close friend in the years 1887 to 1890, during their first stay in Florence: the city where, from 1900 to 1916, he would live with his family, acquiring great prestige as an art restorer and imitator.

### Edoardo Gelli
### *Portrait of Bruna Pagliano*
Oil on canvas, 170.5 × 126 cm

A significant example of the style adopted by Gelli in portraying exponents of the high bourgeoisie, this painting, dated 1904, was rendered spectacular by the frame with its sinuous *Art Nouveau* decorations. The Ligurian artist had been trained at the school of Antonio Ciseri, whence the clear construction of his drawing. However, instead of continuing the austere formalism of his teacher, he soon adapted to the themes favoured by the market-place, specialising in the genres of moralistic painting and historical-military subjects.

### Room 24

#### Pointillism, Symbolism and social themes

*The spiritualistic movements that characterised European culture in the last two decades of the 19th Century – from the symbolism of Gustave Moreau and Odilon Redon to the 'D'Annunzianism' of Sartorio and Michetti – engendered the crisis in the principles of objective reality that is to underlie the naturalistic optimism of the informative painting of the century's final years. These orientations arose as reactions to the inadequacies of Positivism and Verismo and, revealing the feeling of mystery, regarded light and colour as the means to overcome the materiality of things. It was on the basis of these premises, therefore, that the divisionist painting of Nomellini, Previati, Kienerk, the more intensely literary ones of Adolfo Tommasi and Antony De Witt, as well as the same formal disintegration evident in the Medardo Rosso's sculptures, would integrate a contradictory range of values, from mysticism to social intervention, conceived as indivisible categories of the new lyrical spiritualism.*

### MEDARDO ROSSO
#### *Laughing woman*
Bronze, h. 59 cm

The woman's physiognomy, as in other plastic 'snapshots' by the sculptor, arises from a background that defines the perspective and circumscribes the relationships amongst figure, environment and atmosphere, according to compositional canons anticipating the solutions of the new century. The work is dated 1891, according to the author's own indications at the first Italian show on Impressionism in Florence in 1910. It was organised with the intention of countering the dusty luminism of French painters with the formal synthesis of Cézanne's painting, by which even the vigorous definition of sculptural planes of Rosso seemed to abide.

### PLINIO NOMELLINI
#### *Little Bacchus*
Oil on canvas, 121 × 94 cm

This painting was presented at the 1910 Venice Biennial and probably depicts Nomellini's own son, transfigured by the artist's fantasies of Pan. On that occasion, Vittorio Pica underscored the painter's capacity to unify "purposeful audacity in technique with noble grace in composition", recognising the work as the culmination of the symbolist vein already brilliantly enunciated in *Ditirambo*, also exhibited in Venice in 1905. Although contained within his experimentation on the *tocco diviso* (divided brush strokes), the aestheticism with which Nomellini evokes the appearance of the young god remains evident and recalls the classicism of Sartorio and De Carolis.

## Gaetano Previati
### In the meadow
Oil on canvas, 61 × 55 cm

Carried out between 1880 and 1890, the painting was exhibited at the 10th Biennial of Venice (1912) and acquired by the Minister Credaro for the Florence Modern Art Gallery, which thereby came into possession of one of the Emilian painter's most significant works. The painting, also known as *Morning and Children in the meadow*, signals the decisive stage in Previati's conversion to the technique of pointillism and demonstrates the artist's vocation for wide and luminous spaces and a variety of chromatic combinations that correspond perfectly to the high concept of 'decoration' as conceived by symbolist poetics.

## Rooms 25, 26
### Study collections
*These two rooms are given over to holding temporary exhibitions of the works conserved in the museum's inventory, new acquisitions, especially significant collections and small showings of subjects akin to the themes of 19th and 20th-century art in the Gallery's holdings.*

### The collection of Emilio Gagliardini

*Composed of for forty-three paintings, most of which are by the most famous exponents of* macchiaioli *painting (Fattori, Lega, Signorini, Borrani, Abbati, Banti, Cabianca, D'Ancona, Di Tivoli, Costa and Sernesi), this collection, for it aesthetic value and historical significance, represents one of the most excellent and well-known examples of Italian collecting of our century. The critical rigor and the taste with which the collector performed his selections make viewing this collection a required and irreplaceable step for studying and understanding the important Tuscan realist movement. Created by the industrialist Emilio Gagliardini in the second post-war period, the collection offers the opportunity to admire a series of masterpieces that had remained unseen for some time. Some of them hold particular significance within the overall production of their respective authors. Paintings, like* Horses in Tombolo *by Fattori,* The spring roses *by Lega and* Children in the sun *by Signorini, represent focal points within the whole collection and evince a goal in the creative parable of these artists. Their current arrangement in the Modern Art Gallery of Pitti Palace, possible by virtue of the commodate consenting their exhibition to the public, further enrich the Florentine collections with extraordinary testimonies to the schools of Castiglioncello and Piagentina. Together with works of such renowned Maestri, the collection has included a number of artists from the generation immediately following the* macchiaioli. *From the 'Leghorn School' come a number of paintings already well-known to the public, such as Oscar Ghiglia's* The Mirror *and Nomellini's* Noon.

## ODOARDO BORRANI
### *The mournful news*
Oil on canvas, 110 × 138 cm

The subject of the painting still belongs to the climate of the Risorgimento and represents a young girl, seated at a table lighted by an oil lamp, reading the newspaper to two women emotionally moved by the news of the death of Vittorio Emanuele II. Borrani worked on the painting in 1880, and in it appeals to a solemn and intense composition that demonstrates his having transcended the formal *macchiaioli* tradition in favour of themes and atmospheres drawn most likely from French contemporary painting.

## TELEMACO SIGNORINI
### *Expulsion of the Austrians from the village of Solferino*
Oil on canvas, 61.5 × 120 cm

This is the largest of the five works painted by Signorini between 1859 and 1861 in a theme from the Risorgimento. It was exhibited at the Promotrice of Florence in 1861 and later at the first National Exhibition, where it received a medal and was acquired by Isabella Falconer. The reality of the scene, accented by the extraordinary effect of the storm, follows from the studies that Signorini carried out directly on the grounds of war, even being arrested under suspicion of espionage.

## GIOVANNI FATTORI
### Horses in the pine wood of Tombolo
Oil on canvas, 85 × 174 cm

The painting is from the artist's most prolific years, between 1866 and 1867. While living in the vicinity of Leghorn, Fattori experimented with a style based on the study of space and rigorous construction of natural elements. It was this that allowed him to overcome the compositional aspects without however neglecting the effects of lighting and its incidence on the landscape, in accordance with the rural spiritualism of Millet and the Barbizon painters.

## PLINIO NOMELLINI
### Noon
Oil on canvas, 198 × 198 cm

In this work of monumental dimensions, Nomellini develops one of the subjects that best fit his sensibilities, refined as they were by literary interests and a cult of the emotions that would frequently lead him to depict his family in scenes of subtle emotional involvement. The artist had just risen from the table in order to capture the beautiful tree-filtered light of a summer's midday; thus confirming the talent of this, 'the solar painter' in exploiting the technique of the *tocco diviso* to render powerful luminous irradiation.

## Room 27

### Figurative Tuscan culture surrounding "Il Marzocco" and "Leonardo"

*The 20th Century commences in Florence with a vitality that assimilates the drive for emancipation from the aesthetics of the late 19th Century and the strong aspirations of its artists to appropriate the newly arisen European tendencies in antagonism to the cultural sediment of the century just ended. In the magazine "Il Marzocco", this appeal to progress was concretised in the cosmopolitan vision of Ugo Ojetti and aesthetic eclecticism represented by the 'D'Annunzian' milieu, which would attract young artists like Soffici and Costetti, and others like Armando Spadini, bound to each other by an intellectual aristocracy, declared in the elegant pages of "Leonardo" and the refined circle of their supporters, headed by Giovanni Papini.*

ARMANDO SPADINI
*Confidences*
Oil on canvas, 107 × 100 cm

This work, which can be dated to between 1919 and 1922, documents the period in which the artist, leaving behind the works that he himself defined as "sketches and impressions", begins to manifest a clear tendency toward demanding composition, thus reacting to the criticism levelled at him by the theorists of the return to order, who demanded monumentality and formal rigour in art. This poetic change earned Spadini admission to the group of Plastic Values in the Florentine Primaverile of 1922, where his painting was praised for its healthy character and freedom from 'cerebralism'.

OSCAR GHIGLIA
*Portrait of Giovanni Papini*
Oil on canvas, 66 × 57 cm

This incomplete portrait was executed in the second decade of the 20th century, when Papini became interested in the painting of the Leghorn artist, writing an article in "Vita d'arte" in 1908 that regarded precisely Ghiglia's work as a portrait-artist and his sound knowledge of post-impressionism French art. After sharing the enthusiasm of the artistic and literary adventures linked to "Leonardo" and "La Voce", the two would pass on to a dignified, though hostile estrangement that would for a long time place them on diametrically opposed sides of the debate regarding avant-garde futurism and the autonomy of art.

## Room 28

### European influences on Tuscan art of the second decade of the 20th century

*On the occasion of the show of the "Leghorn impressionists" of 1891, Giovanni Fattori expressed concern and disappointment upon seeing that his young pupils had distanced themselves from the solid structures created by the* macchiaioli *tradition and given themselves over to rash combinations of tones, following the example of the contemporary post-impressionist currents. The exhibition, that brought together Nomellini, Muller and Kienerk, amongst others, actually signalled that the provincial post-*macchiaioli *approach had been surpassed, thanks to the timely awareness by these painters of the Secessionist movement and the figurative results born of critical reflections on impressionist art. On the other hand, Fattori could not know to what extent his own work, carried to its extreme, as essential and analogical as the painting of Cézanne, would influence some artists of the early 20th century, mainly Oscar Ghiglia and other Tuscans who, by the same means and thanks to the critical zeal of Soffici and Ojetti, learned to understand the spirit of the European avant-garde.*

LORENZO VIANI
*Self-portrait*
Oil on canvas, 98 × 67 cm

This self-portrait, dated between 1910 and 1912, corresponds to the description of the restless artist offered by Ettore Cozzani, director of the magazine "L'Eroica", on which Viani collaborated as xylographer in 1914: "a strange scruffy and impetuous sort of savage ... a provocative and sarcastic rebel". Concerning the style, the painter addresses Mitteleuropean culture, interpreting in an original and unembellished fashion the *fauve* and expressionist languages, with references to Nolde, Die Brücke, Munch and Barlach, whom Viani had purposely chosen so as to underscore the nonconformist and anarchical positions that he would hold throughout his life.

GIUSEPPE VINER
*The mine*
Oil on canvas, 128 × 143 cm

The painter, strongly tied to the land of his origins, very often worked on subjects that illustrated the scenes and events related to the quarries of Carrara, achieving spectacular results through their resolution in an abstracting and chromatically vibrant style, very akin to some of the figurative aspects of the Viennese Secession. The controlled balance between nature and decoration present in this painting is moreover the result of Viner's training, beginning at the Industrial Arts School of Florence and continuing through his work as decorator in Tuscany, where the ornamental fashion of Galileo Chini was held in the utmost regard.

## GALILEO CHINI
### *Peace*
Oil on canvas, 199 × 126.5 cm

This was carried out, along with the two other paintings, *Indolence* and *Faith*, between 1911 and 1914, during Chini's travels in Siam, where he had gone to fresco the throne room of the Royal Palace in Bangkok. On his return from East China he would accentuate the evocative aspects of his divisionist formation, participating in the Venice Biennial of 1914 with a series of paintings wholly comparable to the most significant examples of European Symbolism, and from then on cultivating a style of great literary suggestion, which called for the collaboration of modernist poets and musicians believing in the syncretism of the arts.

## GIOVANNI COSTETTI
### *Girl on the balcony (At the terrace)*
Oil on cardboard, 50 × 33 cm

The painting probably originates from the years in which the artist became especially interested in the works of German Expressionism which he had opportunity to view at the Third Show of the Secession in Rome in 1915 and the Venice Biennial of 1922, where the figurative current was amply represented. Indeed, a drawing by Munch exhibited in Rome, entitled *The two*, even seems to have constituted a certain precedent for this painting, which moreover indicates its having been executed between 1915 and 1920.

## Room 29
### Legacy of Mai Sewell Costetti

*This room is dedicated to the paintings of Giovanni Costetti bequeathed to the Gallery by the painter's widow, a Norwegian citizen, journalist and ceramist. Her last will and testament stipulated that the works left in her possession were to be donated to the museums of the cities most linked to her husband's activities: Florence, Reggio Emilia, Settignano and Bergen. Of the thirty works received, this selection represents the most important, and most suitable to delineating Costetti's personality: idealist, tending towards mysticism, but also attentive to the evolution of the 20th-century aesthetic aimed at recovering the values of Cézanne and the return of order.*

## GIOVANNI COSTETTI
### *The good smile (The French woman)*
Oil on canvas, 120 × 95 cm

Dated to around 1903, the painting depicts perhaps the painter Beatrice Ancillotti and was exhibited for the first time at the Biennial of Venice in 1912, entered with the title of *The good smile*. The work represents a high level of the artist's adhesion, in his youth, to the symbolist culture and international secessionism of the early part of the century, a culture which he could have become directly acquainted with during his stay in Paris in 1900. In those same years, Costetti collaborates on the magazine "Leonardo" and keeps the company of artists and writers – D'Annunzio, De Carolis, Andreotti and Kienerk – that further stimulate his interest in the European horizon, as also evident in this portrait, very akin to certain pastels by Fernand Knopff.

## GIOVANNI COSTETTI
### *Self-portrait with pupil Domenico Candia*
Oil on cardboard, 70 × 58 cm

This is one of the numerous portraits that Costetti performed using as a model his pupil, Domenico Candia, who himself exhibited for the first time, together with his teacher, in the Florentine Primaverile of 1922. Possibly done in that same year, the work demonstrates the attention that Costetti devoted to the renaissance tradition and his awareness of fixing within a portrait, through erudite references, an almost heroic moment, which was in any event, relevant to his own experience and the culture of the moment and saw him as the interpreter of the European avant-garde.

## Room 30
### Acquisitions at the Florentine Primaverile of 1922

*In 1922 Florence hosted important exhibitions dedicated to the art of the 17th and 18th Centuries, a fact that underscored the renewed interest in studying those centuries which had until then been despised. It was also the site of an important, wide-ranging contemporary art review aimed at recapitulating the national artistic research of the post-war era and, almost in syntony with the rediscovery of Caravaggio and Mattia Preti, finding the way to rejoin tradition indicating, amongst others, the 19th century Italians - commemorated through the homage of Lega and Signorini - as an ulterior area for aesthetic inquiry. The choice of artists invited to the Tuscan Primaverile substantially reflected this planned return to the form and noble models of Italian art. Thus, amongst the choices were the much appreciated 'purified naturalism' of Baccio Maria Bacci, the architectural sense of Libero Andreotti, the impressive realism of Evaristo Boncinelli, the inlays of pure colour by Arturo Checchi and the devotion of Fattori's pupils to Cézanne, which the review gathered together for the first time, trenchantly recording the contributions of the new generation within the Tuscan setting.*

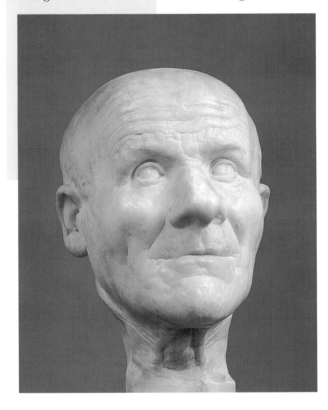

### EVARISTO BONCINELLI
#### *Head of old man (Contadino)*
Marble, h. 32 cm

This version in marble was cast from the plaster mould, also in the collection of the Modern Art Gallery, displayed at the First Tuscan Winter Exhibition of 1914-1915. The sculptor, who suffered from psychic imbalance and tended to represent human misery, sculpted the face of the old man with a sharp realism that finds its roots in the more Hellenic examples of Roman sculpture and the rough and vivid figures of Etruscan art. These would be the models recovered in the 20th Century through the expressive force that its artists would couple with a return to the strong original substance of Italian art.

### RENATO NATALI
#### *Quarter (via Buontalenti)*
Oil on canvas, 190 × 150 cm

The painting stands out in monumental form amongst the many 'masquerades balls' and 'brawls' that Natali imagined by uniting observation of reality with the signs and colours matured during his experiences with the Tuscan post-*macchiaioli* and avant-garde Paris, where the painter moved in 1914, also adhering to the graphic tastes of Leonetto Cappiello. The scenographic cut of the painting is indeed sustained by a graphic layout of great solidity, while the colour defines the form, exalting its expressive value with effective emergence of tones that recall the pictorial expressiveness of the *peintres de rues* of the 19th and 20th centuries.

# The Bourbon Quarters or New Palatine

Laura Baldini Giusti

The name Bourbon Quarters or New Palatine refers to the part of the courtyard's left wing that originally, at the end of the sixteenth century, was the second-floor apartment of the young princes. Here, in these airy rooms full of light, the many sons of Ferdinando I and Cristina of Lorraine spent their days, with their nannies and tutors.

This custom of providing living space in the palace for the scions of the reigning family would remain constant, with few exceptions, in both the Medici and Lorraine periods.

The apartment looked then rather different than it does today, both with respect to its decoration and to the arrangement of the rooms. In particular, in place

of the three rooms that now look out towards the Boboli Gardens, there was a large covered terrace, where the young princes perhaps practiced the art of fencing, as the court pages did on the other, matching terrace on the opposite side of courtyard. Both terraces were walled in around the middle of the seventeenth century and sub-divided into several rooms.

The last of the Medici to live in the apartment was Ferdinando II's second son, His Serene Highness Child Prince Francesco Maria, who was born in 1660.

The apartment was then left abandoned for a long time, there being no more children born to the Medici, and was uninhabited for many years.

No major changes were made even after the end of

the Medici dynasty. The Lorraines preferred the right wing of the palace and more or less ignored the rest of the building.

Under the Kingdom of Etruria, the apartment took on a role more or less analogous to its function in the past. Queen Maria Luisa allocated it as a residence for Count Odoardo Salvatico, the Chief Counsellor of the Cabinet Secretariat. Pasquale Poccianti was commissioned to oversee the recovery and restoration of these rooms, neglected for decades.

With the return of the Lorraines, the apartment immediately regained its original role, and was assigned to the Crown Prince, Archduke Leopoldo.

The restoration work began in this period (1814), once more directed by Poccianti. Ferdinando III entrusted him with the construction of a new, secondary staircase (replacing Ammannati's beautiful "snail" staircase), as well as with the arrangement of the palace's entire second floor: the Crown Prince's Quarters, previously known as the Salvatico Quarters, the Archduchess' Quarters along the façade, and the Winter Quarters in the right wing.

The rooms' appearance changed radically. The decorated wooden planking – perhaps analogous to what can still be seen today, decorated with elaborate friezes, in the only three rooms in this wing that were not altered – were replaced or covered with vaults and matting and painted with educational, historical or celebratory themes. The new decoration of the apartment was completed by the white and gilded stuccowork, the wall panelling, the monochrome painting of friezes and baseboards, and the mock-Venetian floors. The result – as had already been the case with the Napoleonic Quarters on the first floor – conformed completely to the neo-classical canons then in vogue.

The work went on for several years. Poccianti's *Account*, written in 1825, describes the state of all the work underway in the Pitti Palace, and clearly indicates that by then there remained little to do: the ornamentation of the walls, vault and fresco in the Ballroom (work which was never actually completed), some stuccowork in the Chapel, the double doors of mahogany.

The architect not only oversaw the architectonic work but also concerned himself with the choice of the decorative themes, even deciding on the pictorial subjects and the way of representing them. The considerable documentation available makes very clear the wide decision-making authority granted to Poccianti, as well as the inferior position in which the painters were obliged to operate. Poccianti even dictated the choice of poses and of the clothing worn by painted figures, thus reducing the painters to mere executors of a figurative plan subject to the Chief Architect's meticulous examination, leaving very little room for their own imaginations.

The work in the entire wing was completed by 1830, although a number of rooms, among which the Ballroom, were left without the planned decoration. This was perhaps due to the fact that Leopoldo, who succeeded to the throne after the death of Ferdinando III, had moved into other quarters in the palace, before then going into exile in 1859.

The Savoy period left few significant traces in these rooms, which retain their neo-classical look and are a perfect framework for some of the most prestigious works in the Pitti's Modern Art Gallery.

On the opposite page: *Modern Art Gallery, Room 17.*
Above and below:
*Giuseppe Bezzuoli*, Alexander in Apelle's Study, *a fresco on the vault in Room 12.*
*Modern Art Gallery, Room 12.*

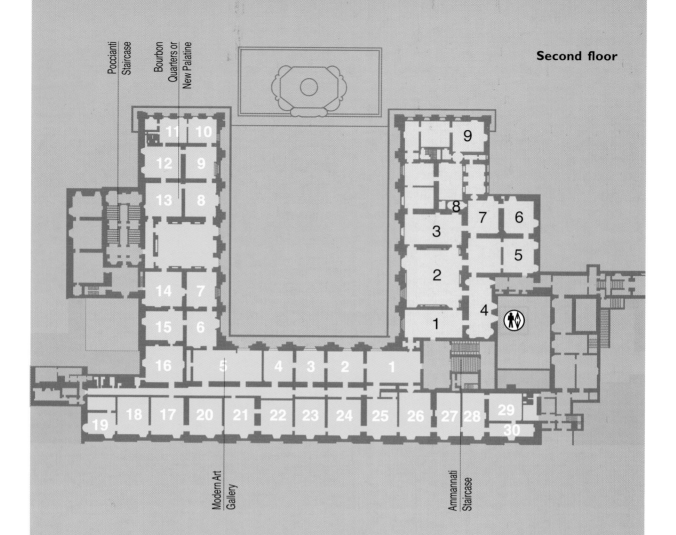

Poccianti Staircase

Bourbon Quarters or New Palatine

Modern Art Gallery

Ammannati Staircase

## THE WINTER QUARTERS OR APARTMENT OF THE DUCHESS OF AOSTA
(VISITS BY APPOINTMENT ONLY)

| | |
|---|---|
| 1 | THE FOOTMAN'S ROOM |
| 2 | THE FLEUR-DE-LIS ROOM OR BALLROOM (TEMPORARY EXHIBITS) |
| 3 | THE MUSIC ROOM |
| 4 | THE MUSES GALLERY |
| 5 | THE RED ROOM |
| 6 | THE KING'S STUDIO |
| 7 | KING'S BEDRROM |
| 8 | THE BATHROOM (FORMERLY THE CHAPEL) |
| 9 | THE BEDROOM |

# The Winter Quarters or Apartment of the Duchess of Aosta

LAURA BALDINI GIUSTI

When Archduke Ferdinando became Grand Duke of Tuscany in 1790, taking the name Ferdinando III, one of the first works he commissioned was the creation of the Winter Quarters in the right wing's second-floor rooms, the same rooms that he had shared with his brother Francesco when they were boys.

Maria de' Medici, daughter of Francesco I and Giovanna of Austria, was the first to live in this apartment, at the end of the sixteenth century. At the time, the apartment included the large Drama Room, the same size as the White Room below it. Ottavio Rinuccini's *Euridice* was performed here for the first time, with music by Jacopo Peri, in honour of Maria's marriage to Henry IV of France.

After Maria's departure, the apartment was given to her half-brother don Antonio, the natural son of Francesco I and Bianca Cappello. Later, it was occupied by Ferdinando II and Vittoria della Rovere and, later still, from 1658 on, by Prince Cardinal Leopoldo, brother of the Grand Duke.

Leopoldo, a man of culture and a scientist, founder of the Cimento Academy, arranged his enormous collection of manuscripts, rare books, mathematical instruments, sculptures, drawings, and paintings in this apartment. Its appearance was luxurious. The walls of the drawing room (partitioned to create the Footmen's Antechamber) were covered with red taffeta and its ceiling was painted red and embellished with gilded intaglios. In the other rooms, adorned with fine objects and works of art, the wallcoverings were of brightly coloured silk, embellished with silver-and-gold thread.

After Leopoldo's death, in 1675, the apartment was occupied by Francesco Maria, brother of Cosimo III, and then by his widow, Eleonora Gonzaga. The wallcoverings and furniture were changed during this period: deep red became the dominant colour and velvet replaced the silk, giving the apartment a decidedly more austere overall appearance.

Under Peter Leopold, after the end of the Medici dynasty and the period of the Lorraine Regency, the apartment was given over to Archdukes Francesco and Ferdinando and then later, in 1775, to the Archduchess. These arrangements were not preceded by any major work on the apartment. A limited amount of restoration was done, the more worn wallcoverings were replaced, and the furnishings were adapted to the needs of the new tenants. The only significant intervention was the subdivision of the drawing room above the Bona Room (indicated as "H" on the seventeenth-century floor plan), under the direction of Niccolò Gaspare Paoletti.

The first major changes were not made until 1790. Once again, Ferdinando III entrusted the project to

D.M. Marmi, Second-floor Apartments, ca 1662. The original Drama Room is subdivided into two rooms, marked "T" ("Footmen's Antechamber") and "S".

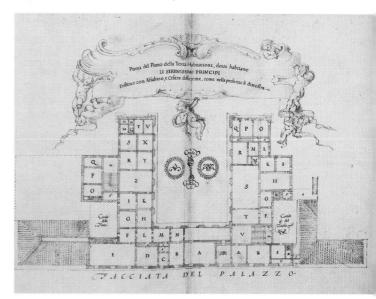

*Winter Quarters, Music Room*

*Winter Quarters, Red Room.*

Paoletti, who began his work in the old Drama Room. He eliminated the Footmen's Antechamber and, on the other side, built the Music Room, which was frescoed by Giuseppe Terreni. The ceiling was modified in order to adapt it to the new subdivision, but was left substantially unchanged.

The decorations of the doors, walls and ceilings were renewed in the all of the quarter's rooms, the work being done mainly by Terreni, with the assistance of many other artists. Among the main undertakings were the creation of the gilded stucco niche for the stove in the Bedroom and the renovation of the decorations in the little chapel, most likely attributable to the stucco artist Francesco Visetti.

The colours of the wallcoverings were made lighter and more in keeping with the taste of the period. The red seventeenth-century velvet was replaced with green and yellow silk *amouerre* and with white satin, patterned with stripes, flowers and little knots. The Quarters' baroque look, still present in the temporary arrangement done in 1775, has by now completely disappeared.

The work on the Quarters was interrupted

*Winter Quarters, King's Bedroom, with the large stove in the niche, decorated with gilded stuccowork.*

*Winter Quarters, King's Studio.*

*Winter Quarters, detail of the Chapel vault.*

during the Napoleonic interval and was begun again in 1815, under the direction of Pasquale Poccianti, who created the Guardroom, the Ballroom and the Muses Room. Luigi Catani designed the ornamentation, "to make it easy for the stucco workers". Various sculptors – Giovannozzi, Santarelli, and Spedolo – supplied the models for the bas-reliefs and other plastic decorations. An "orchestra" was made above the Guardroom, facing the Ballroom, with three camouflaged openings made of wooden panels decorated like the walls.

In the other rooms, which after the death of Ferdinando III were assigned to his widow, Grand Duchess Maria Ferdinanda, the pictorial decoration of the walls and vaults was continued. The work was done by Catani, as well as by other painters working in the Pitti at the time, such as Antonio Marini and Giuseppe Castagnoli.

As compared to the public rooms, characterised by strongly-coloured stuccowork and representations with classical themes, the Grand Duchess' private rooms were done in soft shades, the doors were decorated with flowers and garlands, the backgrounds were blue and pink, the overall effect still being that of eighteenth-century taste.

*Winter Quarters, Ballroom.*

*Winter Quarters, Muses Gallery.*

*Winter Quarters, Bedroom, detail of the vault and overall view.*

After the end of the Lorraine Grand Duchy and the annexation of Tuscany to the Kingdom of Italy, and during the period when Florence was the country's capital (1865 – 1869), the Pitti Palace became the residence of the Savoys. The Winter Quarters were among the apartments given to Vittorio Emanuele II and hence became called "His Majesty the King's Apartment".

*Winter Quarters, Bathroom (formerly the Chapel).*

No major work was done on the apartment during this period, apart from changes to the wallcoverings and furnishings, giving the rooms their definitive appearance, just as we see them today. Only one of the rooms underwent a radical alteration: Cardinal Leopoldo's seventeenth-century chapel, renovated at the end of the eighteenth century, was made into a spacious bathroom connected to the King of Italy's bedroom.

The sovereigns occupied these rooms for only a short time and they bear more the stamp of the younger branch of the Savoy family, the Aosta, whose residence they were from the first years of their reign and who continued to live here with considerable continuity even when most of the palace had become offices of the State Administration. This is the reason why the Winter Quarters are also known as the "Duchess of Aosta's Apartment", a testimony to a daily life lived here until 1946, when the history of the Pitti as a royal residence came to a definitive end.

Three of the descendants of Amedeo Aosta, brother of King Umberto I, lived in the Pitti.

His grandson Amedeo, son of his eldest son Emanuele Filiberto and heir to the title, was given the Winter Quarters. After his death in 1931, his widow Anna Elena of France, Duchess of Aosta, continued to live there until the Second World War.

Vittorio Emanuele, Count of Turin, brother of Emanuele Filiberto, was given the Meridian Quarters, which he held until his death (1946).

The other brother, Luigi, Duke of the Abruzzi, had the mezzanine above the Winter Quarters, previously assigned to the Prince of Naples.

# The Prince of Naples' Quarters

LAURA BALDINI GIUSTI

In 1871, a small set of rooms was prepared in the Pitti Palace for Umberto and Margherita of Savoy's eldest son, Vittorio Emanuele, born on November 11, 1869, and given the title of Prince of Naples. Some of the mezzanine rooms above the Winter Quarters were chosen for the purpose and were connected to the these quarters by a small staircase. In Cardinal Leopoldo's time, these rooms were the Library, the Gallery of Various Mathematical Instruments, and the Armoury. In the Lorraine period, they were used as service rooms.

When the apartment was re-done for the young Prince, it was completely renovated and re-furnished, in a more sober style than was used for the quarters below it. Painted wallpaper was chosen to replace the luxurious wallcoverings, and only in the drawing room do they resemble silk damask, the effect of which was reproduced with a particular printing technique, while simple lozenge motifs on soft pastel background shades were used in the other rooms. The furnishings also confirm the moderate tone of these rooms. The Prince's bedroom is large and airy, with his wet nurse's sofa bed, his cradle, the large mirror, and the "imitation tapestry" carpet that covers the central table. The servant's room is more austere, similar to many "bourgeois" interiors depicted in mid-nineteenth-century paintings.

The last tenant in this apartment, as in the Winter Quarters, was also an Aosta. It was assigned to Luigi, Duke of the Abruzzi (1873 – 1933), Amedeo d'Aosta's third child, remembered for his voyages in Alaska and in the Arctic, during which he made a number of significant scientific and astronomical observations.

*Prince of Naples' Quarters, bedroom.*

# Costume Gallery

CATERINA CHIARELLI

Established in 1983, the Costume Gallery is located in the elegant Meridian Building, annexed to the south side of the Pitti Palace, facing the Boboli Gardens. Grand Duke Peter Leopold entrusted construction of the building to Gaspare Maria Paoletti, who began work in 1776; it was completed approximately a half century later by Pasquale Poccianti. A comfortable and secluded villa, it was chosen as a residence by all the reigning houses, from Lorraine to Savoy, including the French interrugnum. The frescoed vaults are an extremely significant heritage of Tuscan historical romanticism, while some of the façade rooms, used for exhibitions, still have period neo-classical decorations and wallcoverings. The rooms, smaller than the monumental spaces characteristic of the palace's official apartments, are ideally

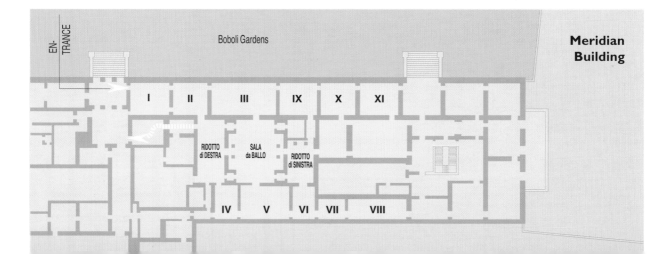

suited to be "inhabited" by mannequins wearing, appropriately, historical clothing.

The gallery is currently the only museum in Italy devoted to the history of fashion and has a patrimony consisting of more than six thousand pieces, including very old clothing, theatrical costumes and refined and decorative accessories. Most of the pieces have been donated, a few have been purchased, while some of the costumes, a small collection of very old textile fragments, and a similar

*View of some rooms of the museum.*

collection of sacred paraments, were already in the possession of the Monuments and Fine Arts Office. The funeral clothing used for Cosimo I de' Medici, Eleonora of Toledo and her son Don Garzia, restored in the museum's restoration laboratory, has been added to the collection.

It naturally being impossible to exhibit everything at the same time, for reasons having to do with both conservation and lack of space, the works are normally kept in storage and displayed in rotation. The selections exhibited in the display cases are thus changed on an average of every two months, so that, over time, the public has the opportunity to see the entire collection, which is often presented in the context of theme exhibitions. This periodic rotation renders the museum a living institution in which ideas and initiatives are constantly simmering. It enables the museum to exhibit the largest possible number of works, thus also satisfying both scholars' needs and donors' understandable expectations.

The restoration laboratory and the storage department, two indispensable aspects of the gallery's organisation, are connected to the museum spaces. All the works are first examined in the restoration laboratory before being exhibited or stored. It is in fact in the laboratory, after a careful examination of an object's state of conservation, that the decision is made whether to place it in storage, or, if it has been altered or is deteriorating, to undertake a more complete restoration. The storage department is the gallery's other fundamental component. Located on the Villa's first floor, in rooms that are constantly air-conditioned and appropriately set up for textile conservation, the storage department has been undergoing a complete re-organisation for the past three years, so as to make it accessible to visitors.

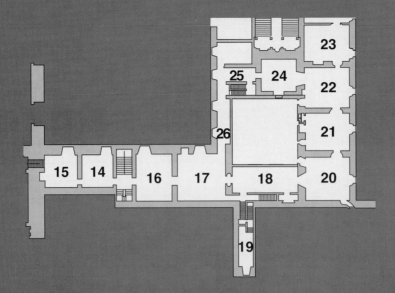

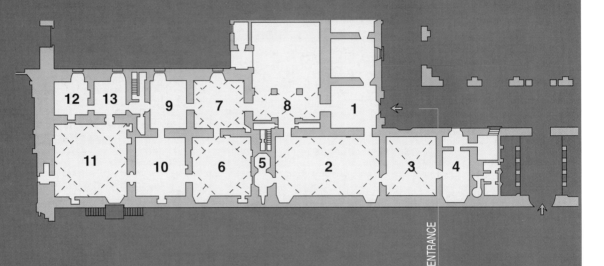

ENTRANCE

| | | | |
|---|---|---|---|
| 1. | LUCA PITTI ROOM | 13. | ROOM OF IVORIES AND RELIQUARIES |
| 2. | ROOM OF GIOVANNI DA SAN GIOVANNI | 14. | CAMEOS ROOM |
| 3. | LORENZO ROOM | 15. | JEWELS ROOM |
| 4. | GROTTICINA | 16-17. | SALZBURG TREASURE |
| 5. | CAPPELLINA | 18. | LOGGETTA |
| 6. | PUBLIC HEARING ROOM | 19. | TESORETTO |
| 7. | ROOM OF CRYSTALS AND SEMIPRECIOUS STONES | 20. | EXOTIC ROOM |
| 8. | COURTYARD OF AJAX | 21. | CHINESE PORCELAIN ROOM |
| 9. | AMBERS ROOM | 22. | JAPANESE PORCELAIN ROOM |
| 10. | PRIVATE HEARING ROOM | 23. | DONATIONS ROOM |
| 11. | THIRD HEARING ROOM | 24. | CASTINGS ROOM |
| 12. | IVORIES ROOM | 25. | CASTINGS HALLWAY |
| | | 26. | RELIQUARIES HALLWAY |

# Silverworks Museum

MARILENA MOSCO

The history of this museum is linked to the history of the Medici. As much as the artists who executed the works, it was their love of all things beautiful that has made this place and the treasure it contains one of the richest and most prestigious museums of decorative art in all Europe. The silver works for which the museum is named come, for the most part, from the House of Lorraine, being part of the so-called "Salzburg Treasure", that is to say, the collections of the bishops of Salzburg and Wurzburg that Fernando II of Lorraine 'plundered' during the Napoleonic era (exactly as Napoleon was doing in Italy) and had brought to Florence on his return.

Thus, the museum is named for the original 19th-century exhibition of precious "silverworks" in the Room of Giovanni da San Giovanni. However, it could just as rightly be called the Museum of the Grand-ducal Treasure: officially established only in 1919, it gathers together all the treasures collected by the Medici and Lorraine grand dukes.

The precious and semiprecious stone vases originally belonged to Piero and Lorenzo il Magnifico; after being stored in a number of sites, they were placed in the Gems Room of the Uffizi, to be transferred later to the Silverworks Museum. Similarly, the rock crystals commissioned by Francesco I from Milanese workshops, together with the renowned lapis lazuli vase designed by Bernardo Buontalenti and the rock crystal coffer by Valerio Belli were also originally on display in the famous Tribuna of the Uffizi. The fantastic vases of polished ivory, the war spoils of prince Matías de' Medici, figured in the Uffizi inventory of 1633, while the ivory figures, commissioned from the German sculptor Baldassare Stockamer, belonged to Cardinal Leopoldo's fabulous collection, held in Pitti Palace. Prince Ferdinando is instead responsible for some of the crystal, amber and ivory pieces, while it was grand duke Cosimo II who charged the sculptor Giovanni Battista Foggini with the by-now renowned *stipo,* or decorated cabinet.

Finally, it was with the advent of the Lorraine in 1737 that Anna Maria Luisa de' Medici, in an act of foresight and wisdom, bequeathed the family inheritance to the city of Florence, in her words: "for State embellishment, public use and to attract the curiosity of Foreigners", also donating her private collection of jewelled *galanterie*, considered rarities today. Partly transferred to Vienna by the Lorraine, these jewels were then returned to Italy after the First World War, precisely when the grand-ducal patrimony, administered by the House of Savoy, became property of the Italian state.

Covering twenty-five rooms, the museum occupies the left wing of Pitti Palace, added during the 17th Century to the original 15th-century core and used as Summer Apartments by the grand dukes. The rooms overlooking the square of Piazza Pitti, once used as hearing rooms, contain magnificent frescoes celebrating the patronage of the Medici, while those at the back, which the palace royalty took as their private quarters, were unadorned and now hold beautiful collections of rare and precious works.

The mezzanine, frescoed by several 17th-century artists, is given over to the Lorraine collections, gems, jewellery and exotic curiosities.

*Ottavio Vannini,* Lorenzo amongst the artists, *detail, Room of Giovanni da San Giovanni.*

## Luca Pitti Room

The entrance hall is also called the Luca Pitti room, because of the 15th-century Terracotta bust (wall opposite the entrance) of the famous Florentine banker who originally had the palace built. The hall also contains an interesting *Portrait of a lady*, a work from the Florentine School done sometime before 1598, the year in which the houses then surrounding the old palace were demolished, as can be seen in the upper right corner of the painting.

The *Medici Family tree*, on the opposite side, illustrates the first and second branches of the family. The eight terracotta busts, from the 18th Century, depict the family's most illustrious members.

*Medici Family Tree, 1699, ink on paper, 152 × 136.6 cm.*

*Workshop of Giovan Battista Foggini, Bust of grand duke Francesco i de' Medici, 1723-1725, terracotta.*

*Room of Giovanni da San Giovanni.*

## Room of Giovanni da San Giovanni

This room takes its name from the Valdarno painter who designed the room's decoration in 1635 on the occasion of the marriage of Ferdinando II to Vittoria della Rovere, which is frescoed on the ceiling. The vault and wall of the entrance depict the advent of Islam in the person of Mohammed II (first panel), the flight from Constantinople conquered by the Turks and the expulsion of the poets (Homer and Sappho) and philosophers (Plato and Aristotle) from Mount Parnassus (second panel) and their arrival in the Florence of Lorenzo il Magnifico (third panel). With the quatrain verses annotating the scenes at the frescoes' base, the Tuscan painter, strives to provide a counterpoint to Rafael's Parnassus, now in the Vatican, with a representation of Instinct, represented by the satyrs, overcoming Culture.

The other frescoes decorating the room are more in keeping with the donor's intent, which was to celebrate Medici patronage. Here we find the work of the Florentine painters Cecco Bravo, Ottavio Vannini and Francesco Furini. On the left wall, frescoed by Cecco Bravo, is a portrait of Lorenzo il Magnifico meeting Apollo and the Muses (fourth panel), conversing with Prudence while banishing War and Envy and bringing on the reign of Peace and Plenty (fifth panel). On the wall opposite the entrance, Vannini depicts Lorenzo il Magnifico surrounded by a group of artists, amongst whom, Giuliano da Sangallo, to the left with a model of the villa at Poggio a Caiano and, to the right, young Michelangelo, presenting the classically inspired bust of *Faun* (seventh panel).

Lastly, on the right wall, done by Francesco Furini, Lorenzo can be seen at the foot of Plato's statue before the villa at Careggi, the site of the neo-Platonic cenacle evoked by the portraits of Marsilio Ficino and Pico della Mirandola and allegories of Astronomy and Poetry (ninth panel). The next panel depicts the allegory of Lorenzo's death, with the three Parcae receiving the thread of the life and the swan recovering Lorenzo's memory from Lethe, the river of forgetfulness. Lorenzo is immortalised by the tree of Fame, whilst at the bottom the clouds of war gather with the return of Mars (tenth panel).

## Lorenzo Room

The Lorenzo Room, also called the *Sala Buia* (Dark Hall) or Hearing Room of the Grand duchess, is the ideal continuation of the celebration of Lorenzo il Magnifico begun in the Room of Giovanni da San Giovanni. The left-hand wall bears his portrait, attributed to Luigi Fiammingo, from the school of Bronzino, and death mask, while the showcases in the centre hold the Semiprecious stone vases that belonged to his collections.

The Roman passion for marble and semiprecious stones spread to Florence and particularly enthralled Lorenzo's father, Piero de' Medici, who began the collection of ancient vases, thus explaining the abundance of these objects combining exquisite execution with rare and varied materials (jasper, amethyst, sardonyx). Generally of classical Roman or Venetian manufacture, they were decorated in Lorenzo's time and stamped with his initials. After the fall of the Medici in the time of Charles VIII, Lorenzo's son, Giovanni, later Pope Leo X, salvaged them and brought them to Rome. Clement VII then had them returned to Florence, where they became reliquaries, conserved in the Church of San Lorenzo in a cabinet designed by Michelangelo expressly for this purpose. In 1785, when the cult of relics was superseded by the advent of illuminism, they were emptied and transferred to the Gems Room in the Uffizi and thence, already empty, moved to the Silverworks Museum at the beginning of the 20th Century. The mountings are by Florentine or Flemish goldsmiths. One of these, Giusto da Firenze decorated the beautiful Red jasper vase, in the long showcase on the left, noteworthy for the cast and engraved gilded silver mounting decorated with red, white and green enamel and gold filigree base, set with blue, gold, violet and silver enamels. The vase, probably manufactured in Venice in the 13th Century, originally bore the Medici symbol of six balls arranged in a circle. The same showcase also holds the light-speckled and veined Double-handled Roman vase with brown sardonyx cover bearing a beauti-

ful gilded silver mounting with the coat of arms of Lorenzo il Magnifico in the base's centre; the faun heads, after the style of Buontalenti, on the upper handle joints were added later, during the time of Francesco I.

The two small showcases along the left wall display crystals and ancient vases, mostly Roman or Byzantine, amongst which a sardonyx libation *simpulum* from the Imperial period (Inv. Gemme 1921, No. 532) and two small chalcedony Roman-art goblets from the First Century A.D., mounted in enamelled gold by the grand duke's workshops in the late 16th Century (Inv. Gemme 1921, No. 576, 602).

The earliest Medici's passion for the antique is testified to by the small porphyry statue of *Venus* (Inv. Sculture 1914, No. 1067), carried out by Pier Maria Serbaldi, a sculptor quite famous in the time of Lorenzo il Magnifico who was cited by Vasari for having reintroduced the antique custom of using red porphyry in sculpture.

Lastly, the two right-hand showcases contain reliquaries and chalices from the 14th and 15th Centuries. Worthy of note is the Limoges enamel triptych (15th Century, Inv. A.S.E., No. 96) representing the Passion and Crucifixion, probably by an artist in the circle of the Penicaud, and a Silver reliquary chest with appliqué at the borders and gilded silver medallions. The relic contained within is visible through the small rock-crystal fenestration, while the upper portion opens up like a cover. It is one of the few examples of 14th-century Rhenish art remaining from the once rich antique reliquary collection.

*Rhenish Art*, Reliquary, 14th C, partially gilded silver and rock crystal, 16.7 × 11.5 × 15.2 cm, Inv. A.S.E., No. 258.

*Venetian manufacture and Florentine goldwork (Giusto da Firenze)*, Vase, 13th C, 15th C mount, red jasper, enamelled silver-gilt mount, h. 27 cm, initialled "Laur. Med.", Inv. Gemme 1921, No. 638.

## Grotticina

The Lorenzo Room leads into the *Grotticina*, or Small Grotto, named so because it was once covered with shells like the Buontalenti Grotto in Boboli Gardens. Today the right side is still embellished by a 17th-century Fountain surrounded by sponge and sculptures of cupids, the work of the Florentine Andrea Peruzzi.

The room, formerly for the exclusive use of the Grand duchess, now goes by the name of the Frames Room because it contains many of the frames from the storerooms of Pitti Palace, now on display after their recent restoration.

Opposite the entrance is the Frame with sunflower, attributed the Dutchman Vittorio Crosten, active in the court of Cosimo III during the late 17th Century. An exquisite example of the elaborate frames of baroque art, its thick swirling-leaf volutes curl inward and unfold outward to intertwine and terminate in jutting bellflowers resting on the inner layer, in turn formed by arrays of laurel leaves. In the centre of the room, a semiprecious stone table base vies for the visitor's attention.

## Cappellina

High on the left wall, the beautifully carved limewood relief by the Englishman Grinling Gibbons was presented to Cosimo III in 1682 by king Charles II of England as a token of the friendship and peace between England and Tuscany.

Once through the Room of Giovanni da San Giovanni, we come to the Cappellina or small chapel, decorated by Michelangelo Cinganelli in the third decade of the 17th Century. The two lateral windows used to allow outside onlookers to follow the religious functions. On the altar to the left is the gilded silver Reliquary of the holy cross, attributed a Parisian goldsmith after the design of Etienne Delaune (1555-1650). The piece, which once belonged to Christine of Lorraine, framed a portrait within an oval crystal, but was transformed into a reliquary during the 17th Century with the addition of the cross, symbols of the passion, cherubs and, at its crown, the cupids and resurrected Christ.

*Andrea Peruzzi, Fountain, 17th C.*

*Grand-ducal workshops, attributed to Vittorio Crosten, Frame with Sunflower, late 17th C, carved and gilded wood, 149 × 115 cm, s.n.*

*Grand-ducal workshops, design by Etienne Delaune, Reliquary of the Holy Cross, ca 1632, silver gilt and brass, semiprecious stone, enamel and crystal decorations, h. 75 cm, Inv A.S.E., No. 227.*

## Public Hearing Room

The following room, whose central wall contains the inscription "Rado tu parla e sii breve et arguto" (Speak seldom and be brief and witty), was decorated in 1639 by the perspective artists, Angelo Michele Colonna and Agostino Mitelli, providing proof to Ferdinando II de' Medici of their talents, already evident in Palazzo Spada in Rome.

The two were masters of illusionism who devised effects of limitless perspective, with real and false windows (note the trompe l'oeil on the wall toward the façade), colonnades and arcades where curious characters appear, such as the boy chasing the monkey on the entrance wall and, on the opposite side, the chamberlain and dame reminiscent of the ladies painted by Veronese in the Maser villa. In the room's centre is the large Stipo d'alemagna, a decorated cabinet of carved ebony with painted and semiprecious stone intarsia panelling. The cabinet, destined to hold precious stones in its various drawers was carried out in 1628 in Augsburg (hence its name, meaning "German cabinet"). The archduke of Tyrol presented it to Ferdinando II de' Medici during one of his visits to Innsbruck. The coloured semiprecious stone panelling on the outside is miniated with biblical scenes and stories from the life of Christ, while the insides of the drawers are decorated with semiprecious stone intarsia. When open, the doors reveal a rotating four-sided drum: two with small amber statues, one with semiprecious stone panels and the last with a painting of Virgin and Child.

It is interesting to compare the German mosaic work on the cabinet with the Florentine intarsia of the *prie-dieu* in front: the base of this latter bears a semiprecious stone panel with the floral motifs typical of Florence, while its upper portion contains a tiny mosaic, the work of Giovanni Battista Calandra from the early 17th Century.

*Augsburg workshops, Decorated "German cabinet", 1628, ebony and semiprecious stones, 260 × 137 × 93 cm (base h. 56 cm), Inv. O.D.A. 1911, No. 1541.*

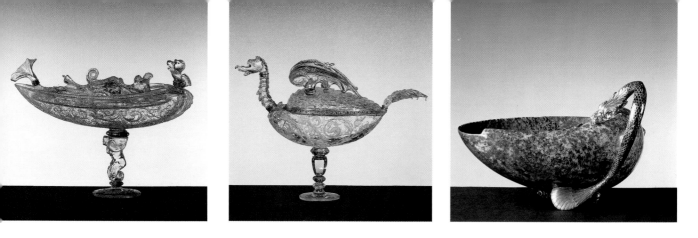

## Room of Crystals and Semiprecious Stones

The door on the left leads to the following room containing masterpieces of 16th and 17th-century Milanese and Tuscan craftwork. The articles found here were originally destined for the showcases of the Tribuna of the Uffizi and were rarely used for table settings.

Most of the finest pieces found in the room were carried out by Milanese master craftsmen, particularly, the Saracchi and Miseroni brothers and their workshops.

After witnessing the skill of the Milanese, Francesco I de' Medici, a passionate admirer of beautiful materials, decided to establish a shop in Florence for the manufacture of semiprecious stones. To this end, he called upon Ambrogio and Stefano Caroni and Giorgio di Cristofano Gaffurri, who set up shop in the *Casino di San Marco*, built by Buontalenti (today seat of the Appeals Court).

The vases and goblets made in the Milanese shops are characterised by their bizarre, typically mannerist forms: richly carved fish, birds, monsters and dragons. The mounts – gold or silver gilt adorned with enamelling, precious stones or cameos – are the work of Flemish, Dutch and French goldsmiths who had taken refuge in Italy because of the difficulty of working in their respective countries, torn, as they were by religious wars. Amongst these, the Dutchman Jacques Bylivelt, the Flemish Hans Domes and Frenchman Odoard Vallet, all worked in the *Casino di San Marco*.

A dolphin, symbol of wisdom and prudence, forms the cover of the Boat-shaped rock crystal and enamelled gold vase upheld by a pillar in the form of a siren.

A typical creation of the Saracchi brothers is the Rock crystal vase in the form of a dragon, whose cover is carved in relief to represent the animal's winged back. Bands of enamelled gold unite the two main parts of the body, the lower part of which is engraved with plant motifs. The vase, with its strange and extravagant forms, is a fine example of the inventive fantasy typical of mannerism. It was replicated several times in Florence as well by the Caroni and Gaffurri.

The famous Lapislazuli flask with gold chain and mounting is a masterpiece of Florentine craft and Flemish gold work, done in around 1581 to 1583. The brilliant architect Bernardo Buontalenti devised the two unique handles formed by winged, fish-tailed sphinxes, on which the goldsmith Jacques Bylivelt set two elegant female figures united by a band of enamelled gold. The original gold chain was replaced with the current gilded copper one. The harmony of the work's design and execution bespeaks of collaborative effort between Caroni, who realised Buontalenti's design, and Bylivelt, who did the gold work.

The Snake-handled lapislazuli goblet appealed to Francesco I's taste for refined objects inspired by nature. It was executed by the goldsmith Giovan Battista Cervi, working in the *Casino di San Marco* on commission from the grand duke.

Also noteworthy is the beautiful Rock crystal goblet with handles depicting two grotesque masks facing one another and whose bottom is engraved with sea gods in combat.

Another of the museum's masterpieces is the Rock crystal bowl by Valerio Belli, whose name is engraved with the date 1532 in the cover's central panel. The enamelled ovals bear the name and em-

*French manufacture, Boat-shaped Vase, mid-16th C, rock crystal, enamelled gold, 25.5 × 34 cm, Inv. Bargello 1917 (III), No. 16.*

*Milan workshop of the Saracchi brothers, Dragon-shaped vase, late 16th C, rock crystal and enamelled gold, h. 23 cm, Inv. Bargello 1917 (III), No. 14.*

*Florentine manufacture and Giovan Battista Cervi, Bowl with snake handle, mid-16th C, lapis lazuli, gold with enamel, 8 × 15 cm, Inv. Gemme 1921, No. 413.*

*Bernardo Buontalenti (design), Jacques Bylivelt (goldwork), Gian Stefano Caroni (stonework), Flask, late 16th C, lapis lazuli, gold and enamel, h. 40.5 cm, Inv. Gemme 1921, No. 802.*

blems of Pope Clement VII who commissioned the work from Belli, the finest engraver of the time, to give to Francesco I on the occasion of the marriage of Caterina de' Medici to Henry II of France. The eight panels represent scenes of Christ's Passion, engraved from behind and backed with silver leaf, a procedure that endows the work with transparency.

A work that has instead been attributed to the Saracchi workshop is the red jasper Dragon-shaped vase with cover in the form of a darting-tailed dolphin. The vase was once adorned with many more precious stones than the four rubies and three pearls remaining today.

Lastly, the two beautiful Rock crystal vessels deserve special attention: the first, from the Milanese shop of Annibale Fontana, bears graceful engravings of garlands, festoons and acanthus leaves and a grotesque mask handle; the second was executed from a single block of crystal so perfect (only a single vein) that it called for no engraving, but only a ruby-studded enamelled gold mount reminiscent of South American masks. To date, this is the only known work of the goldsmith Odoard Vallet (1618).

## Ambers Room

The right-hand exit of the Crystals Room leads to the Courtyard of Ajax – named for the 2nd-century B.C. Roman marble sculpture depicting Ajax sustaining the body of Patroclus, located under the vault decorated in 1624 by Cosimo Lotti, a student of Bernardino Poccetti – while the left side exits into to the Ambers Room, originally the bedroom of the grand duke Gian Gastone (portrayed on the door).

Yellow amber is a fossil resin of plant origin found mainly in the lignite de-

posits formed from ancient coniferous forests along the Baltic coast. In fact, it was amber mainly from northern countries, especially Königsberg, that was used to fashion the altars collected by Maria Maddalena of Austria, wife of Cosimo II de' Medici, both intensely religious. Other pieces here, mainly secular, belonged to Ferdinando II, such as the the Wine-making fountain to the right of the entrance, or to Prince Ferdinando, such as the Amber chest with ivory relief, topped by the statue of Saint Casimir and decorated with the Medici shields, which was carried out in Gdansk, Poland, a city specialized in the manufacture of amber and ivory objects. The Amber altar, signed and dated 1619 by the great engraver Georg Schreiber from Königsberg, is made up of three parts decorated with ivory reliefs representing the *Crucifixion* with the Virgin and Saint John. It has been placed at the centre of a number of other altars, all from Königsberg, displayed in the grand showcase built in 1728 expressly to hold these ambers by the Florentine engraver Giuseppe Gonnelli, who decorated it with plant and marine motifs in allusion to the origins of the material itself.

*Odoard Vallet, Vase, 1618, rock crystal, enamelled gold with emeralds and rubies, h. 38 cm, Inv. Gemme 1921, No. 490.*

*Milan workshop of the Saracchi Brothers, Dragon-shaped vase, late 16th C, jasper, pearls, rubies and gold with enamel, h. 21 cm, Inv. Gemme 1921, No. 493.*

*North-west Germany, Wine-making fountain, mid-17th C, amber and gilded bronze, h. 78 cm, Inv. Bargello 1917 (I), No. 95.*

## Private Hearing Room

This room is known as the Columns Room in reference to the grandiose columns painted by the Bolognese perspective artists Angelo Michele Colonna and Agostino Mitelli in an attempt to stupefy the observer and attract her eye to the ceiling fresco exalting Alessandro Magno. Alessandro is also portrayed in the lower panels as peacemaker and Maecenas on a par with Ferdinando II de' Medici. Between two columns on the ceiling a gentleman looks out with a telescope, echoing Galileo's invention, and a boy plays with a parrot, a novelty from the New World. The room contains five exquisite semiprecious stone mosaics worth examining closely, particularly the 17th-century Semiprecious and soft-stone mosaic table on touchstone backing in the left corner of the wall toward the façade. It serves as testament to the evolution of Florentine craftsmanship from the early 16th-century geometric principles of Roman origin to the naturalism of the 17th Century, evident in the floral motifs at the corners.

## Third Hearing Room

This room, which Mitelli finished decorating in 1640, concludes the series of reception rooms in the Summer Apartments of the grand dukes, who reserved the back quarters for personal use. The walls are hung with portraits of the grand dukes. The tables – the great ancient jasper wheel in the centre, the one decorated by Dionigi Nigetti with sphinxes, and the two with harpies by Giovan Battista Balatri (17th Century) – serve to evoke the sumptuousness of the palace decorations during the 16th and 17th-Centuries.

A dazzling example of late baroque Tuscan furniture is the ebony and semiprecious stone Elector's cabinet, executed by the Florentine Giovan Battista Foggini on commission from Cosimo III who presented it to his daughter Anna Maria Luisa de' Medici for her marriage to Giovanni Guglielmo, the Palatine Elector. The celebrative intent of the *stipo*, or decorated cabinet, is well evident in the brass and semiprecious stone figure of the Elector seated on an arms trophy. The figure is crowned by the quartered Medici and Palatine coats flanked by the allegorical figures of Magnanimity and Strength.

German manufacture, Ornamental polyhedron, probably rom late 16th C, turned ivory and gold decorations, h. 28.6 cm, Inv. Bargello 1879, No. 133.

"Master of the Furies", Curtius riding his horse into the abyss, 17th C, ivory, h. cm 57, Inv. Bargello 1879, No. 36.

## Ivories Room

Numerous articles collected by the Medici grand dukes are on display here. Prince Ferdinando himself loved to work the lathe (note the turned vase in the right-hand showcase, Inv. Bargello 1879, No. 45). This material's fascinating origins, its rarity, preciousness, beauty, malleability and resistance, as well as the structural properties that make it well-suited to sculpture, all explain how it came to replace brass during the 17th Century, especially in countries like Saxony and Denmark, where the art of lathing was more highly developed. Even many princes practiced this art, amongst whom the duke of Coburg, who had two master turners in his service: Marc Heiden and Johann Eisenberg, the authors of the phantasmagorical series of turned vases in the most disparate and fascinating shapes. The vases were looted in 1638 during the Thirty Years' War by prince Matias de' Medici who had them brought to Florence.

Another masterpiece is the ivory sculptural group located in the room's centre: Curtius riding his horse into the abyss, carried out in the 17th Century by the German "Master of the Furies".

The marquetry that was so successful in Florence in the 15th Century, with the masterpieces by Giuliano da Maiano in Palazzo Vecchio, returns in a different form in the 17th Century, through the work of the Flemish master artisan, Leonardo van der Vinne, author of the beautiful Decorated cabinet inlaid with exotic wood, ivory, mother of pearl and gilded brass on the left-hand wall. According to the 1667 Medici inventory, this *stipo* was topped, not only by a brass and alabaster statue of Mars, but by ten other gilded brass statuettes carried out by the court silversmith, Marcantonio Merlini. In the 19th Century, however, the originals were substituted with the current small brass vases.

## Ivories and Reliquaries Room

This room contains a number of works by the German artist Balthasar Stockamer who studied classical and baroque sculpture in Rome, taking inspiration for several pieces that he would complete in the mid-17th Century for cardinal Leopoldo de' Medici, for example, *David Seated* (Inv. Bargello 1879, No. 150, from a brass by Susini), *Hercules and Hydra* (Inv. Bargello 1879, No. 151, from a brass by Algardi) and especially the Crucifixion (inspired by Pietro da Cortona). Apart from these rather lofty works, there are also others in the naturalist genre, inspired by the more commonplace, such as the the caged pony by the Sicilian Filippo Planzone (Inv. Bargello 1879, No. 198), and Maddalena of Austria's dog, inspired by the pet that Cosimo II gave his wife, who liked to surrounded herself with dogs in the villa at Poggio Imperiale.

Balthasar Stockamer, Crucifixion, 1666-1668, ivory, h. 88.7 cm, Inv. Bargello 1879, No. 79.

Florentine manufacture, Dog, 17th C, ivory (dog) and ebony (box), 6 × 18 cm, Inv. A.S.E., No. 187.

## Cameos Room

The passageway to the stairs leading to the mezzanine is hung with the painting *Vase of flowers*, done in *scagliola*, a coloured imitation marble reintroduced in Florence in the 18th Century by Ignazio Hugford and Cristiano Lamberto Gori, which still today is the pride of Florentine artisans. The right wing of the mezzanine is given over to cameos, mosaics and jewels once belonging to members of the Medici house, from Cosimo I up to Anna Maria Luisa. The gems and stones, incised or in relief, served to glorify the Medici family and offer visual testimony to the culture of the classical world, held to be a paragon to be emulated.

The cameos – stones worked in relief with wheels and abrasives mixtures of sand or diamond powder and water – include the famous onyx Cameo of Cosimo I, displayed in the central showcase, which portrays the grand duke with his wife, Eleonora of Toledo, and four children. The central *tondo* must have contained a medal with the city of Florence, which has been lost, as also the figures of the couple's other three children. The cameo, carried out by Giovanni Antonio de' Rossi between 1557 and 1562, is one of the most important works of its kind from the 16th Century.

In the same showcase, one can admire the seven amethyst or green jasper-backed panels with gold reliefs by Giambologna representing the Feats of Francesco i de' Medici and the Oval with Panorama of Piazza della Signoria. The semiprecious stone intarsia work with gold purfling and stamped gold bas reliefs was carried out in 1599 by Bernardino Gaffurri (the gold reliefs were executed by Jacques Bylivelt in 1600). The architectural elements visible in the background are miniated in ground silver engraved with the figures at the windows, the small man exiting the door of the Customs Office, Cellini's *Perseus* and Giambologna's *Rape of the Sabine Women*. Standing out in its centre are the *Equestrian Monument to Cosimo I,* the *Neptune Fountain, Marzocco, David, Hercules and Cacus*, all in gold relief. A curious feature of the work is that it shows the

*Bernardino Gaffurri (mosaic), Jacques Bylivelt (gold bas relief), Oval with panorama of Piazza della Signoria, 1599, 18 × 25.5 cm, Inv. Gemme 1921, No. 823.*

*Giovanni Antonio de' Rossi, Cosimo I's Cameo, 1557-1562, onyx, 18.5 × 16.5 cm, Inv. Bargello 1917, No. 1.*

ancient terracotta and *pietra serena* pavement of Piazza della Signoria, which the Florence Town Council recently proposed, unsuccessfully, bringing back.

The wall is hung with a Roman mosaic with minute *tesserae*, carried out in 1615 by the master Marcello Provenzale, specialized in this technique. Also interesting is the Diamond-eyed turquoise mask, surrounded by an oak branch alluding to Vittoria della Rovere (whose surname means "oak"), visible in the showcase leading to the adjacent room (a similar branch is present over the doorframe).

In the wall showcases the various cameos on display are arranged according to type (the Medici, popes, kings, emperors, mythological scenes, divinities). The showcase opposite the entrance holds the *Triumph of Phillip II of Spain* by Domenico Romano, who has been identified as Domenico dei Cammei, an artist working in Rome in 1550.

## Jewels Room

This room is given over to Anna Maria Luisa de' Medici's famous collection of jewelled *galanterie* (tokens of esteem presented to a lady). Only a portion of the original set remains, as Francesco Stefano of Lorraine sold many of them. The rest was transferred to Vienna to be returned to Italy only in 1921. In addition, the collection surely contains many 16th-century jewels given by Ferdinando I de' Medici to his niece Eleonora for her marriage to Vincenzo Gonzaga in Mantua, and which were returned to Florence after her death in 1611. The series of minuscule animals on display here also likely belonged to this group: the dragonfly, frog, lizard, spider, dragon and possibly also the Rooster pendant (in the showcase opposite the

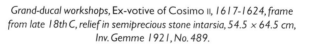

*Grand-ducal workshops, Ex-votive of Cosimo II, 1617-1624, frame from late 18th C, relief in semiprecious stone intarsia, 54.5 × 64.5 cm, Inv. Gemme 1921, No. 489.*

*German art,* Drinking horn, *14th-15th C, buffalo horn with silver-gilt and enamel mounting, 28 × 32 cm, Inv. Bargello 1917 (II), No. 1.*

*Paul Hübner (Augsburg),* Ewer and basin, *1585-1590, silver gilt and reliefs, ewer h. 45 cm, basin diam. 61 cm, Inv. A.S.E., No. 8-9.*

entrance), formed by two irregular pearls, two rubies, diamonds and enamelled gold, thought to have been executed by a Flemish goldsmith in Florence in about 1570-1580.

The German-made Gondola pendant is from the same period. Done in enamelled gold, diamonds, rubies and pearls, it represents a gondola with a couple in love, two musicians and two oarsmen – a tiny masterpiece of goldwork. The other jewels in the showcase are of 16th or 17th-century Flemish or Dutch manufacture, while the 18th century German trinkets in the next case provide good examples of the attention typically paid by illuminists to so-called "Arti per via" (street arts) and the world of crafts and peasants revolving round the European courts.

Curiosities are not lacking, such as the cherry stone carved with a hundred miniature heads, by Properzia de' Rossi (16th Century) in the first showcase on the left and, in the long display case on the opposed side, several semiprecious stone mosaics, such as the cornelian with Savonarola's profile, done by Giovanni delle Corniole between 1498 and 1516.

One of the walls is hung with the outstanding ex-voto of cosimo II, with stone intarsia in relief representing the devotion of the grand duke in the act of petitioning Saint Carlo Borromeo to cure his illness.

## Salzburg Treasure

The first two rooms of the opposite wing of the mezzanine – whose vaults were frescoed in the time of Ferdinando II with allegories of Prudence, Fame and Justice by Cecco Bravo and the Coronation of Juno, attributed to Ottavio Vannini – contain the Treasure of ferdinando III of lorraine, which the grand duke took to Florence from the principalities of Salzburg and Würzburg, where he had been exiled during the Napoleonic period.

In the first room, apart from a sheet-silver altarpiece of the Virgin and Child with stories from the Virgin's life (1598), the showcase on the right also contains five ostrich egg and briar double chalices (Inv. Bargello 1917 (II), No. 4, 7, 8, 17, 18). The design of these cups, in which the upper, inverted cup acted as drinking bowl, while the lower one was used to hold the wine, was intended to safeguard against being poisoned: it was even said that the materials themselves offered protection. Also interesting is the Drinking horn, made of buffalo horn and silver gilt in Germany in the 15th Century. The horn

rests on an eagle, probably symbolising Christ, to whom the wounded pelican at the horn's tip also alludes.

In the centre of the room stands the Portable altar, with crucifix and alabaster figures of the Virgin and Saint John with scenes of the Passion carved in coral. This was probably the work of a German artist, dated to before 1753 by the Salzburg inventory.

The second room of the Salzburg treasure contains the beautiful series of fifty-four silver-gilt bowls from the table of the archbishop of Salzburg. Fashioned by the goldsmiths Cornelius Erb and Paul Hübner in Augsburg between 1580 and 1590, they depict the Seasons, Elements, Virtues and Months with the signs of the Zodiac. The allegories present on the bowls (which were meant to hold sweets and comfits) are quite reminiscent of works of the Italian Renaissance, Giambologna in particular.

The Gilded silver ewer and basin (used for washing one's hands), also by Erb and Hübner, bear the stamp of Augsburg and are engraved with Orpheus enchanting the animals. In the showcase to the left opposite the entrance is the Grotesque decorated flask bearing the heraldry of archbishop Wolf Dietrich von Raitenau, signed and dated by its author, Hans Karl in 1602.

In the centre of the room we find the *Necessaire* of Ferdinando III of Lorraine, containing toiletries and breakfast articles bearing his initials which were made for him by Parisian goldsmiths between 1768 and 1769.

*Hans Karl, (Salzburg),* Flask, *1602, enamelled gold, h. 22.5 cm, signed and dated, Inv. A.S.E. 1912, No. 1.*

## Loggetta

The ceiling of this gallery passageway are completely frescoed with panels representing Man's undertakings, such as the foundry – redolent of similar vaults in the Uffizi corridors – and the lunettes with two large cages of real and imaginary animals suggested by stories of the New World.

The portion of the ceiling overlying the 17th-century *Portrait of Montezuma*, by an anonymous painter, is illustrated with *The Discovery of America*. The four vases at the corners are also of Mexican inspiration.

Through the doorway to the right is the so-called *Tesoretto*, or small treasure, containing 16th, 17th and 18th-century collections of small gems formerly held in the Uffizi and recently moved for exhibition here. The ceiling is completely covered with late 18th-century grotesque-figure frescoes, attributed to Michelangelo Cinganelli.

## Exotic Room

The varied articles on display here come from many faraway lands and attest to the Medici's frequent contacts with merchants, heads of foreign states, travellers and explorers who during the 15th Century would bring back objects of art and crafts never before seen in the western world.

The Ivory horns from the Congo, used for sounding the recall, the special Mogul art Mother-of-pearl boxes, the 14th-century celadon pitcher and plate (Inv. Bargello 1917, No. 102), a gift of the Bey of Tunisia to Lorenzo il Magnifico, all serve as testaments to the enormous breadth of the collection. However, especially noteworthy for their fan-

*Mexican art (Teotihuacan), Mask, classical period (250-600 a.d.), jade, 15.8 × 17.3 × 5 cm, Inv. Gemme 1921, No. 824.*

ciful, often bizarre mannerist or baroque representations are the Nautili or Oriental shells displayed on the right-hand wall, many of which bear Chinese decorations, though they were mounted in Holland, Flanders or other northern European countries.

An exquisite example of Nordic goldwork is the Mother-of-pearl and silver-gilt ewer, carried out for Francesco I de' Medici at the end of the 16th Century, formed by two nautilus shells bound together and adorned with high-relief heads set amongst volutes alternating with rubies and turquoise. The spout has the form of winged dragon with a snake coiled about extending to strike a horse's head just below the vessel's neck, which is closed by an eel-shaped cover with plant-motif engravings, while another snake forms its handle.

The Mother-of-pearl and gilded silver goblet upheld by a base

*French art, Goblet with three-dolphin base, 16th C, nautilus shell with figures engraved in China, mounted on silver gilt, 17 × 16 cm, Inv. Bargello 1917 (v), No. 20.*

formed by three dolphins was decorated with plant and landscape motifs in Canton. A similar one can be found in the same showcase (Inv. Bargello 1917 [v], No. 21). This was worked by a French goldsmith active around 1560 in the court of Caterina de' Medici, who presented it to her niece, Christine of Lorraine, who in turn brought it to Florence. The showcase just opposite holds the Antropomorphic statuettes and busts in the bizarre style of Giuseppe Arcimboldo. It is made of shells applied to a papier-mâché backing, probably done by court artisans in the mid-17th Century. In the showcase to the left of the entrance are some Mexican artefacts, such as the Teotihuacan (250-600 B.C.) Jade mask, which in 1621 already figured as part of the collection of Francesco I's son.

It is instead to Ferdinando I that we owe the Mexican mitre with infula executed in a typically pre-Columbian mosaic of feathers providing an interesting indigenous interpretation of Christian iconography, such as the Passion and Crucifixion.

### Porcelain Room

Next we come to the Chinese porcelain collection containing specimens of a wide variety of types and ages: from the Ming dynasty, the White-Blue style, the so-called "Blanc de Chine" (showcase to the right of the entrance), the "green family", frequently bearing war or society scenes (showcase opposite the entrance) and finally the "pink family", characterized by the presence of peony, a motif taken up in 18th-century Italy in the manufacture of Doccia (showcase to the left of the entrance).

The Japanese porcelain collection includes Chinese and Japanese *Imari* styles, named for the Japanese port whence pieces destined for exportation to the West were shipped. They are clearly recognizable by the red, gold and blue decorations also found on the large ornamental vases (showcase to the left).

In the room's centre, a group of lacquer articles exemplifies the typical oriental work in vogue in Europe during the 18th Century.

### Donations Room

The last section of the museum holds an eclectic collection of donations to the museum: jewels from the 17th to the 20th Century, articles in the 18th-century floral style, as well as 19th century neoclassical pieces, including tiny precious mosaic sets, 18th and 19th-century Sicilian and Neapolitan goldwork and the spectacular amethyst and diamond-studded Cartier Diadem from 1900.

The displays in the last two rooms include fifty-eight plaster casts of the large decorative silver plates that were given each year to Cosimo III and successors for the feast of Saint John. Executed by several baroque Roman sculptors, they were melted down by the French in 1799: all that remains are the casts for the manufacture of Doccia porcelain. The same room also contains 17th and 18th-century silver services, which the Bourbon family of Parma brought to Florence in 1801.

*Japanese art,* Vase, ca 18th C, porcelain, Inv. M.P.P., No. 12299.

*Chinese art,* Plate, ca 18th C, porcelain, Inv. A.C.E., No. 1216.

*Cartier (Paris),* Diadem, ca 1900, amethysts, diamonds set in platinum, diam. 20 cm, h. cm 7.5.

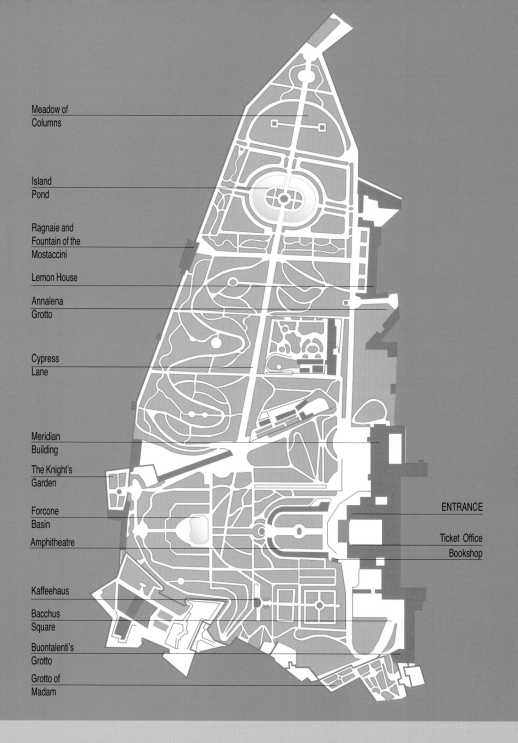

Meadow of
Columns

Island
Pond

Ragnaie and
Fountain of the
Mostaccini

Lemon House

Annalena
Grotto

Cypress
Lane

Meridian
Building

The Knight's
Garden

Forcone
Basin

Amphitheatre

Kaffeehaus

Bacchus
Square

Buontalenti's
Grotto

Grotto of
Madam

ENTRANCE

Ticket Office
Bookshop

## Notes on the vegetation

Boboli is the consummate garden *alla italiana*. Its paths are lined by high hedges composed of holm-oaks (*Quercus ilex*) in their upper portions and various shrub species below (*Viburnum tinus, Laurus nobilis, Phillyrea latifolia, Rhamnus alaternus, Myrtus communis*). The inner copses are also made up mostly of holm-oaks, though a number of deciduous plants are also represented: the plane trees (*Platanus acerifolia*) of the Forcone and the Meadow of Columns, as well as a *Ginkgo biloba*, an *Acer monspessulanum* and two *Liriodendron tulipifera*. The cedars include, amongst the predominant Atlantic and deodar species, a single specimen of *Cedrus libani* in the Lower Botanical Garden.

The potted citrus collection is amongst the largest in Europe, and the roses in the gardens of the Island's Lemon House include many exquisite varieties, such as 'Chapeau de Napoléon', 'Madame Pierre Ogier', 'Complicata', 'Tuscany Superb', 'Variegata di Bologna', 'Ferdinand Pichard' and 'Cardinal de Richelieu'. The Upper Botanical Garden also holds an interesting collection of aquatic plants, including *Euryale ferox, Glyceria acquatica, Victoria regia, Hybiscus militaris, Dion spinolosum* and *Pandanus utilis*.

# Boboli Gardens

LITTA MEDRI
GIORGIO GALLETTI

Camellia Garden.

Garden of the Island, citrus trees and roses.

Garden of the Lemon House, autumn blossoms.

The Ragnaia della Stella.

*Due to their very nature, these historical gardens require constant restoration and maintenance. A schedule has therefore been established which provides for their seasonal, yearly and long-term care through periodic renovation and upkeep. Clearly, the architectural components and plant-life are involved more frequently than the inorganic structures of the garden and its decorations, and although the different types of work are not necessarily interdependent, they have been planned for during the same period of time. Moreover, the need to safeguard sculptural works from degradation by atmospheric agents and vandalism often requires housing the originals indoors and replacing them with copies for display. Thus, the gardens' furnishings are necessarily in an incomplete and constantly changing state.*

## The 16th Century

The present-day Boboli Garden complex is the result of the union of the hill-side garden beyond the villa that Eleonora of Toledo, wife of Duke Cosimo I de' Medici, acquired in 1550 from the Pitti family, and the great expanse of land, originally given over to agriculture, bordered by the ramparts that the self-same Cosimo I built during the war against Siena (1546-48) and the 14th C wall, its Roman Gate and the houses in via Romana. Already in the Late Middle Ages the area was known as "Boboli", a toponym used at the time to indicated wooded areas. The initial project envisaged the transformation of the *Orto de' Pitti* ('Pitti Orchard') into a garden setting worthy of the regal palace that Cosimo planned to realise there.

The original project was by Niccolò Pericoli, known as 'Il Tribolo' (Florence 1500-50), the Duke's favoured artist and creator of the Medici gardens in Villa in Castello. Upon the death of Il Tribolo, supervision of the work passed on to Davide Fortini, who was in turn succeeded by Giorgio Vasari from 1554 to 1661 and, finally by Bartolomeo Ammannati (ca 1560-83). With the advent of Francesco I (1574), the artist Bernardo Buontalenti rose to eminence, and it was he who completed the Grand Grotto (also called Buontalenti's Grotto, 1583-93).

Despite the succession of overseers, Il Tribolo's original design was followed closely: as in the Gardens of Castello, the hill and valley behind the palace were subdivided into a grid of perpendicular compartments, filled with either abundant grape-vines and olive trees, or copses crossed by high espaliers, according to a typically Tuscan layout, termed *ragnaie*, that is, copses criss-crossed by frameworks hung with bird-hunting nets called *ragne*. The stone quarry at the foot of Belvedere Hill was transformed into a semi-eliptical open space which followed the design of Roman hippodromes, though copses of various tree species were planted in place of the usual tiered stands. The area was called the Amphitheatre, and later, the wings of the palace courtyard (1561) would be designed by Bartolomeo Ammannati to fit this structure's U shape. Thus, the Pitti Palace and Boboli Gardens were to become a single indivisible architectural unit.

The Ocean Fountain, first documented in 1577 as standing in the Amphitheatre's arena, was sculpted by Giambologna on a huge granite slab brought from Elba Island by order of Cosimo I de' Medici, moulded by Il Tribolo and later moved to the centre of the Island. The Grotto of Madam, work of Davide Fortini and Marco del Tasso (1553-55) dates back to the gardens' origins. A dwarf fruit-tree grove, considered particularly precious by Cosimo I, was planted nearby.

The Grand Grotto was begun under Vasari's supervision (1557) and brought to completion by Ammannati and Buontalenti between 1583 and 1593. The first stage in the gardens' history ended under Ferdinando I (Grand Duke, 1587 to 1609).

*Agnolo Bronzino,* Portrait of Eleonora of Toledo with her son Giovanni, *1454 ca, oil on canvas, 115 × 96 cm, Florence, Uffizi.*

*Perspective map, known as 'the chain', 1470, Florence, Museo "Firenze com'era".*

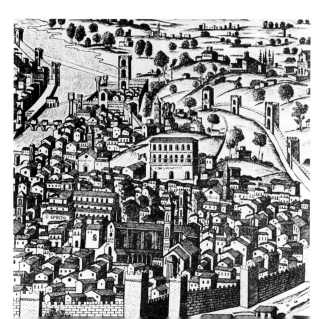

*Stefano della Bella, Scenes from* Atlantis *from the ballet on horseback* Il mondo festeggiante, *erformed in the Amphitheatre in 1661, engraving, Florence, Gabinetto Disegni e Stampe degli Uffizi.*

## The 17th Century

Under Cosimo II (Grand Duke from 1609 to 1621) the gardens were expanded beyond the walls erected during the war against Siena. The work of extending the grounds, of which we have documents dating back to 1612, was overseen by Gherardo Mechini and Giulio Parigi. The garden's axis became the wide Cypress Lane that leads to the striking Island Pond, begun in 1612 and completed sometime before 1620. South of the lane, three large labyrinths were planted, as well as a walkway covered by holm-oak branches (the *Cerchiata grande* or 'Large Latticework') which is crossed midway by Cypress Lane and yet two more long, covered passages parallel to it (*Cerchiate piccole* or 'Small Latticework').

The *ragnaie* surrounding the Amphitheatre once provided a spectacular sequence of perspectives: first, the large *Ragnaia* of the Island, which hid the Island Pond from view, creating a surprise effect, and then the *Ragnaia della Pace* ('of Peace') under the 14th century walls, animated by bird troughs and a very long water 'chain', still in existence today and known as the

*Romolo Ferrucci del Tadda,* Fountain of the Mostaccini, *pietra forte, 1619-21, detail.*

Fountain of the Mostaccini. The spectacular culmination of the garden was the Island Pond, also designed by Giulio Parigi, which was begun in 1612 and described for the first time in 1620 by the poet Raffaello Chiabrera. The Island was originally conceived of as a garden for the cultivation of citrus fruit and flowers. In all probability, a Venus fountain once stood in its centre but was removed by order of Grand Duke Ferdinando II in 1636 and substituted with Giambologna's Ocean Fountain. It was Cosimo II who also had the idea of transforming the Amphitheatre into a masonry structure, though the actual work of this modification was begun only in 1630 under Grand Duke Ferdinando II, according to a project attributed rather uncertainly to Giulio Parigi and completed in 1636 under the guidance of Alfonso Parigi il Giovane. The current location of the statue of *Plenty* (begun by Giambologna and completed by Pietro Tacca) dates back to 1636 and represents the idealised end point of the line of sight which runs from Pitti Palace along the length of the axis formed by the Amphitheatre and Forcone Basin.

*Map of the Gardens from Francesco Maria Soldini's Descrizione, 1789.*

## The 18th Century

With the death of Gian Gastone de' Medici in 1737, the Medici dynasty came to a close and the Grand Duchy passed to the House of the Habsburg-Lorraine, who governed through a regent until 1765. Although the gardens fell into disuse during these years, a number of radical alterations were undertaken under the direction of Ignazio Pellegrini, such as the construction of a carriageable path linking Bacchus Square to the Amphitheatre and a large chapel that was, however, never completed.

Instead, under the Grand Duke Leopoldo de Lorraine (1765 to 1790), numerous modifications were performed on the gardens' sculptural, architectural and water works, as well as on its stone structures and veg-etation. New buildings, designed to harmonise with the age-old landscape were also added, amongst which, the Kaffeehaus (1775) and Lemon House (1777-78), both designed by Zanobi del Rosso, and the Meridian Building, begun in 1776 by Niccolò Gaspero Paoletti. Outstanding works of classical sculpture were brought from the Villa Medici in Rome, such as the two *Daci Prisoners*, numerous torsos and the Egyptian obelisk, placed in the Amphitheatre's centre in 1790. Further contributions by Pietro Leopoldo were the remodelling of the Meadow of Columns, the creation of a botanical garden near the Specola (currently the Lower Botanical Garden) and the *jardin potager*, intended for the cultivation of exotic vegetables, fruits and flowers (the Upper Botanical Garden).

*Zanobi del Rosso, The Lemon House, 1777-78.*

## The 19th and 20th Centuries

During Napoleon's reign (1799-1814) the gardens once again underwent a period of decline. The intention of the Grand Duchess, Elisa Baciocchi, was to turn Boboli into an English-style garden, a plan never realised for lack of funds. Instead, as the traditional techniques of pruning were abandoned, the espaliers and copses consequently grew wild with overgrowth.

The restorative works ordered by the Lorraines once again re-established the rigorously formal setting that the gardens had had since their origins. The most significant works of this period were the entranceway dubbed 'Annalena', executed after the design of architect Giuseppe Cacialli between 1815 and 1820, the gateway to the Lemon House (1818), and the large Tepidarium of the *jardin potager* (1816), also designed by Cacialli.

In 1834, under Grand Duke Leopoldo II, the gardens suffered the most traumatic remodelling of its long history: the destruction of the labyrinths to make way for a wide carriageable lane, a project undertaken by Pasquale Poccianti, and the diversion of many of the straight paths of the *ragnaie* into curving lanes, after the fashion of the time.

Sometime between 1841 and 1850 the *jardin potager* was transformed into a botanical garden by Filippo Parlatore. Since then Boboli has remained largely unchanged, except for several restorations and the rather sporadic addition of new tree species. The open-air shows held in the gardens during the current century have enjoyed world renown. It is enough to recall *A Midsummer Night's Dream*, directed by Max Reinhart (1933), Jacques Copeau's rendition of *As You Like It* (1938), *The Tempest*, directed by Giorgio Strehler (1948), Luchino Visconti's *Troilus and Cresida*, (1949) and *The Fairy Queen*, directed by Luca Ronconi (1987).

*View of Boboli Gardens from Pitti Palace in a period image.*

## Amphitheatre (Anfiteatro)

Once inside the main entrance of Pitti Palace, one passes through the wide Ammannati courtyard, closed off on three sides by the inner façades of the building and on the fourth by a single storey topped by the Artichoke Fountain (Fontana del Carciofo, 1639-41), the work of Francesco Susini. The middle archway on this side leads to the 17th C Grotto, in whose centre rises the colossal porphyry statue of *Moses*, its base immersed in an elliptical basin.

The entrance to the gardens is to the Grotto's right. The magnificent sight of the Amphitheatre is the first to greet the arriving visitor at the end of the entrance ramp. The masonry foundation was built between 1630 and 1634, after a design by architect Giulio Parigi, and inaugurated in 1637 on the occasion of the coronation of the Grand Duchess of Tuscany, Vittoria della Rovere, wife of Ferdinando II, with the 'Carosello', a choreographic succession inspired by *Gerusalemme Liberata*. The large arena is surrounded by the six-tiered stands and a balustrade interrupted by twenty-four aedicules which originally held statues, mostly classical, while those on the lateral foundations were of dogs and other animals.

The present arrangement, in which statues alternate with terracotta urns painted to resemble marble, dates back to the work of Giuseppe Cacialli in 1818. In place of the stands, the original Amphitheatre had terraces of beech, oak, ash, olive, fir, cypress and plane-trees. The cavea, which had been buried during the Lorraine period to construct the carriageable path linking the Bacchus entranceway with Meridian Square, was transformed into a garden decorated with box hedges and potted citrus.

In the Amphitheatre's centre stands the Egyptian Obelisk, brought from the Villa Medici in Rome and set in its current position in 1790, as planned by Niccolò Gaspero Paoletti. The large ancient granite basin also found here was placed in 1840, after the design of Pasquale Poccianti.

## Forcone Basin (Vasca del Forcone)

Leaving the Amphitheatre behind, we continue along the first landing of the ramp to find two Roman statues, an *Emperor* and a togaed citizen, and in the centre, *Ceres*, a Roman copy of the original Greek statue. Further up we come to the Forcone Basin. This large mixtilinear basin is the result of the modifications carried out by Zanobi del Rosso (1777-78) on the original, rectangular one that acted as a collecting basin for the irrigation waters transported via the aqueduct of Arcetri to the entire area of the gardens. At the centre of the basin stands the bronze statue of *Neptune*, by Soldo Lorenzi, which depicts him brandishing his trident over a cliff on which four marin demi-gods are crouching. The sculptural composition, executed in 1571 for a flower garden once situated to the north of the Palace, was set in its current location in about 1635. The terracing of the surrounding semicircle was originally executed in the 17th century; their present form is the result of 18th century modifications.

Continuing our ascent, to the left we can admire the spectacle of Fort Belvedere with its imposing walls and behind, Pitti Palace with Florence as its backdrop. Finally, we come to the colossal statue of *Plenty* (*Abbondanza*), begun by Giambologna in 1608 and completed by Pietro Tacca and Sebastiano Salvini (1636-37). At first, conceived of as a portrait of Giovanna of Austria, wife of Francesco I, which

would crown a column in Piazza San Marco, it was moved to Boboli in 1636 to represent the prosperity of the Tuscan State, as symbolised by the golden ears of wheat in her left hand and the Cornucopia in her right.

Amongst the trees on the terraces, of particular interest are the plane-trees (*Platanus acerifolia*) planted in the Napoleonic era and pruned to form candelabra.

*The Knight's Villa and Garden.*

*A photo of the Kaffeehaus and a print by Aniello Lamberti.*

## The Knight's Garden (Giardino del Cavaliere)

Continuing towards the right, we come to the two tenail tiers that lead to the Knight's Garden, offering an enchanting view of the Florentine hills. This garden takes its name from the rampart, known as the 'Bastion of Cavaliere Malatesta' (Malatesta the Knight), which was designed by Michelangelo in 1529. The medicinal plants originally cultivated here, called *semplici*, were replaced by exotic varieties in 1612 when the garden was remodelled after a design by Giulio Parigi.

In this same year the Knight's Lodge (*Casino del Cavaliere*) was built. This is a large room originally utilised to store pots, but subsequently used first by Cardinal Leopoldo de' Medici as a meeting place for scholars and scientists and then in the late 18th C by Cosimo III for the French lessons of his son, Gian Gastone. Today it houses the Porcelain Museum (*Museo delle Porcellane*).

The current arrangement of the garden and its spectacular entranceway date back to the 1792 remodelling by Giuseppe del Rosso, who designed the lower stairway flanked by the two statues of *Muses*, the tenail tiers with circular ramps, as well as the entrance gate overlooked by the marble-painted sandstone *Sphinxes* (by Giovan Battista Giovannozzi, currently in storage) and the garden's box partitions. At the

cross-roads of the two main paths, we find the Fountain of the Monkeys *(Fontana delle Scimmie):* the marble *putto* are thought to be by either Pierino da Vinci or Stoldo Lorenzi (17th C), while the bronze monkeys are attributable historically to Pietro Tacca (17th C). To the right and left, just under the pillars, are the white marble sculptures of *Jupiter with Eagle* and *Flora*, both attributed to Giovan Battista Caccini (16th C). Lastly, each May the blooming of the 'Banksiae', 'Bourbon' and 'Tea' roses, together with the peonies provides an especially beautiful sight.

## Kaffeehaus

Walking out of the Knight's Garden and along the tree-lined path at the foot of Fort Belvedere, we come to the Kaffeehaus. This singular building, designed as a resting place for the Court during their walks through Boboli, was constructed at the wish of Pietro Leopoldo between 1774 and 1775 after the design of Zanobi del Rosso in an airy ro-

coco style. Its original colouring was white and green. The decorations within are by the painters Giuseppe del Moro, Giuliano Traballesi and Pasquale Micheli.

On the lawn opposite the Kaffeehaus stands the Fountain of Ganymede; the current figure of Ganymede is a cast of the original marble sculpture executed by Stoldo Lorenzi in the latter half of the 16th C.

*The Cypress Lane.*

*Romolo Ferrucci del Tadda,* Fountain of the Mostaccini, *pietra forte, 1619-21.*

## Cypress Lane (Il Viottolone)

From the Kaffeehaus we take a path which, passing Forcone Basin, leads to the beginning of Cypress Lane. This large path (i.e. *Viottolone*) makes up the symmetry axis of the expanded gardens, as ordered by Cosimo II and carried out by Giulio Parigi. Planting of the cypresses began in 1612, at the same time as the addition of the labyrinths that used to follow them on the southern side. The entrance onto the lane is flanked by *Aristogiton* on the right and *Harmodius* (cast) on the left, two Roman sculptures copied from Greek originals and restored by Domenico and Giovan Battista Pieratti in 1635. The beginning of the *Viottolone* is still marked by the two citrus groves first planted from 1612 to 1614 according to the traditional arrangement of espaliers of bitter oranges, bordered by a rare red, white and green mosaic marble pavement. The lane is flanked by numerous sculptures, some classical, such as *Mercury with Child Bacchus* (Roman copy of original by Polycletus, replaced by cast), *Young Nero* (Roman art), others from the late 16th C, such as *Hygieia* and *Aesculapius* and *Hyppolytus,* both by Giovanni Caccini and reproduced as copies (ca 1608). The exceptional sculptural group, *Autumn* and *Winter* by Pietro Francavilla (late 16th C) serves to highlight one of the loveliest spots in Boboli, the cross-roads of the *Viottolone* and La Cerchiata ('Latticework'), where a long line of holm-oaks have been pruned to form a continuous 'tunnel'. This was cultivated between 1612 and 1614 together with the two minor latticeworks running alongside the *Viottolone*. From the northern tract, one can reach the Upper Botanical Garden (open only in summer months), created from about 1841 to 1850 by Filippo Parlatore in place of the *jardin potager*, where the visitor can admire the two aquatic-plant pools.

## Ragnaie and Fountain of the Mostaccini

Walking left along the *Cerchiata*, we then continue down the path formed by the 14th C wall and high espalier of holm-oak and evergreen hedge that is all that remains of the large *Ragnaia della Pace*, designed for bird-hunting with nets. One of the main features of the *ragnaie* were the drinking troughs for birds, a well-preserved example of which is the Fountain of the Mostaccini, formed by a long cascading chain of water gushing from sixteen large, monstrous masks (called *Mostaccini*, perhaps in reference to the moustaches) and terminating below in another water chain devoid of any decoration. The fountain was most likely built between 1619 and 1621 by Romolo Ferrucci del Tadda, author of other animal sculptures found in the gardens. To the left stands the large bust of *Jupiter* (ca 1560) by Giambologna, marking the start of another, typically straight path of the *ragnaie*.

*Roman copy of original Greek statue of* Harmodius, *white marble, 5th C (cast).*

*Roman copy of original Greek statue of* Mercury with Child Bacchus *by Polycletus, (cast).*

*Giovan Battista Caccini,* Hygieia, *ca 1608 (cast).*

*Giovan Battista Caccini,* Aesculapius and Hyppolytus, *ca 1608 (cast).*

## Island Pond (Vasca dell'Isola)

*(Accessible only in May and June)*

Towards the end of the *Viottolone* to the left one can see the sculptural group, the *Saccomazzone* by Orazio Mochi and Romolo Ferrucci del Tadda (17th C), while Giovan Battista Capezzuoli's *Gioco della Pentolaccia* ('the clay-pot game') (18th C) stands on the right. We thus come to the Island Square (*Piazzale dell'Isola*). The pond itself is made up of a large oval basin with the small island in its centre. The island can be reached by two paths running parallel to the *Viottolone*. The open space of the square is bordered by a tall espalier of hedge and holm-oak with numerous niches holding 17th C statues, mostly from the Florentine school and nearly all depicting peasants or hunters, according to an aesthetic sense for themes befitting the gardens' bucolic atmosphere.

Noteworthy examples are the *Moor Hunter* by Giovan Battista Pieratti, the *Hunter with Sparrow-hawk* by Domenico Pieratti, and the *Youth* by Giovan Simone Cioli. The pond's borders were originally equipped with a continuous series of water jets. Now, on its northern and southernmost points, we find the two Fountains of Loves executed respectively by Giovan Battista and Domenico Pieratti, and Cosimo Salvestrini and Giovan Francesco Susini between 1623 and 1624, and at the eastern and western ends, the Harpies Fountains, late 18th C copies by Innocenzo Spinazzi of the 17th C originals, probably designed by Giulio Parigi.

*View of the Island Pond.*

Access to the Island is through two gates upheld by paired sandstone columns topped by the marble *Capricorns* symbolising Cosimo I de' Medici that were partly restored or redone in the 18th C by Giovan Battista Capezzuoli. Immersed in the pond's waters we can see *Perseus*, restored by Giovan Battista Pieratti, and *Andromeda*, attributed to this same artist. In the island's centre we find Giambologna's 1576 Ocean Fountain (*Fontana dell'Oceano*), originally located in the Amphitheatre's arena and moved here in 1636. The colossal *Ocean*, an early 20th C copy by Raffaello Romanelli of the original now held in the Museo del Bargello, rises above the pedestal, about which are arranged the Nile, Ganges and Euphrates rivers. The pedestal is adorned with sculpted bas-reliefs depicting mythological scenes: the *Rape of Europa*, *Diana Bathing* and the *Triumph of Neptune*. The fountain's basin is made from a single granite block, transported from the Island of Elba by order of Cosimo I and sculpted by Il Tribolo in 1550. The surrounding garden, with nearly two hundred potted citrus trees, maintains the original design, while an ancient rose collection has recently been reconstructed within the flower-beds. The surrounding flower-beds are adorned with 17th and 18th C varieties of bulbous plants.

*Perseus on horseback, white marble, 1636-37, restored by Giovan Battista Pieratti.*

*Giovan Battista Pieratti, Andromeda, white marble, 1636-37.*

## Meadow of Columns (Prato delle Colonne)

Continuing onto the wide semicircle which links the Island Pond with the area of the Roman Gate (*Porta Romana*), we come to the Meadow of Columns. The gravel path parallel to the *Viottolone* divides the meadow into two sectors, in the centre of which stand the two red porphyry columns, of uncertain origins, placed here between 1775 and 1779. Their layout is by Gaspero Niccolò Paoletti, who also executed the bases and crowns, made up of capitals topped by marble urns. Along the hedges ringing the meadow are twelve colossal busts, some original Roman sculptures, others, Roman copies of Greek originals, and still others, classical elements contaminated by late-Renaissance insertions.

Among the most noteworthy are the *Bearded Hero* from the Villa Medici in Rome, and so-called *Trajan* and *Pyrrhus*. The Meadow once held *Aesculapius*, from the Villa in Pratolino, attributed to Stoldo Lorenzi, and *Saturn*, by Gherardo Silvani (1621), both currently in storage. Along the small path leading to the Roman Gates we find the sculptural group of grotesque figures called the *Caramogi*, by Romolo Ferrucci del Tadda (1619-20), while opposite these is the *Owl Game* (1780), by Giovan Battista Capezzuoli, based on the original work of Romolo Ferrucci del Tadda. Near the Roman Gate stands Vincenzo Danti's *Perseus* (1577), and at its base, the beautiful Roman sarcophagus depicting the *Trials of Hercules*, by Lisippus (2nd C).

*View of the Meadow of Columns.*

*Roman Art, copy of original by Lisippus, sarcophagus with the Trials of Hercules, white marble, 2nd C.*

*Michelangelo Naccherini, Adam and Eve, detail with the mosaic vault of the Annalena Grotto in the background.*

## Annalena Grotto

In 1817 the architect Giuseppe Cacialli created the small Annalena Grotto beside the entranceway in via Romana. The fine sculptural group of *Adam and Eve* (1616) by Michelangelo Naccherino (1550-1622) was taken from one of the hanging gardens at the top of the *Viottolone* and placed in the grotto.

The neo-classical architecture of the Grotto is reminiscent of the series of modifications carried out by Cacialli between 1815 and 1820 in order to enhance and enlarge the entrance in via Romana.

The interior decoration with sponges and large masks shows evident traces of Bernardo Buontalenti's marvellous innovations in the Grand Grotto, however with a measured distancing from this latter evincing Cacialli's personal reflections on Renaissance decorative models and their reinterpretation in a contemporary manner.

The ceiling, made up of bright sea-blue panels with yellowish orange bordering, depicts the attributes of the god of the seas, Poseidon, with his entourage: tridents, shells and corals, surrounded by minute concretions simulating the stalactites of a natural grotto and abundant *Haliotis lamellosa*, the shells of a very common species rich in mother of pearl. A recent restoration has brought out the vivacious tones of the ceiling and the warm hue of the Pratolino sponges which, suspended from the ceiling, provide a pleasant contrast to the white marble of the large masks, created in the same period by Ottaviano Giovanozzi after the design of the grotto's architect, Giuseppe Cacialli.

## Lemon House (Limonaia)

Flanking the garden's borders along the Lemon House path are the *Peasant with spade* and Harvest Fountain, both by Valerio and Giovan Simone Cioli (1599-1608) .

Just down the path we come to the Lemon House, built from 1777 to 1778 after the design of Zanobi del Rosso as a substitute for the former Menagerie and its collection of rare animals which was dismantled by order of Grand Duke Pietro Leopoldo de Lorraine. The rococo façade preserves its original colours, and the building is still used today to store the collection of nearly five hundred potted citrus plants, one of the most typical characteristics of Tuscan gardens. The Medici held citrus trees in high esteem, both for their therapeutic and aromatic value, as well as for their unique beauty. Still today many rare and unique varieties are cultivated here. The box flower-bed opposite the Lemon House reflects the original 18th C design, and is now used to cultivate ancient varieties of roses, camellia and bulb plants. The wall is topped by classical statues depicting the *Muses*, a *Bagpiper* and *Dwarf.* Also worthy of note is the beautiful wrought-iron gate designed by Giuseppe Cacialli in 1817.

## Meridian Building (Palazzina della Meridiana)

Continuing along the Lemon House path to Pitti Palace, on the left we find the Meridian Building, at present housing the Costume Museum (Museo del Costume), which Pietro Leopoldo de Lorraine had built to equip the royal residence with more practical apartments than the uncomfortable quarters in Pitti Palace. It was begun around 1776 by Niccolò Gaspero Paoletti and completed in 1832 by architect Pasquale Poccianti. The ramps leading to the Chestnut grove and *Viottolone* were also added by Paoletti to the sloping grounds in front of the building, once used as a stone quarry. In the centre of the first ramp stands the winged horse, called *Pegasus* (late 16th C), restored by Aristodemo Costoli in 1865. Looking out the parapet towards Palazzo Pitti, one can view the Camellia Garden, an 19th C camellia collection in a garden created during the 17th C.

*View of the hill opposite the Meridian Building.*
*Nicolò Gaspero Paoletti and Pasquale Poccianti,* Meridian Building, *1766-1832.*
Pegasus, *by unknown late 16th C artist restored by Artistodemo Costoli in 1865.*

*Valerio and Giovan Simone Cioli,* Harvest Fountain, *white marble, 1599-1608.*

*Roman Art,* pair of Muses, *white marble, 2nd C.*

*Roman Art*, Daci Prisoners, *porphyry and white marble, 2nd C.*
*Valerio Cioli*, Dwarf Morgante, *white marble, 1560.*

## Bacchus Square (Piazzale di Bacco)

Walking past Pitti Palace towards the exit, we come to the wide Bacchus Square, which gets its name from the singular statue situated near the exit gate. Though known to the Florentines as 'Bacchus', the statue is actually the *Dwarf Morgante*, depicted by Valerio Cioli astride a turtle (currently replaced by a copy). Entering the wide carriageable path, we find the *Daci Prisoners*, porphyry Roman statues from the Villa Medici collection in Rome, and dating back to the 2nd C (the white marble heads were likely added in the 16th C). The two white marble bases are also worthy of note: sculpted with trophies, barbarians, Dioskouroi and Victories, likely taken from a Roman triumphal arch from the 3rd C.

## Buontalenti's Grotto or Grand Grotto (Grotta del Buontalenti or Grotta Grande)

Along the boundary of the gardens, on the northern side of Bacchus Square, we come to this grotto, also known as the Grand Grotto. Its current appearance is the result of modification of the original plant nursery built by Giorgio Vasari between 1557 and 1560 in the last section of the corridor linking Palazzo Vecchio and Pitti Palace, which was also designed by Vasari together with the façade and loggia of the entrance with its columns in red Monterantoli stone and while marble bases and capitals.

Between 1583 and 1587 the nursery was transformed into a grotto according to the design of Bernardo Buontalenti.

In 1587 Giovanni Battista del Tadda decorated the façade with the 'rustic' figures, *Peace* and *Justice* (or *Harmony*?), as well as the emblems of Cosimo I and a *Capricorn* and *Turtle*.

In the niches flanking the entrance are Baccio Bandinelli's statues of *Apollo* and *Ceres* (1552-56). The interior walls of

*Giorgio Varsari and Bernardo Buontalenti, façade of the* Grand Grotto, *detail and outside view, 1557-60.*

*Giambologna, Venus, 1573.*

the first room were decorated by Pietro Mati in a spongy material with a bas-relief series inspired by the myth of Deucalion and Pyrrha. In 1585 Buontalenti placed Michelangelo's *Prisoners* in the grotto's corners (the originals, now housed in the Museo dell'Accademia, were replaced with white concrete castes in 1924). The ceiling and wall frescoes by the ruins of a cupola were painted by Bernardino Poccetti (1886-87) and depict various animal species. It is said that the circular opening in the vault was once filled by a hollow crystal ball with fish swimming in. Water once gushed forth from encrustations throughout the walls, creating spectacular effects as the wet materials glistened in all their chromatic glory.

In 1587 the sculptural group, *Theseus and Helen*, by Vincenzo de' Rossi was placed in the second chamber, while Giambologna's masterpiece *Venus* was set in the centre of the third, most secretive room on a green African marble bowl upheld by white marble satyrs. The wall frescoes by Bernardino Poccetti portray an arbour with birds flying about its vines. Giovan Battista del Tadda (1589) created the mountain-shaped fountains in the corner niches, while the terracotta anthropomorphic masks in the vault's cornice are by Gualtieri di Jacopo Gonnelli (1585-86).

*View of the first chamber's interior.*

### Grotto of Madam (Grotticina di Madama)

Leaving Buontalenti's Grotto towards the left, we encounter the Grotto of Madam, Boboli's oldest.

It was commissioned by Eleonora of Toledo and carried out between 1553 and 1555 under the direction of Davide Fortini. The interior is decorated with a spongy material and stalactites. The sculptures are by Baccio Bandinelli and Giovanni di Paolo Fancelli. The vault frescoes have been attributed to Francesco Ubertini, known as 'Il Bachiacca' (1554-55), while the splendid two-coloured terracotta floor is the work of Santi Buglioni.

*Davide Fortini, Grotto of Madam, sculpture by Baccio Bandinelli and Giovan Paolo Fancelli, white marble and pietra serena, 1553-55.*

# Porcelain Museum

MARILENA MOSCO

The elegant building in the middle of the garden on the Knight's Hill was designed by Giuseppe del Rosso and built in 1790, replacing the old Medici Casino, where Cardinal Leopoldo had once presided over meetings of the Cimento academicians and where the young son of Grand Duke Cosimo III, Gian Gastone, used to take his French lessons. Since 1973, this building has been the home of the porcelain collections that once belonged to the Medici, to the Lorraines, to Maria Luisa di Borbone Parma, to Elisa Baciocchi and to the Savoys.

The first room is devoted to Italian and French porcelain. Worthy of attention are the small biscuit statues, with renderings of the King of Naples' clothing, inspired by the

gouaches depicting Royal costumes donated to the Lorraine Grand Duchy by the Ferdinando IV di Borbone, King of Naples, and executed in porcelain in 1784, by Filippo Tagliolini in the Royal Naples Porcelain Factory. Also noteworthy are the pieces from the Doccia Factory – founded in 1737 by Carlo Ginori – and characterised by their white and blue decorations and by the bouquets of tulips and oth-

The Knight's Villa and Garden.

Meissen manufacture, bowl, ca 1720.

er flowers, a common motif on various eighteenth - and nineteenth century services.

The Vincennes Factory, founded in 1740 and then moved to Sèvres, mostly uses the colour blue (notice the large vase) but also pastel colours such as pink and green, edged with gold and often framing subjects taken from prints by François Boucher (notice the *Flowerbox*).

Elisa Baciocchi's service is displayed in the two central cases. It was made by Sèvres and presented to her by Emperor Napoleon in honour of her appointment to the Grand Duchy of Tuscany. A Sèvres porcelain portrait of Napoleon can be seen on the wall in front of the entrance.

The second room contains examples of Viennese porcelain. The group in biscuit, depicting *Empress Maria Theresa of Austria and her son Peter Leopold,* is particularly noteworthy.

Notice should also be taken of the beautiful neoclassical service, showing views of Vienna taken from prints published by the Artaria publishing house, collected by the Lorraines and brought to Florence to decorate the Medici villas.

*Doccia manufacture, L. Ginori Lisci, Cup, 1865.*

The third room contains an exhibition of Meissen porcelain, as well as some pieces from the Nymphenburg, Frankental and Worcester porcelain factories, taken from the collections in the Ducal Palace in Parma. The Meissen factory, the first factory devoted to the manufacture of porcelain, was opened by Augustus II of Saxony in 1710 and specialised in the creation of original pieces. Particular notice should be taken of the tea service and butter dish given to Gian Gastone de' Medici, and of the vase and services with Chinese motifs, Meissen products that were part of the birth of a new fashion, exoticism, of which a later and famous manifestation was the Porcelain Room in the Capodimonte Palace in Naples.

*Royal Naples Porcelain Factory, Tea-pot, ca 1800-1805.*

*Royal Naples Porcelain Factory, Coffee-pot, ca 1785-1790.*

# Carriage Museum

FAUSTA NAVARRO

Housed in the rooms of the Pitti Palace's Meridian Building, the museum contains fine examples of carriages used by the Lorraine and Savoy courts in the eighteenth and nineteenth centuries and, in the cabinets along the walls, antique harnesses.

The oldest carriage, a coupé used for drives in the city, elegantly decorated with rocaille, is datable to the middle of the eighteenth century. Its original owner is unknown, but given the quality of the carriage's manufacture, it was certainly a noble and refined gentleman. Ferdinando III of Lorraine was very fond of carriages and, upon his return from exile (1816 – 1818), he commissioned the construction of six luxurious berlins for himself and his court. The museum contains three of these carriages, among which is the most

important of the six, the Grand Duke's personal carriage, made to be drawn by three pairs of horses (six-in-hand), and the work of various specialised artisans, from Busi and Dani, makers of leather goods, who directed the overall work, to Cioci and Gori, bronze workers, to Paolo Sani, a carver, to the painter Antonio Marini. The latter painted triumphant quadrigas on the carriage's gilded box. The quadrigas depict Lorenzo the Magnificent and Poliziano, Cosimo I and Giorgio Vasari, Cosimo II with Galileo, and Ferdinando III in glory, surrounded by cupids bearing symbols of abundance, all of which was intended to signify not only the continuity between the two reigning Medici and Lorraine houses but also the enlightened nature and the patronage of the rulers of Tuscany. The sedan

On the previous page:
*Ferdinando III of Lorraine's carriage.*

Above and on the right:
*Silver carriage.*

chair is older than Ferdinando's carriage, dated 1793, and was ordered by Ferdinando III for his wife, Grand Duchess Maria Luisa di Borbone. The same sovereign also commissioned the 1822 sedan chair, used to carry the wife of Crown Prince Leopoldo from the Meridian Building to the baptistery for the baptism of her first son. But the museum's most important piece is the silver carriage, like something out of an ancient fairy tale. At the beginning of the nineteenth century, it belonged to the King of Naples, Ferdinando II di Borbone, and was later brought to Florence by the Savoys, who added to it their own coat-of-arms, as a sign of its new ownership.

The following lists refer to the distribution of the works in the various rooms at the time of publication. Any changes to these lists have been dictated by the restoration-, conservation- or administrative needs that are part of the management of museums as rich and complex as these.

# Palatine gallery list of works

## FOOTMEN'S ANTECHAMBER

**Antonio Domenico Gabbiani**
*Ritratto di Ferdinando de' Medici*
Olio su tela, cm 191 × 134
Inv. 1890 n. 2731

**Ferdinand Richter**
*Ritratto di Gian Gastone de' Medici, granduca di Toscana*
Olio su tela, cm 320 × 240
Inv. 1890 n. 3805

## CASTAGNOLI ROOM

**Sodoma**
*San Sebastiano*
1515 ca
Olio su tela, cm 204 × 145
Inv. 1890 n. 1590

## ALLEGORIES ROMM

**Cristofano Allori**
*La Maddalena nel deserto*
Olio su rame, cm 29 × 43
Inv. 1890 n. 1344

**Cristofano Allori**
*Madonna col Bambino*
Olio su rame, cm 14 × 12
Inv. 1890 n. 1498

**Cristofano Allori (attr.)**
*Gesù bambino addormentato sulla croce*
Olio su tavola, cm 34 × 43
Inv. 1890 n. 1358

**Bronzino (scuola del)**
*Ritratto di Cosimo I de' Medici*
Olio su tavola, cm 57 × 45
Inv. 1912 n. 212

**Bronzino (scuola del)**
*Ritratto di donna*
Olio su tavola, cm 45 × 38
Inv. 1912 n. 204

**Bronzino (scuola del)**
*Ritratto di donna*
Olio su tavola, cm 61 × 48
Inv. 1912 n. 328

**Bronzino (scuola del)**
*Ritratto di donna*
Olio su tavola, cm 48 × 40
Inv. Poggio Imperiale 1860 n. 548

**Annibale Carracci (attr.)**
*Ritratto di Antonio Carracci*
Olio su tela, cm 22 × 19
Inv. 1912 n. 250

**Annibale Carracci (scuola di)**
*Riposo nella fuga in Egitto*
Olio su tavola, cm 23 × 27
Inv. 1912 n. 350

**Cigoli**
*Santa Maria Maddalena nel deserto*
Olio su tela, cm 114 × 87
Inv. 1890 n. 2173

**Cesare Dandini**
*Ritratto di giovane*
Olio su tela, cm 55,5 × 45,5
Inv. 1890 n. 2189

**Cristofano dell'Altissimo**
*Ritratto di Clarice Ridolfi Altoviti*
Olio su tavola, cm 64 × 51
Inv. 1912 n. 327

**Cristofano dell'Altissimo**
*Ritratto di una gentildonna di Casa Ruini*
Olio su tela, cm 51 × 64
Inv. 1912 n. 315

**Lavinia Fontana**
*Ritratto di una gentildonna di Casa Ruini*
Olio su tela, cm 90 × 74
Inv. O.D.A. 1911 n. 536

**Anastagio Fontebuoni**
*San Giovanni nel deserto*
Olio su rame, cm 29 × 24
Inv. 1890 n. 1465

**Artemisia Gentileschi**
*Madonna con il Bambino*
Olio su tela, cm 118 × 86
Inv. 1890 n. 2129

**Giovanni da San Giovanni**
*Gesù servito dagli angeli*
Olio su rame, cm 35 × 43
Inv. 1890 n. 1529

**Giovanni da San Giovanni**
*Nozze mistiche di santa Caterina*
Olio su tela, cm 178 × 146
Inv. 1890 n. 1565

**Giovanni da San Giovanni**
*La Pittura che dipinge la Fama*
1634 ca
Affresco su embrice, cm 53 × 38
Inv. 1890 n. 1533

**Giovanni da San Giovanni**
*Prima notte di nozze*
Olio su tela, cm 231 × 348
Inv. 1890 n. 2120

**Giovanni da San Giovanni**
*Venere che pettina Amore*
Olio su tela, cm 229 × 173
Inv. 1890 n. 2123

**Benedetto Luti**
*Ritratto di giovinetta*
Pastello su carta, cm 33 × 26
Inv. 1890 n. 819

**Benedetto Luti**
*Testa di cherubino*
Pastello su carta, cm 32 × 27
Inv. 1890 n. 821

**Onorio Marinari**
*David*
Olio su rame, cm 43 × 34
Inv. 1890 n. 1555

**Maso da San Friano**
*Ritratto e Elena Gaddi Quaratesi*
Olio su tavola, cm 24 × 17
Inv. 1890 n. 1552

**Livio Mehus**
*Il genio della Scultura*
Olio su tela, cm 70 × 79
Inv. 1890 n. 5337

**Livio Mehus**
*Maddalena in estasi*
Olio su rame, cm 45,8 × 34,5
Inv. O.D.A. 1911 n. 516

**Livio Mehus**
*Maddalena penitente*
Olio su rame, cm 46,6 × 34,5
Inv. O.D.A. 1911 n. 517

**Gregorio Pagani**
*Tobiolo risana Tobia*
Olio su tela, cm 99 × 81
Inv. 1890 n. 1539

**Frans Pourbus il Giovane**
*Ritratto di Elisabetta di Francia bambina*
Olio su tela, cm 52 × 43
Inv. 1890 n. 2403

**Frans Pourbus il Giovane**
*Ritratto di Luigi XIII fanciullo*
Olio su tela, cm 51 × 41
Inv. 1890 n. 2400

**Camillo Procaccini**
*Natività*
Olio su tela, cm 48 × 39
Inv. 1912 n. 319

**Carlo Antonio Sacconi**
*Ritratto del padre Giunta Servita*
Olio su tela, cm 146 × 117
Inv. 1890 n. 1582

**Carlo Antornio Sacconi**
*Ritratto di un bey di Tunisi*
Olio su tela, cm 115 × 93
Inv. 1890 n. 2370

**Scuola bolognese del XVIII secolo**
*Ritratto virile*
Olio su carta incollata su tela, cm 40 × 33
Inv. 1912 n. 310

**Scuola fiorentina del XVI secolo**
*Ritratto di Bianca Cappello*
Olio su tavola, cm 66 × 51
Inv. 1890 n. 2317

**Scuola fiorentina del XVI secolo**
*Venere e Adone*
Olio su tavola, diam. cm 17
Inv. 1890 n. 6266

**Scuola tedesca del XVI secolo**
*Ritratto d'uomo*
Olio su tavola, cm 40 × 29
Inv. 1912 n. 334

**Giusto Suttermans**
*Ritratto del signor Puliciani*
Olio su tela, cm 64 × 49
Inv. 1890 n. 1059

**Giusto Suttermans**
*Ritratto di Carlo, arciduca d'Austria*
Olio su tela, cm 67 × 52
Inv. 1912 n. 293

**Giusto Suttermans**
*Ritratto di Caterina Puliciani*
Olio su tela, cm 63 × 49
Inv. 1890 n. 1071

**Giusto Suttermans**
*Ritratto di Cosimo III de' Medici*
Olio su tela, cm 72 × 58
Inv. 1890 n. 2875

**Giusto Suttermans**
*Ritratto di Margherita de' Medici, moglie di Odoardo I di Parma*
Olio su tela, cm 64 × 50
Inv. 1912 n. 298

**Giusto Suttermans**
*Ritratto di un gentiluomo*
Olio su tela, cm 73 × 59
Inv. 1890 n. 769

**Giusto Suttermans**
*Il senato fiorentino presta giuramento a Ferdinando II de' Medici*
Olio su tela, cm 101 × 138
Inv. 1890 n. 9692

**Giorgio Vasari**
*La visione del conte Ugo*
Olio su tavola, cm 49 × 78
Inv. 1890 n. 8685

**Giorgio Vasari (scuola del)**
*Natività della Vergine*
Olio su tavola, cm 49 × 78
Inv. 1890 n. 8684

**Volterrano**
*Amore dormiente*
1665 ca
Affresco su intonaco su stuoia, cm 73 × 43
Inv. 1912 n. 107

Volterrano
*Amor venale*
Affresco su lavagna, cm 64 × 45
Inv. 1912 n. 105

Volterrano
*La burla del pievano Arlotto*
1640 ca
Tempera su tela, cm 107 × 150
Inv. 1890 n. 582

Volterrano
*Ritratto di Antonio Baldinucci*
Pastello su carta, cm 48 × 38
Inv. 1890 n. 2578

Emilio Zocchi
*Michelangelo fanciullo*
1861
Marmo, h. cm 60
Inv. O.D.A. 1911 n. 453

## ROOM OF THE FINE ARTS

Cristofano Allori
*Adorazione dei Magi*
Olio su tela, cm 337 × 220
Inv. 1890 n. 8741

Federico Barocci
*Testa dell'Annunziata*
Carta incollata su tavola, cm 37 × 26
Inv. 1912 n. 261

Federico Barocci
*Testa di angelo*
Carta incollata su tavola, cm 36 × 26
Inv. 1912 n. 251

Cigoli
*Madonna col Bambino che legge*
Olio su tela, cm 146 × 114
Inv. 1912 n. 430

Cigoli
*Martirio di santo Stefano*
1597
Olio su tela, cm 480 × 287
Inv. 1890 n. 8713

Cigoli
*San Francesco in adorazione*
1600 ca
Olio su tela, cm 140,5 × 114,5
Inv. 1912 n. 46

Carlo Dolci
*La Vergine appare a san Luigi di Tolosa*
Olio su tela, cm 340 × 228
Inv. 1890 n. 747

Jacopo da Empoli
*Madonna del soccorso*
Tavola, cm 262 × 177
Inv. 1890 n. 9383

Giulio Romano
*Sacra Famiglia*
Olio su tavola, cm 35 × 24
Inv. 1912 n. 247

Jacopo Ligozzi
*Apparizione della Madonna a san Francesco*
Olio su tela, cm 259 × 173
Inv. 1912 n. 289

Jacopo Ligozzi
*Santa Caterina d'Alessandria trasportata dagli angeli*
Tela, cm 133 × 106
Inv. 1890 n. 8044

Peter Paul Rubens
*Cristo risorto*
Tela, cm 183 × 155
Inv. O.D.A. 1911 n. 479

Francesco Salviati
*Ritratto d'uomo*
Olio su tavola, cm 22 × 18
Inv. 1912 n. 274

Scuola fiamminga del XVI secolo
*Ritratto di uomo*
Tavola, cm 30,5 × 21,5
Inv. 1912 n. 424

Scuola fiorentina del XVI secolo
*Ritratto di dama*
Olio su rame, cm 30 × 20
Inv. 1912 n. 433

Scuola fiorentina del XVI secolo
*Ritratto di giovinetta*
Olio su tavola, cm 24 × 18
Inv. 1912 n. 283

Giusto Suttermans
*Ritratto di Vittoria della Rovere come santa Margherita*
Olio su rame, cm 29,5 × 21,5
Inv. 1890 n. 1038

Jacopo Vignali
*San Silvestro papa battezza l'imperatore Costantino*
Olio su tela, cm 130 × 160
Inv. 1890 n. 8682

## HERCULES ROOM

Borgognone
*La battaglia di Lutzen*
Olio su tela, cm 140 × 275
Inv. O.D.A. 1911 n. 451

Borgognone
*La battaglia di Nordlingen*
Olio su tela, cm 141 × 275
Inv. O.D.A. 1911 n. 452

## DAWN ROOM

Jacopo da Empoli
*L'ebbrezza di Noè*
Olio su tela, cm 207 × 174
Inv. 1890 n. 9413

Jacopo da Empoli
*Sant'Ivo protettore degli orfani*
1617
Olio su tavola, cm 288 × 212
Inv. 1890 n. 1569

Lavinia Fontana
*Ritratto di Francesco Panigarola, predicatore milanese*
Olio su tela, cm 146 × 111
Inv. 1890 n. 807

Jacopo Ligozzi
*Adorazione dei Magi*
1597
Olio su tela, cm 228 × 173
Inv. 1890 n. 8671

Lorenzo Lippi
*Giacobbe al pozzo*
Olio su tela, cm 232 × 342
Inv. 1890 n. 3477

Lorenzo Lippi
*Trionfo di David*
Olio su tela, cm 232 × 342
Inv. 1890 n. 3476

Pietro da Cortona
*Morte di santa Maria Egiziaca*
Olio su tela, cm 97 × 111
Inv. 1890 n. 572

Domenico Pugliani
*Natività della Vergine*
Tavola, cm 58 × 125
Inv. 1890 n. 8416

Giusto Suttermans
*Ritratto del principe Czomanodoff, ambasciatore moscovita*
Olio su tela, cm 232 × 342
Inv. 1890 n. 2371

Giusto Suttermans
*Ritratto di Maria Maddalena d'Austria come santa Maria Maddalena*
Olio su tela, cm 168 × 90
Inv. 1890 n. 563

Jacopo Vignali
*Cristo e la Samaritana*
Olio su tela, cm 87 × 72
Inv. 1890 n. 8030

Jacopo Vignali
*Episodio dalla Gerusalemme liberata*
Olio su tela, cm 189 × 205
Inv. 1890 n. 5054

Volterrano
*Ecce Homo*
Olio su tela, cm 116 × 86
Inv. Poggio Imperiale 1860 n. 152

## BERENICE ROOM

Francesco Albani
*Liberazione di san Pietro dal carcere*
Olio su rame, cm 234 × 235
Inv. 1912 n. 278

Cristofano Allori
*Adorazione dei pastori*
Olio su tela, cm 97 × 78
Inv. 1912 n. 475

Cristofano Allori
*Maddalena penitente*
Olio su tela, cm 145 × 91
Inv. 1890 n. 2174

Cristofano Allori
*San Francesco in preghiera*
Rame, cm 39 × 30
Inv. 1912 n. 290

Giovanni Bilivert
*Angelica e Ruggero*
Olio su tela, cm 116 × 150
Inv. 1890 n. 8034

Giovanni Bilivert
*La castità di Giuseppe*
1619
Olio su tela, cm 240 × 399
Inv. 1890 n. 1585

Giovanni Bilivert
*Sacra Famiglia*
Olio su tavola, cm 180 × 149
Inv. 1890 n. 2177

Francesco Cambi
*Ritratto di Stefano della Bella*
Olio su tela, cm 54 × 45
Inv. 1890 n. 1541

Caravaggio (attr.)
*Il cavadenti*
Olio su tela, cm 101 × 150
Inv. 1890 n. 5682

Carlo Dolci
*Gesù nell'orto*
Tavola, cm 70 × 49
Inv. 1912 n. 288

Carlo Dolci
*San Simone*
Olio su tela, cm 40 × 27
Inv. 1890 n. 1557

Francesco Furini
*Adamo ed Eva nel Paradiso terrestre*
1630
Olio su tela, cm 193 × 242
Inv. 1912 n. 426

Francesco Furini
*La Poesia e la Pittura*
1626
Olio su tela, cm 180 × 143
Inv. 1890 n. 6466

Anton Domenico Gabbiani
*Morte di san Giuseppe*
Olio su tela, cm 116 × 87
Inv. Poggio Imperiale 1860 n. 1029

Luca Giordano
*Adorazione dei Magi*
Tela, cm 199 × 122,5
Inv. Poggio Imperiale 1860 n. 155

Livio Mehus
*Miracolo di san Zanobi*
Olio su tela, cm 147 × 117
Inv. Poggio Imperiale 1860 n. 1216

Orazio Riminaldi
*Martirio di santa Cecilia*
Olio su tela, cm 315 × 171 (con l'ampliamento 333,3 × 217,5)
Inv. 1912 n. 489

Orazio Sammacchini
*Sacra Famiglia*
Olio su tavola, cm 351 × 283
Inv. 1912 n. 240

Filippo Tarchiani
*La Madonna e la novizia*
Tela, cm 116 × 139
Inv. 1890 n. 2167

Hans van Aachen (attr.)
*Sacra Famiglia*
Tela, cm 30 × 24
Inv. 1912 n. 284

Volterrano
*Santa Caterina da Siena*
Tavola, cm 25 × 18
Inv. 1890 n. 1518

**PSYCHE ROOM**

Salvator Rosa
*Albero stroncato e uomo seduto*
Olio su tela, cm 33,5 × 27
Inv. GDSU n. 19173

Salvator Rosa
*Battaglia*
1640 ca
Olio su tela, cm 234 × 350
Inv. 1912 n. 133

Salvator Rosa
*Empedocle che cade
nella voragine*
Tavola, cm 88 × 63
Inv. GDSU n. 19152

Salvator Rosa
*Filosofo in un bosco*
Olio su tavola, cm 86 × 63
Inv. GDSU n. 19151

Salvator Rosa
*Marina con arco naturale*
Olio su tela, cm 15 × 44
Inv. 1890 n. 1325

Salvator Rosa
*Marina con le torri*
Olio su tela, cm 102 × 127
Inv. 1912 n. 312

Salvator Rosa
*Paesaggio con arco naturale
e cascata*
Olio su tela, cm 65 × 49
Inv. 1890 n. 1319

Salvator Rosa
*Paesaggio con due figure*
Olio su tavola, cm 29 × 50
Inv. GDSU n. 19149

Salvator Rosa
*Il ponte rotto*
Olio su tela, cm 102 × 127
Inv. 1912 n. 306

Salvator Rosa
*La selva dei filosofi*
Olio su tela, cm 149 × 223
Inv. 1912 n. 470

Salvator Rosa
*Studio di albero con uomo*
Olio su tavola, cm 34 × 27
Inv. GDSU n. 19174

Salvator Rosa
*Uomo seduto in un bosco*
Olio su tavola, cm 28 × 50
Inv. GDSU n. 19150

**ROOM OF FAME**

Jan Both
*Paesaggio al tramonto*
Olio su tela, cm 163 × 122
Inv. 1912 n. 411

Paul Brill
*Caccia al cinghiale*

Olio su tela, cm 88 × 116
Inv. 1890 n. 1076

Paul Brill
*Caccia all'Airone*
Tela, cm 95,5 × 127
Inv. 1890 n. 598

Abraham Bruegel
*Uccelli morti*
Olio su tela, cm 48 × 30
Inv. 1890 n. 7601

Michelangelo Cerquozzi (attr.)
*Paesaggio con contadini*
Olio su tela, cm 50 × 66
Inv. 1912 n. 458

Giacomo Ceruti
*Ragazzo con cesta di pesci*
Olio su tela, cm 56 × 37
Inv. 1911 n. 301

Andries Daniels, Hendrik
van Balen
*Sacra Famiglia in una ghirlanda*
Tavola, cm 106 × 85
Inv. 1912 n. 467

Jan Davidsz de Heem
*Festone di fiori e frutta*
Olio su tela, cm 57 × 81
Inv. 1890 n. 1261

Jan Davidsz de Heem
*Natura morta di fiori e frutta*
Olio su tela, cm 60 × 73
Inv. 1890 n. 1244

Frans Floris de Vriendt
*Adamo ed Eva*
Olio su tavola, cm 176 × 150
Inv. 1890 n. 1082

Jean Paul Gillemans
*Natura morta*
Olio su tela, cm 46 × 66
Inv. O.D.A. 1911 n. 499

Anton Goubau
*Il suonatore del villaggio*
Olio su tavola, cm 50 × 75
Inv. 1890 n. 1041

Theodor Helmbreker
*Cucina rustica*
Tela, cm 67 × 91
Inv. Petraia n. 9

Bartolomeo Ligozzi
*Natura morta con pappagallo*
Tela, cm 107 × 74,5
Inv. 1890 n. 1774

Otto Marseus van Schrieck
*Fiori e farfalle*
Olio su tela, cm 60 × 50
Inv. O.D.A. 1911 n. 551

Otto Marseus van Schrieck
*Natura morta con funghi e
farfalle*
1655
Olio su tela, cm 38 × 48
Inv. 1890 n. 5268

Otto Marseus van Schrieck
*Piante e roditori*
Olio su tela, cm 81 × 67
Inv. O.D.A. 1911 n. 500

Otto Marseus van Schrieck
*Rettili, farfalle e piante nei pressi
di un albero*
Olio su tela, cm 60 × 47
Inv. O.D.A. 1911 n. 502

Otto Marseus van Schrieck
*Sottobosco con animali*
Olio su tela, cm 62 × 49
Inv. O.D.A. 1911 n. 503

Otto Marseus van Schrieck
*Vaso con fiori e farfalle*
Rame, cm 32 × 25
Inv. O.D.A. 1911 n. 529

Filippo Napoletano
*Calvario*
Tela, cm 92 × 135
Inv. 1890 n. 574

Filippo Napoletano
*Combattimento di cavalieri*
Tela, cm 107 × 122
Inv. 1890 n. 3857

Filippo Napoletano
*Due conchiglie*
Olio su tela, cm 39 × 56
Inv. 1890 n. 6580

Filippo Napoletano
*Nettuno e Anfitrite*
Tela, cm 117,5 × 169,5
Inv. O.D.A. 1911 n. 496

Filippo Napoletano
*Paesaggio*
Olio su rame, cm 31 × 39
Inv. 1890 n. 4981

Filippo Napoletano
*Paesaggio campestre*
Tela, cm 93 × 120
Inv. Poggio a Caiano n. 304

Clara Peeters (attr.)
*Fiori e frutta*
Olio su tavola, cm 42 × 41
Inv. O.D.A. 1911 n. 549

Frans Pourbus il Vecchio
*Orfeo*
Tavola, cm 129 × 188
Inv. 1890 n. 5409

Marco Ricci
*Marina con figure*
Olio su tela, cm 49 × 74
Inv. 1890 n. 6798

Marco Ricci
*Paesaggio*
Olio su tela, cm 75 × 98
Inv. 1890 n. 5770

Marco Ricci
*Paesaggio con arco naturale*
Olio su tela, cm 67 × 97
Inv. 1890 n. 7160

Josef Roos
*Pastore e armenti in un paesaggio*
Olio su tela, cm 73 × 87
Inv. 1890 n. 8750

Gottfried Schalcken
*La Fama*
Olio su tela, cm 69 × 60
Inv. 1890 n. 1192

Scuola fiamminga del XVII secolo
*Paesaggio montuoso*
Olio su tela, cm 75 × 99
Inv. 1912 n. 498

Scuola italiana del XVI secolo
*Flagellazione di Cristo*
Olio su rame, cm 35 × 25
Inv. Poggio Imperiale 1860 n. 525

Scuola tedesca del XVII secolo
*Paesaggio con contadini*
Tela, cm 56,8 × 85,2
Inv. 1912 n. 463

Scuola tedesca del XVIII secolo
*Paesaggio con cacciatori*
Olio su tela, cm 57 × 85
Inv. 1912 n. 456

David Teniers il Giovane
*Baccanale*
Tavola, cm 36 × 48
Inv. 1890 n. 1040

Willem van Aelst
*Cacciagione e ortaggi*
Olio su tela, cm 84 × 102
Inv. Poggio Imperiale n. 3533

Willem van Aelst
*Natura morta con fiori*
Olio su tela, cm 73 × 58
Inv. O.D.A. 1911 n. 508

Willem van Aelst
*Natura morta con frutta*
Olio su tela, cm 73 × 58
Inv. O.D.A. 1911 n. 509

Willem van Aelst
*Natura morta con vasellame,
frutta e cacciagione*
Olio su tela, cm 190 × 134
Inv. O.D.A. 1911 n. 561

Adriaen van der Cabel
*Marina al tramonto*
Olio su tela, cm 45 × 99
Inv. 1890 n. 535

Adriaen van der Cabel
*Veduta costiera*
Olio su tela, cm 50 × 99
Inv. 1890 n. 533

Jan van Kessel
*Natura morta con frutta
e frutti di mare*
1653
Olio su tela, cm 31 × 44
Inv. 1890 n. 1119

Pieter van Laer
*Pastore e animale*
Olio su tela, cm 56 × 54,5
Inv. 1890 n. 1226

Maria van Osterwick
*Vaso di fiori*
Olio su rame, cm 38 × 30
Inv. 1890 n. 1308

Jan Philipp van Thielen,
Erasmus Quellyn
*Madonna col Bambino
in una ghirlanda di fiori*
Olio su tela, cm 81 × 61
Inv. 1890 n. 1191

Gaspard van Wittel
(Gaspare Vanvitelli)
*Riviera di Chiaia a Napoli*
Olio su tela, cm 50 × 105
Inv. 1890 n. 9288

Gaspard van Wittel
(Gaspare Vanvitelli)
*Veduta di Firenze dalle Cascine*
Olio su tela, cm 45 × 75
Inv. 1890 n. 9292

Gaspard van Wittel
(Gaspare Vanvitelli)
*Veduta di Marino*
Olio su tela, cm 74 × 98
Inv. 1890 n. 9295

Gaspard van Wittel
(Gaspare Vanvitelli)
*Veduta di Napoli*
Olio su tela, cm 50 × 98
Inv. 1890 n. 9290

Gaspard van Wittel
(Gaspare Vanvitelli)
*Veduta di Verona*
Olio su tela, cm 48 × 105
Inv. 1890 n. 9289

Nikolaus Veerendael
*Vaso di fiori*
Olio su tavola, cm 30 × 23
Inv. 1890 n. 1079

## POCCETTI
## CORRIDOR

Federico Barocci
*Ritratto di un ecclesiastico*
Olio su tela, cm 51 × 49
Inv. 1912 n. 407

Niccolò Cassana
*Ritratto di un pittore*
Olio su tela, cm 74 × 61
Inv. 1912 n. 188

Niccolò Cassana
*Ritratto d'uomo*
Olio su tela, cm 70 × 52
Inv. 1912 n. 481

Bartolomeo Cavarozzi
*San Gerolamo nello studio*
Olio su tela, cm 116 × 173
Inv. 1912 n. 417

Jusepe de Ribera
*Martirio di san Bartolomeo*
1628-30
Olio su tela, cm 145 × 216
Inv. 1912 n. 19

Gaspard Dughet
*Paesaggio con due uomini
in primo piano*
Olio su tela, cm 51 × 87
Inv. 1912 n. 441

Gaspard Dughet
*Paesaggio con fauno danzante*
Olio su tela, cm 51 × 87
Inv. 1912 n. 416

Gaspard Dughet
*Paese con fauni e ninfe*
Olio su tela, cm 51 × 87
Inv. 1912 n. 421

Gaspard Dughet
*Paese con ruderi*
Olio su tela, cm 52 × 87
Inv. 1912 n. 436

Domenico Feti
*La dramma perduta*
Olio su tavola, cm 75 × 44
Inv. 1912 n. 30

Domenico Feti
*Gli operai della vigna*
Olio su tavola, cm 75 × 44
Inv. 1912 n. 26

Domenico Feti
*Santa Margherita vince
il demonio*
Olio su tavola, cm 60 × 43
Inv. 1890 n. 9262

Francesco Furini
*Ila e le ninfe*
1635 ca
Olio su tela, cm 230 × 261
Inv. 1890 n. 3562

Peter Lely
*Ritratto di Oliver Cromwell*
Olio su tela, cm 73 × 61
Inv. 1912 n. 408

Andrea Pozzo
*Ritratto del gesuita Pietro
Pinamonti*
Olio su tela, cm 68 × 53
Inv. 1912 n. 496

Scipione Pulzone (attr.)
*Ritratto del cardinale Ferdinando I
de' Medici*
Olio su tavola, cm 69 × 56
Inv. 1912 n. 492

Jacob Pynas
*Predica di san Giovanni Battista*
Olio su tela, cm 89 × 117
Inv. 1912 n. 431

Matteo Rosselli
*I tre fanciulli nella fornace*
Olio su tela, cm 176 × 216
Inv. 1890 n. 3560

Rosso Fiorentino
*Ritratto di Francesco
da Castiglione*
Olio su tavola, cm 50 × 38
Inv. 1912 n. 249

Peter Paul Rubens
*Ritratto del duca di Buckingham*
Olio su tavola, cm 65 × 50
Inv. 1912 n. 324

Peter Paul Rubens
*Ritratto di Catherine Manners,
duchessa di Buckingham*
Olio su tavola, cm 64 × 46
Inv. 1890 n. 761

Schiavone
*Adorazione dei pastori*
Olio su tela, cm 116 × 162
Inv. 1890 n. 905

Giusto Suttermans (scuola di)
*Ritratto di un gentiluomo
in armatura*
Olio su tela, cm 70 × 52
Inv. 1912 n. 485

Jan van Scorel
*Stimmate di san Francesco*
Olio su tavola, cm 69 × 54
Inv. 1912 n. 482

## PROMETHEUS ROOM

Mariotto Albertinelli
*Sacra famiglia*
Olio su tavola, diam. cm 86
Inv. 1912 n. 365

Cristofano Allori
*Ritratto di un uomo in nero*
Olio su tela, cm 91 × 67
Inv. 1912 n. 72

Andrea del Sarto (attr.)
*Madonna dell'Umiltà*
Tempera su tavola, cm 20 × 12
Inv. O.D.A. 1911 n. 1154

Andrea del Sarto (scuola di)
*L'Arcangelo e Tobia*
Tavola, cm 42 × 29,5
Inv. 1912 n. 292

Andrea del Minga (da cartone
di Baccio Bandinelli)
*La cacciata dal Paradiso*
Tavola, cm 212 × 172
Inv. 1912 n. 378

Andrea del Minga (da cartone
di Baccio Bandinelli)
*Creazione di Eva*
Tavola, cm 198 × 167
Inv. 1912 n. 367

Bachiacca
*La Maddalena*
Olio su tavola, cm 51 × 42
Inv. 1912 n. 102

Jacopo Bassano
*Ritratto di uomo*
Tela, cm 30 × 24,5
Inv. 1912 n. 335

Domenico Beccafumi
*Sacra famiglia*
Olio su tavola, diam. cm 88
Inv. 1912 n. 359

Sandro Botticelli
*Madonna col Bambino
e san Giovannino*
Tela, cm 134 × 92
Inv. 1912 n. 357

Sandro Botticelli
*Madonna col Bambino,
san Giovannino e angeli*
Olio su tavola, diam. cm 115
Inv. 1912 n. 348

Sandro Botticelli
*Ritratto di gentildonna
("La bella Simonetta")*
Olio su tavola, cm 61 × 40
Inv. 1912 n. 353

Sandro Botticelli
*Ritratto di giovane con
"mazzocchio"*
1470 ca
Olio su tavola, cm 51 × 34
Inv. 1912 n. 372

Francesco Botticini
*Adorazione del Bambino*
1485
Tempera su tavola, diam. cm 123
Inv. 1912 n. 347

Bronzino (scuola del)
*Ritratto di Cosimo I de' Medici*
Olio su tavola, cm 77 × 60
Inv. 1912 n. 403

Bronzino (scuola del)
*Ritratto di donna*
Olio su tavola, cm 60 × 40
Inv. Poggio a Caiano n. 18

Bronzino (scuola del)
*Ritratto di Piero il Gottoso*
Olio su tela, cm 73 × 59
Inv. 1890 n. 2122

Jacopo de' Boateri
*Sacra famiglia*
Olio su tavola, cm 58 × 47
Inv. 1912 n. 362

Jacopino del Conte
*Ritratto di uno Scarlatti*
Tavola, cm 85 × 70
Inv. 1912 n. 238

Jacopo del Sellaio
*Madonna adorante
il Bambino Gesù*
Tavola, diam. cm 99
Inv. 1912 n. 364

Jusepe de Ribera
*San Francesco*
1643
Olio su tela, cm 103 × 77
Inv. 1912 n. 73

Fra' Bartolomeo
*Ecce Homo*
Affresco, cm 60 × 38
Inv. 1912 n. 377

Franciabigio
*La calunnia di Apelle*
Tavola, cm 37 × 47
Inv. 1912 n. 427

Giacinto Gemignani
*Rebecca al pozzo*
Olio su tela, cm 94 × 144
Inv. 1912 n. 368

Girolamo Genga
*Ritratto virile*
Tavola, cm 55 × 49
Inv. 1912 n. 382

Domenico Ghirlandaio
(scuola di)
*Epifania*
Olio su tavola, diam. cm 99
Inv. 1912 n. 358

Ridolfo del Ghirlandaio
*Madonna col Bambino*
Olio su tavola, cm 60 × 39
Inv. 1912 n. 363

Ridolfo del Ghirlandaio
*Santi Pietro e Paolo*
Olio su tavola, diam. cm 105
Inv. 1890 n. 6063

Giulio Romano (copia da)
*"Madonna della lucertola"*
Olio su tavola, cm 149 × 110
Inv. 1912 n. 57

Francesco Granacci
*Sacra Famiglia con san
Giovannino*
Olio su tavola, cm 68 × 58
Inv. 1912 n. 345

Filippino Lippi (scuola di)
*Madonna col Bambino
e san Giovannino*
Tavola, diam. cm 87
Inv. 1912 n. 349

Filippo Lippi
*Madonna col Bambino
ed episodi della vita di sant'Anna
("Tondo Bartolini")*
1450 ca
Tempera su tavola, diam. cm 135
Inv. 1912 n. 343

Valerio Marucelli
*Assunzione della Maddalena*
Marmo, cm 56 × 34
Inv. 1912 n. 346

Baldassare Peruzzi
*La danza di Apollo e le Muse*
Olio su tavola, cm 35 × 78
Inv. 1912 n. 167

Piero di Cosimo
*Ritratto di Caterina Sforza*
Tavola, cm 47 × 36
Inv. 1890 n. 604

Pontormo
*Adorazione dei Magi*
1520
Olio su tavola, cm 85 × 191
Inv. 1912 n. 379

Pontormo
*Martirio di san Maurizio
e delle legioni tebane*
1529-30
Olio su tavola, cm 65 × 73
Inv. 1912 n. 182

Frans Pourbus il Giovane
(scuola di)
*Ritratto di donna*
Tavola, cm 21 × 18
Inv. 1912 n. 260

Guido Reni
*Bacco fanciullo*
Olio su tela, cm 87 × 70
Inv. 1912 n. 47

Cosimo Rosselli
*Natività*
Olio su tavola, diam. cm 116
Inv. 1912 n. 354

Francesco Salviati
*Ritratto d'uomo*
Olio su tavola, cm 74 × 56
Inv. 1912 n. 361

Santi di Tito
*Ritratto di Don Giovanni
de' Medici*
Olio su tavola, cm 56 × 38
Inv. 1912 n. 287

Bartolomeo Schedoni
*Madonna col Bambino*
Olio su tavola, cm 25 × 19
Inv. 1912 n. 360

Scuola dell'Italia settentrionale
*Ritratto d'uomo*
Tavola, cm 55 × 49
Inv. 1912 n. 382

Scuola dell'Italia settentrionale
del XVI secolo
*Madonna col Bambino
e due santi*
Olio su tavola, cm 63 × 46
Inv. 1912 n. 309

Scuola emiliana del XVI secolo
*Madonna col Bambino
e san Giovannino*
Olio su tavola, cm 59 × 47
Inv. 1912 n. 299

Scuola ferrarese
*La maga col putto*
Olio su tavola, cm 81 × 65
Inv. 1890 n. 5064

Scuola fiorentina del XV secolo
*Ecce Homo*
Tavola, 60 × 38
Inv. 1912 n. 369

Scuola fiorentina del XVI secolo
*Madonna col Bambino
e san Giovannino*
Olio su tavola, diam. cm 85
Inv. 1912 n. 199

Scuola fiorentina del XVI secolo
*Madonna col Bambino,
san Giovannino e angeli*
Olio su tavola, diam. cm 112
Inv. 1912 n. 342

Scuola fiorentina del XVI secolo
*Ritratto di donna*
Rame, cm 21 × 16
Inv. 1912 n. 273

Scuola fiorentina del XVI secolo
*Ritratto di donna*
Olio su tavola, cm 86 × 67
Inv. 1912 n. 351

Scuola umbra del XV secolo
*Epifania*
Olio su tavola, cm 57 × 44
Inv. 1912 n. 341

Luca Signorelli
*Sacra famiglia con santa Caterina*
Olio su tavola, diam. cm 99
Inv. 1912 n. 355

Giorgio Vasari
*La Pazienza*
Olio su tela, cm 177 × 101
Inv. 1912 n. 399

## CORRIDOR OF THE COLUMNS

Christoph Ludwig Agricola
*Paesaggio al tramonto*
Olio su rame, cm 41 × 33
Inv. 1890 n. 1137

Christoph Ludwig Agricola
*Paesaggio con doppio arcobaleno*
Olio su rame, cm 41 × 33
Inv. 1890 n. 1130

Jan Asselijn (attr.)
*Paesaggio montano con cascata*
Olio su tela, cm 47 × 54
Inv. 1890 n. 1045

Adriaen Frans Boudewyns
*Paesaggio*
Olio su tela, cm 36 × 52
Inv. 1890 n. 1227

Bartholomeus Breenbergh
*Cristo e l'adultera*
Olio su rame, cm 33 × 45
Inv. 1890 n. 1266

Paul Brill
*Marina*
Olio su tela, cm 31 × 45
Inv. 1890 n. 1133

Paul Brill
*Paesaggio con caccia al cervo*
1595
Olio su rame, cm 21 × 28
Inv. 1890 n. 1129

Paul Brill
*Paesaggio con caccia alla lepre*
Olio su rame, cm 20 × 28
Inv. 1890 n. 1136

Paul Brill
*Paesaggio montano*
Olio su tela, cm 30 × 43
Inv. 1890 n. 1126

Jan Brueghel dei Velluti
*Orfeo agli Inferi*
1594
Olio su rame, cm 27 × 36
Inv. 1890 n. 1298

Jan Brueghel dei Velluti
*Paesaggio*
Olio su rame, cm 13 × 17
Inv. 1890 n. 1274

Michelangelo Cerquozzi (attr.)
*Paesaggio con figure*
Olio su rame, cm 21 × 14
Inv. 1890 n. 1283

Pieter de Molyn il Vecchio
*Paesaggio con ponte*
Olio su tavola, cm 39 × 60
Inv. 1890 n. 1290

Jean de Momper
*Paesaggio con vaccaro*
Tela, cm 18 × 26
Inv. 1890 n. 1054

Jean de Momper
*Paesaggio fluviale*
Tela, cm 17 × 34
Inv. 1890 n. 6205

Jean de Momper (attr.)
*Paesaggio con bovaro*
Olio su rame, cm 14 × 18
Inv. 1890 n. 1175

Lodewijk de Vadder (attr.)
*Paesaggio con cacciatori*
Olio su tela, cm 47 × 55
Inv. 1912 n. 459

Anastagio Fontebuoni
(da Adam Elsheimer)
*Predica di san Giovanni Battista*
Olio su rame, cm 19,5 × 25,5
Inv. 1912 n. 366

Frans Francken II Giovane
*Trionfo di Nettuno e Anfitrite*
Olio su tavola, cm 51 × 70
Inv. 1890 n. 1068

Frans Francken il Vecchio
*Allegoria del Genio*
Olio su tavola, cm 52 × 70
Inv. 1890 n. 1061

Frans Franken II
*Crocifissione*
Rame, cm 22 × 28
Inv. 1890 n. 1121

Pietro Mera
*Pan, siringa e ninfe*
Rame, cm 28 × 39
Inv. 1890 n. 1147

Pietro Molyn il Vecchio
*Paesaggio*
Tavola, cm 38,5 × 60
Inv. 1890 n. 1290

Filippo Napoletano
*Mulino*
Rame, cm 30 × 23
Inv. 1890 n. 1214

David Ryckaert
*Le tentazioni di sant'Antonio*
Tela, cm 83 × 59
Inv. 1890 n. 1144

David Ryckaert III
*Le tentazioni di sant'Antonio*
Olio su tavola, cm 58 × 83
Inv. 1890 n. 1091

Mathys Schoevaerts
*Paesaggio*
Olio su tela, cm 21 × 37
Inv. 1890 n. 1112

Scuola olandese del XVII secolo
*Paesaggio con Venere e Amore*
Rame, cm 26 × 33
Inv. 1912 n. 461

David Teniers il Vecchio
*L'Alchimista*
Olio su tela, cm 44 × 58,5
Inv. 1890 n. 1067

Willem van Aelst
*Natura morta con uccelli*
Olio su tela, cm 22 × 27
Inv. 1890 n. 1209

Jan Frans van Bredael
*Paesaggio*
Tavola, cm 37 × 29
Inv. O.D.A. 1911 n. 72

Jan Frans van Bredael
*Paesaggio*
Tavola, cm 37 × 29
Inv. O.D.A. 1911 n. 73

Eglon Hendrik van der Neer
*Paesaggio*
Tavola, cm 28 × 41
Inv. 1890 n. 1205

Eglon Hendrik van der Neer
*Paesaggio*
Tavola, cm 28 × 41
Inv. 1890 n. 1213

Abraham van Diepenbeeck
*Madonna dell'Apocalisse*
Olio su tela, cm 73 × 54
Inv. 1890 n. 1105

Jan Frans van Douven
*Ballo in maschera*
Olio su tela, cm 48 × 38
Inv. 1912 n. 478

Jan Frans van Douven
*Ritratto di Anna Maria Lodovica
de' Medici, Elettrice Palatina*
1699
Olio su tela, cm 45 × 33
Inv. 1912 n. 477

Jan Frans van Douven
*Ritratto di Anna Maria Luisa
de' Medici, Elettrice Palatina*
Olio su tela, cm 45 × 33
Inv. 1912 n. 471

Jan Frans van Douven
*Ritratto di Anna Maria Luisa
de' Medici in abito da caccia*
Olio su tela, cm 48,3 × 37
Inv. 1912 n. 472

Jan van Kessel
*Frutta e pesci*
Rame, cm 19 × 24
Inv. 1890 n. 1199

Jan van Kessel
*Lo studio di un naturalista*
Rame, cm 19 × 25
Inv. 1890 n. 1216

Cornelis van Poelenburgh
*Abramo e Isacco*
Rame, cm 11 × 7
Inv. 1890 n. 8263

Cornelis van Poelenburgh
*Adorazione dei pastori*
Rame, cm 38 × 30
Inv. 1890 n. 1224

Cornelis van Poelenburgh
*L'Arcangelo Raffaele e Tobiolo*
Rame, cm 11 × 7
Inv. 1890 n. 8262

Cornelis van Poelemburg
*Danzatore tra rovine antiche*
Olio su rame, cm 44 × 62
Inv. 1890 n. 1200

Cornelis van Poelenburgh
*Due paesaggi*
Olio su rame, cm 11 × 14 ciascuno
Inv. 1912 n. 317

Cornelis van Poelemburg
*Grotte nella campagna romana*
Olio su tavola, cm 10,3 × 16
Inv. 1890 n. 1194

Cornelis van Poelenburgh
*Paesaggio con arco trionfale
e pastori*
Rame, cm 23 × 30
Inv. 1912 n. 479

Cornelis van Poelenburgh
*Paesaggio con bagnanti*
Rame, cm 41 × 56
Inv. 1912 n. 460

Cornelis van Poelenburgh
*Paesaggio con edificio e pastori*
Rame, cm 15 × 21
Inv. 1890 n. 1218

Cornelis van Poelenburgh
*Paesaggio con pastori
e danzatrice*
Rame, cm 22 × 30
Inv. 1912 n. 473

Cornelis van Poelenburgh
*Paesaggio con rovina, gregge
e pastori*
Rame, cm 29 × 40
Inv. 1890 n. 1195

Cornelis van Poelenburgh
*Paesaggio con rovine antiche
e viandanti*
Rame, cm 28 × 41
Inv. 1890 nn. 1176

Cornelis van Poelenburgh
*Paesaggio con rovine e pastore*
Tavola, cm 16 × 21
Inv. 1890 n. 1198

Cornelius van Poelenburgh
*Paesaggio con satiri danzanti*
Olio su rame, cm 45 × 63
Inv. 1890 n. 1221

Cornelis van Poelenburgh
*Paesaggio con un angelo*
Rame, cm 11 × 7
Inv. 1890 n. 1094

Cornelis van Poelenburgh
*Ritrovamento di Mosè*
Olio su tela, cm 45 × 63
Inv. 1890 n. 1203

Cornelis van Poelenburgh
*Ruderi romani*
Rame, cm 16 × 22
Inv. 1890 n. 1197

Cornelis van Poelenburgh
*San Giovanni Battista*
Rame, cm 11 × 7
Inv. 1890 n. 1093

Cornelis van Poelenburgh
*San Giovanni Evangelista*
Rame, cm 11 × 7
Inv. 1890 n. 8265

Cornelis van Poelenburgh
*San Giuseppe e Gesù Bambino*
Rame, cm 11 × 7
Inv. 1890 n. 8260

Cornelis van Poelenburgh
*San Lorenzo*
Rame, cm 11 × 7
Inv. 1890 n. 8264

Cornelis van Poelenburgh
*San Paolo*
Rame, cm 11 × 7
Inv. 1890 n. 8266

Cornelis van Poelenburgh
*San Pietro*

Rame, cm 11 × 7
Inv. 1890 n. 8267

Cornelis van Poelenburgh
*Sant'Anna e la Vergine fanciulla*
Rame, cm 11 × 7
Inv. 1890 n. 8261

Cornelis van Poelenburgh
*San Tommaso d'Aquino*
Rame, cm 11 × 7
Inv. 1890 n. 1095

Cornelis van Poelenburgh
*La verga miracolosa*
Rame, cm 12 × 22
Inv. 1890 n. 1220

Cornelis van Poelenburgh
(seguace di)
*Paesaggio con ninfe e satiro*
Olio su tela, cm 22 × 32
Inv. 1890 n. 1307

Moysesz van Uyttenbroeck
*Paesaggio pastorale*
Tavola, cm 42 × 57
Inv. 1890 n. 1265

Gaspard van Wittel
(Gaspare Vanvitelli)
*Il Tevere a San Giovanni dei
Fiorentini*
1685
Tempera su pergamena, cm 23 × 43
Inv. 1890 n. 4354

Gaspard van Wittel
(Gaspare Vanvitelli)
*Veduta dei "Prati di Castello"*
1685
Tempera su pergamena, cm 23 × 43
Inv. 1890 n. 4355

Gaspard van Wittel
(Gaspare Vanvitelli)
*Veduta di Roma col Tevere*
1685
Tempera su pergamena, cm 29 × 41
Inv. 1890 n. 1247

Gaspard van Wittel
(Gaspare Vanvitelli)
*Villa Medici a Roma*
1685
Tempera su pergamena, cm 29 × 41
Inv. 1890 n. 1256

Hendrik Cornelisz Vroom
*Marina con veliero da guerra*
Legno, cm 33 × 54
Inv. 1890 n. 1055

## JUSTICE ROOM

Jacopo Bassano
*Ritratto di donna*
Olio su tela, cm 109 × 91
Inv. 1912 n. 130

Leandro Bassano
*Ultima cena*
Olio su tela, cm 92 × 135
Inv. 1912 n. 446

Giovanni De Mio
*Riposo durante la fuga in Egitto*

Tela, cm 67 × 93
Inv. 1890 n. 6069

Bonifacio de' Pitati
*Augusto e la Sibilla Tiburtina*
Olio su tela, cm 105 × 124
Inv. 1912 n. 257

Bonifacio de' Pitati
*Gesù e i dottori*
Olio su tela, cm 198 × 176
Inv. 1912 n. 405

Bonifacio de' Pitati
*Riposo nella fuga in Egitto*
Tavola, cm 108 × 151
Inv. 1912 n. 89

Bonifacio de' Pitati
*Ritratto di dama con guanto*
Olio su tela, cm 75 × 58
Inv. 1912 n. 222

Garofalo
*San Giacomo Maggiore*
Olio su tela, cm 84 × 69
Inv. 1912 n. 5

Polidoro Lanciani (attr.)
*Madonna con santa Caterina
e san Giovannino*
Olio su tela, cm 93 × 130
Inv. 1912 n. 17

Pietro Nason
*Ritratto d'uomo*
Olio su tela, cm 70 × 53
Inv. 1890 n. 1017

Scuola veneta del XVI secolo
*Ritratto d'uomo*
Olio su tela, cm 111 × 97
Inv. 1912 n. 389

Scuola veneta del XVI secolo
*Sacra famiglia*
Tavola, cm 91 × 130
Inv. 1912 n. 254

Scuola veneziana
*Ritratto di Costanza Bentivoglio*
1520
Tavola, cm 65 × 76
Inv. 1912 n. 221

Tintoretto
*Ritratto di un giovane*
Olio su tela, cm 110 × 96
Inv. 1912 n. 410

Tintoretto
*Ritratto di un vecchio in rosso*
Olio su tela, cm 109 × 87
Inv. 1912 n. 339

Tintoretto
*Ritratto di uomo*
Olio su tela, cm 104 × 79
Inv. 1912 n. 65

Tiziano Vecellio
*Il Redentore*
1533-34
Olio su tavola, cm 77 × 57
Inv. 1912 n. 228

Tiziano Vecellio
*Ritratto di gentiluomo*
Olio su tela, cm 129 × 98
Inv. 1912 n. 494

Tiziano Vecellio
*Ritratto di Tommaso Mosti (?)*
1520-30 ca
Olio su tela, cm 85 × 66
Inv. 1912 n. 495

Tiziano Vecellio (scuola di)
*Ritratto di Alfonso I d'Este,
duca di Ferrara*
Olio su tela, cm 154 × 123
Inv. 1912 n. 311

Paolo Veronese
*Ritratto di gentiluomo*
Olio su tela, cm 99 × 86
Inv. 1912 n. 108

## FLORA ROOM

Alessandro Allori
*Madonna col Bambino*
1590 ca
Olio su tela, cm 133 × 94
Inv. 1912 n. 442

Francesco Bassano il Giovane
*Scena campestre*
Olio su tela, cm 93 × 122
Inv. 1912 n. 383

Francesco Bassano il Giovane
*Scena rustica*
Olio su tela, cm 93 × 124
Inv. 1912 n. 386

Bronzino
*Ritratto di Laudomia de' Medici*
Olio su tavola, cm 98 × 70
Inv. 1890 n. 8738

Cariani
*Sacra Famiglia*
Olio su tela, cm 78 × 67
Inv. 1890 n. 3349

Cigoli
*Sacra Famiglia*
Tavola, cm 61 × 45
Inv. 1912 n. 239

Melchior d'Hondecoeter
*Animali da cortile*
Olio su tela, cm 107 × 121
Inv. 1912 n. 400

Benedetto Gennari
*David*
Olio su tela, cm 130 × 107
Inv. 1912 n. 143

Michele di Ridolfo
del Ghirlandaio
*Ritratto di gentildonna
con velo bianco*
Tavola, cm 90 × 71
Inv. 1912 n. 28

Michele di Ridolfo
del Ghirlandaio
*Sacra Famiglia con san
Giovannino*
Tavola, cm 116 × 88
Inv. 1912 n. 180

Giovanni da San Giovanni
*Ritratto di un cuoco*
Olio su tela, cm 76 × 76
Inv. 1912 n. 435

Adrian Thomas Key
*Ritratto d'uomo*
Tavola, cm 74 × 101
Inv. 1912 n. 7

Pietro Perugino
*La Maddalena*
1496-1500 ca
Olio su tavola, cm 47 × 34
Inv. 1912 n. 42

Domenico Puligo
*Madonna col Bambino
e san Giovannino adolescente*
Tavola, cm 95 × 70
Inv. 1912 n. 145

Domenico Puligo
*Ritratto di Piero Carnesecchi*
Tavola, cm 106 × 74
Inv. 1912 n. 184

Domenico Puligo
*Sacra conversazione*
Olio su tavola, cm 65 × 89
Inv. 1912 n. 146

Domenico Puligo
*Sacra Famiglia*
Tavola, cm 130 × 95
Inv. 1912 n. 486

Karl Andreas Ruthart
*Animali selvatici*
Olio su tela, cm 104 × 142
Inv. 1912 n. 418

Karl Andreas Ruthart
*Cervo atterrato da belve*
Olio su tela, cm 103 × 143
Inv. 1912 n. 438

Francesco Salviati (attr.)
*Orazione nell'orto*
Olio su tavola, cm 18 × 58
Inv. 1912 n. 385

Spagna
*Sposalizio di santa Caterina*
Olio su tavola, cm 48 × 43
Inv. 1912 n. 499

Lambert Sustris
*Nascita di un bambino*
Tela, cm 76,3 × 97
Inv. 1912 n. 394

Tiziano Vecellio
*Adorazione dei pastori*
Tavola, cm 95 × 115
Inv. 1912 n. 423

Antonie van Dyck
*Riposo nella fuga in Egitto*
Olio su tela, cm 133 × 195
Inv. 1912 n. 437

Giorgio Vasari
*Sacra Famiglia con sant'Anna
e san Giovannino*
Olio su tavola, cm 139 × 102
Inv. 1912 n. 413

Paolo Veronese
*Santa Caterina*
Olio su tela, cm 81 × 64
Inv. 1890 n. 890

## ROOM OF THE CUPIDS

Ludolf Backhuysen
*Marina con vascelli*
Olio su tela, cm 65 × 79
Inv. 1912 n. 464

Paul Brill
*Paesaggio con bestiame*
Olio su tela, cm 98 × 131
Inv. 1912 n. 452

Paul Brill
*Paesaggio con gregge e pastori*
Olio su tela, cm 93 × 139
Inv. 1912 n. 449

Michelangelo Cerquozzi
*Cardatrice di lana*
Olio su lavagna, cm 21 × 23
Inv. 1890 n. 1250

Michelangelo Cerquozzi
*Pastore con cane*
Olio su lavagna, cm 19 × 22
Inv. 1890 n. 1252

Hendrick Jacobsz Dubbels
*Marina*
Olio su tela, cm 69 × 86
Inv. 1912 n. 457

Hieronymus Galle
*Festone di fiori*
Tavola, cm 44 × 67
Inv. 1890 n. 1268

Abramo Hondius
*Caccia al cinghiale*
Olio su tela, cm 80 × 117
Inv. 1890 n. 1304

Jacob Jordaens
*Nettuno crea il cavallo*
Olio su tela, cm 67 × 131
Inv. 1890 n. 1234

Otto Marseus van Schrieck
*Serpente e farfalla in un
paesaggio*
Tela, cm 69 × 53
Inv. O.D.A. 1911 n. 501

Salvator Rosa
*La pace che incendia le armi*
Olio su tela, cm 207 × 137
Inv. 1912 n. 453

Peter Paul Rubens
*Le tre Grazie*
1620-23 ca
Olio su tavola, cm 47 × 34
Inv. 1890 n. 1165

Rachel Ruysch
*Natura morta con fiori e frutta*
1716
Olio su tela, cm 89 × 78
Inv. 1912 n. 455

Rachel Ruysch
*Sottobosco (Natura morta di fiori,
frutta e insetti)*
1716
Olio su tela, cm 89 × 79
Inv. 1912 n. 451

Gottfried Schalcken
*Ragazza con la bugia*
Olio su tela, cm 61 × 50
Inv. 1890 n. 1118

Bartolomeo Schedoni (?)
*Assunta*
Olio su tela, cm 136 × 205
Inv. 1912 n. 231

Willem van Aelst
*Frutta e due vasi di cristallo*
Tela, cm 65 × 49,5
Inv. O.D.A. 1911 n. 498

Willem van Aelst
*Natura morta con frutta e due
vasi di cristallo*
1653
Olio su tela, cm 77 × 102
Inv. 1912 n. 469

Willem van Aelst
*Vasellame (Natura morta con
frutta e vasellame)*
1652
Olio su tela, cm 77 × 102
Inv. 1912 n. 468

Willem van Aelst
*Oggetti da cucina*
1652
Olio su tela, cm 125 × 99
Inv. 1912 n. 454

Willem van Aelst
*Selvaggina e arnesi da caccia*
1652
Olio su tela, cm 125 × 99
Inv. 1912 n. 466

Eglon Hendrik van der Neer
*Ester sviene davanti ad Assuero*
Olio su tela, cm 70 × 54
Inv. 1890 n. 1186

Pieter van Laer
*Scuderia di campagna*
Olio su tela, cm 72 × 52
Inv. 1890 n. 1222

Jacob van Ruysdael
*Paesaggio con cascata*
Tela, cm 52,5 × 62,5
Inv. 1890 n. 8436

Hermann van Swanevelt
*Paesaggio*
Rame, cm 23 × 31
Inv. 1890 n. 2142

Hermann van Swanevelt
*Paesaggio*
Rame, cm 23,2 × 31
Inv. 1890 n. 2143

Hermann van Swanevelt
*Paese*
Olio su tela, cm 108 × 130
Inv. 1912 n. 412

## ULYSSES ROOM

Alessandro Allori
*Predica del Battista*
Olio su rame, cm 39 × 47
Inv. 1912 n. 291

Cristofano Allori
*Cristo a Emmaus*
Olio su tela, cm 69 × 55
Inv. 1912 n. 303

Cristofano Allori
*Ritratto d'uomo*
Tempera su embrice, cm 56 × 37
Inv. 1912 n. 497

Cristofano Allori
*San Giovanni Battista nel deserto*
1620 ca
Olio su tela, cm 158 × 116
Inv. 1912 n. 305

Andrea del Sarto
*Madonna col Bambino e santi*
*("Pala di Gambassi")*
1525-26
Olio su tavola, cm 215 × 175
Inv. 1912 n. 307

Agostino Carracci
*Paesaggio con bagnanti*
Tempera su tela, cm 40 × 49
Inv. 1912 n. 320

Annibale Carracci (copia da)
*Ninfa e satiro*
Tavola, cm 28 × 42
Inv. 1912 n. 480

Pietro Ciafferi
*Ecce Homo*
Olio su tela, cm 47 × 84
Inv. 1912 n. 448

Cigoli
*Ecce Homo*
1604-06 ca
Olio su tela, cm 175 × 135
Inv. 1912 n. 90

Francesco Curradi
*Santa Caterina*
Olio su tela, cm 58 × 44
Inv. 1912 n. 286

Carlo Dolci
*Ecce Homo*
Olio su tela, cm 49 × 39
Inv. 1912 n. 321

Carlo Dolci
*Madonna col Bambino*
Olio su tela, cm 201 × 123
Inv. 1912 n. 302

Carlo Dolci
*Ritratto di Claudia Felicitas*
*in veste di Galla Placidia*
Tela, cm 89 × 70
Inv. 1890 n. 2148

Carlo Dolci
*San Giovanni a Patmos*
Rame, cm 37 × 49
Inv. 1912 n. 465

Carlo Dolci (scuola di)
*Santa Lucia*
Olio su tela, cm 53 × 40
Inv. 1912 n. 295

Francesco Furini
*La Fede*
1645
Olio su tela, cm 65 × 49
Inv. 1912 n. 428

Filippino Lippi
*Morte di Lucrezia*
1470 ca
Olio su tavola, cm 42 × 126
Inv. 1912 n. 388

Anthonis Moor (scuola di)
*Ritratto di gentildonna*
Tavola, cm 88 × 64
Inv. 1890 n. 1841

Giovan Battista Moroni
*Ritratto di gentildonna*
Olio su tela, cm 53 × 45,6
Inv. 1912 n. 128

Giovan Battista Moroni
*Ritratto di prelato*
Tela, cm 52 × 46
Inv. 1912 n. 127

Giovan Battista Moroni
(scuola di)
*Ritratto del vescovo Girolamo*
Olio su tela, cm 93 × 85
Inv. 1912 n. 35

Giovan Battista Moroni
(scuola di)
*Ritratto di un giovane*
Olio su tela, cm 50 × 44
Inv. 1912 n. 120

Giovan Battista Moroni
(scuola di)
*Ritratto di vecchio*
Olio su tela, cm 52,6 × 45,5
Inv. 1912 n. 121

Gregorio Pagani
*Ritratto di un giovane,*
*forse di casa Carafa*
Olio su tela, cm 63 × 52
Inv. 1912 n. 285

Frans Pourbus il Giovane
*Ritratto d'uomo*
Tavola, cm 46 × 35
Inv. 1912 n. 296

Domenico Puligo
*Sacra famiglia*
Tavola, cm 63 × 50
Inv. 1912 n. 294

Raffaello
*Madonna col Bambino,*
*san Giovannino e sante*
*("Madonna dell'impannata")*
1514 ca
Olio su tavola, cm 160 × 127
Inv. 1912 n. 94

Guido Reni
*Carità cristiana*
Olio su tela, cm 116 × 90,5
Inv. 1912 n. 197

Orazio Riminaldi
*Amore vincitore*
Olio su tela, cm 142 × 112
Inv. 1912 n. 422

Salvator Rosa
*Le tentazioni di sant'Antonio*
Olio su tela, cm 125 × 93
Inv. 1912 n. 297

Bartolomeo Schedoni
*San Paolo*
Tavola, cm 57 × 33
Inv. 1912 n. 333

Scuola fiorentina del XVI secolo
*Ritratto d'uomo*
Tavola, cm 69 × 56
Inv. 1912 n. 491

Scuola fiorentina del XVII secolo
*Ritratto di un giovane*

Olio su tela, cm 47 × 42
Inv. 1912 n. 402

Scuola francese del XVI secolo
*Ritratto di Caterina de' Medici*
Tavola, cm 44 × 35
Inv. Poggio Imperiale 1860 n. 441

Scuola veneta del XVI secolo
*Ritratto di gentiluomo*
Tavola, cm 68 × 51
Inv. 1912 n. 493

Scuola veronese del XVI secolo
*Ritratto d'uomo*
Olio su tela, cm 85 × 66
Inv. 1912 n. 69

Agostino Tassi
*Diana e Atteone*
Olio su tela, cm 36 × 45
Inv. 1912 n. 474

Tintoretto
*Madonna con Gesù Bambino*
Olio su tela, cm 151 × 98
Inv. 1912 n. 313

Tintoretto
*Ritratto di Andrea Frizier*
Olio su tela, cm 65 × 85
Inv. 1912 n. 70

Tintoretto
*Ritratto di un francescano*
Olio su tela, cm 62 × 60
Inv. 1912 n. 74

Tintoretto (scuola di)
*Ritratto d'uomo*
Olio su tela, cm 56 × 48
Inv. 1912 n. 330

Giorgio Vasari
*Tentazione di san Girolamo*
1541
Olio su tavola, cm 169 × 123
Inv. 1912 n. 393

Hans von Aachen
*Autoritratto*
Olio su tela, cm 61 × 45
Inv. 1912 n. 329

## EDUCATION OF JUPITER ROOM

Cristofano Allori
*Giuditta con la testa di Oloferne*
1620 ca
Olio su tela, cm 139 × 116
Inv. 1912 n. 96

Giovanni Bilivert
*San Sebastiano*
Olio su tela, cm 92 × 67
Inv. 1912 n. 271

Giovanni Bilivert
*Santa Caterina*
Olio su lavagna, cm 33 × 26
Inv. 1890 n. 1402

Bronzino
*Ritratto di Don Garzia de' Medici*
Tavola, cm 24 × 19
Inv. 1912 n. 279

Bronzino

*Ritratto di Lucrezia de' Medici*
Olio su stagno, cm 25 × 18
Inv. 1912 n. 277

Caravaggio
*Amore dormiente*
1608
Olio su tela, cm 71 × 105
Inv. 1912 n. 183

François Clouet
*Ritratto di Claudio di Lorena,*
*duca di Guisa*
Olio su tavola, cm 29 × 26
Inv. 1912 n. 252

François Clouet
*Ritratto di Enrico II di Francia*
Olio su tela, cm 31 × 23
Inv. 1912 n. 262

Correggio (copia da)
*Testa del Salvatore*
Rame, cm 46 × 36,5
Inv. 1912 n. 259

Giuseppe Crespi
*Ritratto di un vecchio*
Olio su tela, cm 42 × 26
Inv. 1912 n. 308

Bonifacio de' Pitati
*Riposo nella fuga in Egitto*
Olio su tela, cm 84 × 91
Inv. 1890 n. 607

Carlo Dolci
*San Carlo Borromeo*
Olio su tela, cm 93 × 77
Inv. 1912 n. 275

Carlo Dolci
*San Domenico penitente*
Olio su tela, cm 78 × 115
Inv. 1912 n. 406

Carlo Dolci
*San Nicola da Tolentino*
Olio su tela, cm 93 × 77
Inv. 1912 n. 281

Carlo Dolci
*Sant'Andrea davanti alla croce*
1646
Olio su tela, cm 122 × 99
Inv. 1912 n. 266

Giambellino (scuola di)
*Madonna col Bambino,*
*san Jacopo e santa Caterina*
Tavola, cm 87 × 110
Inv. 1912 n. 338

Guercino
*La casta Susanna*
Olio su tela, cm 95 × 116
Inv. 1912 n. 234

Bartolomeo Mancini
*San Francesco Saverio*
Olio su tela, cm 95 × 80
Inv. 1912 n. 280

Bartolomeo Mancini
*Santi Enrico di Baviera*
*e Cunegonda*
Olio su tela, cm 96 × 80
Inv. 1912 n. 276

Filippo Napoletano

*Venditore di chiocciole*
Rame, cm 18 × 13
Inv. 1890 n. 1009

Scipione Pulzone
*Ritratto di Ferdinando I de' Medici*
Rame, cm 17 × 13
Inv. 1912 n. 337

Francesco Salviati
*Deposizione di Cristo nel sepolcro*
1539-40
Olio su tavola, cm 77 × 53
Inv. 1912 n. 115

Scuola veronese del XVI secolo
*Ritratto di uno scultore*
Olio su tela, cm 97 × 67
Inv. 1912 n. 68

Giusto Suttermans
*Sacra Famiglia*
Olio su tela, cm 86 × 109
Inv. 1912 n. 232

Tintoretto (scuola di)
*Deposizione dalla croce*
Olio su tela, cm 95 × 120
Inv. 1912 n. 248

Antonie van Dyck
*Ritratto di gentiluomo*
Olio su su tela, cm 133 × 95
Inv. 1912 n. 258

Antonie van Dyck (maniera di)
*Ritratto di Enrichetta di Francia*
Olio su tela, cm 84 × 68
Inv. 1912 n. 331

Jan Anthonisz van Ravesteyn
*Ritratto di David Heinsius*
Olio su tela, cm 131 × 255
Inv. 1912 n. 255

Veronese (scuola di)
*Gesù si accomiata dalla madre*
Olio su tela, cm 94 × 68
Inv. 1912 n. 136

Veronese (scuola di)
*Le Marie al sepolcro*
Olio su tela, cm 94 × 134
Inv. 1912 n. 134

Veronese (scuola di)
*Resurrezione*
Olio su tela, cm 96 × 120
Inv. 1912 n. 264

Veronese (scuola di)
*Ritratto di fanciullo*
Tavola, cm 20 × 20
Inv. 1912 n. 267

Veronese (scuola di)
*Ritratto di fanciullo*
Tavola, cm 19 × 20
Inv. 1912 n. 268

Andrea Vicentino
*Il festino di Erode*
Olio su tela, cm 96 × 111
Inv. 1912 n. 387

## ILIAD ROOM

Andrea del Sarto
*Assunzione della Vergine*
("Pala Passerini")
Tempera su tavola, cm 397 × 222

Inv. 1912 n. 225

Andrea del Sarto
*Assunzione della Vergine*
("Assunta Panciatichi")
1522-23
Olio su tavola, cm 362 × 209
Inv. 1912 n. 191

Andrea del Sarto
*Madonna col Bambino*
Tempera su tavola, cm 87 × 65
Inv. 1912 n. 476

Federico Barocci (attr.,
copia da Correggio)
*Madonna di san Girolamo*
Olio su tela, cm 205 × 142
Inv. 1912 n. 214

Francesco Bassano il Giovane
*Cristo in casa di Marta*
Olio su tela, cm 81 × 116
Inv. 1912 n. 236

Francesco Bassano il Giovane
*Gesù nell'orto*
Olio su tela, cm 196 × 133
Inv. 1912 n. 443

Leandro Bassano
*Scena pastorale*
Olio su tela, cm 76 × 103
Inv. 1912 n. 450

Giovanni Bilivert
*L'Arcangelo rifiuta i beni di Tobia*
1612
Olio su tela, cm 175 × 146
Inv. 1912 n. 202

Paris Bordone
*Ritratto di Serapica mazziere,
giovane guerriero*
Olio su tavola, cm 58 × 48
Inv. 1912 n. 194

Bronzino (scuola di)
*Ritratto di Francesco I de' Medici*
Tavola, cm 56 × 39
Inv. 1912 n. 206

Annibale Carracci
*Cristo in gloria e santi*
1597-98 ca
Olio su tela, cm 194 × 142
Inv. 1912 n. 220

Carracci (scuola dei)
*Ritratto d'uomo*
Olio su tela, cm 67 × 50
Inv. 1912 n. 189

Carracci (scuola dei)
*Ritratto d'uomo*
Olio su tela, cm 68 × 49
Inv. 1912 n. 193

François Clouet
*Ritratto di Cosimo II*
Olio su tela, cm 192 × 105
Inv. 1890 n. 2445

Carlo Dolci
*Mosè*
Olio su tela, cm 40 × 59
Inv. 1912 n. 213

Carlo Dolci
*San Giovanni Evangelista*
Olio su tela, cm 95 × 79
Inv. 1912 n. 217

Domenichino
*Maddalena*
Olio su tela, cm 88,7 × 76
Inv. 1912 n. 176

Jan Frans Douven
*Ritratto di Giovanni Guglielmo
Elettore Palatino*
Olio su tela, cm 119 × 99
Inv. 1890 n. 993

Fra' Bartolomeo
*Madonna in trono e santi*
Tavola, cm 356 × 270
Inv. 1912 n. 208

Frans Francken il Giovane
*Salita al calvario*
Olio su tavola, cm 54 × 86
Inv. 1912 n. 445

Giovan Battista Franco
*La Battaglia di Montemurlo*
Olio su tavola, cm 137 × 173
Inv. 1912 n. 144

Artemisia Gentileschi
*Giuditta*
1614-20 ca
Olio su tela, cm 117 × 93
Inv. 1912 n. 398

Artemisia Gentileschi
*Maddalena*
1613-20
Olio su tela, cm 146,5 × 108
Inv. 1912 n. 142

Ridolfo del Ghirlandaio
*Ritratto di dama*
1508
Olio su tavola, cm 61 × 47
Inv. 1912 n. 224

Ridolfo del Ghirlandaio
*Ritratto d'uomo* ("L'orefice")
Olio su tavola, cm 43 × 31
Inv. 1912 n. 207

Girolamo da Carpi
*Ritratto dell'arcivescovo Onofrio
Bartolini Salimbeni*
Olio su tavola, cm 90 × 73
Inv. 1912 n. 36

Orazio Marinari
*Tarquinio e Lucrezia*
Olio su tela, cm 92 × 115
Inv. 1890 n. 8037

Simone Pignoni
*Tarquinio e Lucrezia*
Olio su tela, cm 92 × 115
Inv. 1890 n. 8036

Frans Pourbus il Giovane
*Ritratto di Cristina di Francia
bambina*
Olio su tela, cm 50 × 41
Inv. 1890 n. 2407

Frans Pourbus il Giovane
*Ritratto di Eleonora de' Medici,
duchessa di Mantova*
Olio su tela, cm 84 × 67
Inv. 1912 n. 187

Frans Pourbus il Giovane
*Ritratto di Eleonora di Mantova
bambina*
Olio su tela, cm 64 × 49
Inv. 1912 n. 391

Frans Pourbus il Giovane
*Ritratto di Enrichetta Maria
di Francia bambina*
Olio su tela, cm 80 × 61
Inv. 1890 n. 2401

Scipione Pulzone
*Ritratto di Maria de' Medici,
regina di Francia*
Olio su tela, cm 80 × 61
Inv. 1912 n. 192

Scipione Pulzone
*Ritratto di una principessa*
Olio su tela, cm 49 × 38
Inv. 1912 n. 205

Scipione Pulzone
*Ritratto di una principessa*
Tavola, cm 48 × 38
Inv. 1912 n. 210

Scipione Pulzone
*Ritratto di una principessa*
Olio su tela, cm 48 × 38
Inv. 1912 n. 211

Raffaello
*Ritratto di donna* ("La Gravida")
1607 ca
Olio su tavola, cm 66,8 × 52,7
Inv. 1912 n. 229

Scuola francese del XVI secolo
*Ritratto di Caterina de' Medici*
Olio su tela, cm 146 × 105
Inv. 1890 n. 2448

Scuola inglese del XVI secolo
*Ritratto di Elisabetta I d'Inghilterra*
Olio su tela, cm 165 × 129
Inv. 1890 n. 4272

Scuola veneta del XVI secolo
(copia da Tiziano)
*Ritratto di papa Paolo III*
Olio su tavola, cm 139 × 91
Inv. 1912 n. 326

Niccolò Soggi
*Madonna col Bambino in trono
tra due santi*
Olio su tavola, cm 175 × 148
Inv. 1912 n. 77

Giusto Suttermans
*Ritratto dell'imperatore
Ferdinando II*
Olio su tela, cm 64 × 50
Inv. 1912 n. 209

Giusto Suttermans
*Ritratto del principe Mattias
de' Medici*
1660 ca
Olio su tela, cm 75 × 60
Inv. 1912 n. 265

Giusto Suttermans
*Ritratto di Domenico Passignano*
Olio su tela, cm 62 × 46
Inv. 1890 n. 565

Giusto Suttermans
*Ritratto di Eleonora Gonzaga*
Olio su tela, cm 64 × 50
Inv. 1912 n. 203

Giusto Suttermans
*Ritratto di Leopoldo de' Medici*
Olio su tela, cm 70 × 59
Inv. 1890 n. 4343

Giusto Suttermans
*Ritratto di Valdemaro Cristiano, principe di Danimarca*
Olio su tela, cm 71 × 54,5
Inv. 1912 n. 190

Giusto Suttermans
*Ritratto giovanile di Ferdinando II de' Medici*
Tela, cm 78 × 66
Inv. 1912 n. 415

Tiziano Vecellio
*Ritratto di Diego de Mendoza*
Olio su tela, cm 178 × 114
Inv. 1912 n. 215

Tiziano Vecellio
*Ritratto di Filippo II di Spagna*
Olio su tela, cm 185 × 200
Inv. 1912 n. 200

Tiziano Vecellio (copia da)
*Baccanale*
Olio su tela, cm 79 × 90
Inv. 1912 n. 157

Diego Velazques
*Ritratto di Filippo IV a cavallo*
1635 ca
Olio su tela, cm 126 × 91
Inv. 1912 n. 243

Jean Cornelisz Vermeyen
*Ritratto d'uomo*
Olio su tela, cm 74 × 61
Inv. 1912 n. 223

Paolo Veronese
*Il battesimo di Cristo*
1575 ca
Olio su tela, cm 196 × 133
Inv. 1912 n. 186

Paolo Veronese (scuola di)
*Presentazione al tempio*
Olio su tela, cm 117 × 144
Inv. 1912 n. 269

Paolo Veronese (scuola di)
*San Benedetto e altri santi*
Olio su tela, cm 195 × 134
Inv. 1912 n. 196

## SATURN ROOM

Andrea del Sarto
*Annunciazione*
1528
Olio su tavola, cm 96 × 189
Inv. 1912 n. 163

Andrea del Sarto
*Disputa sulla Trinità*
1517
Olio su tavola, cm 232 × 193
Inv. 1912 n. 172

Federico Barocci
*Ritratto di Francesco Maria della Rovere*

Olio su tela, cm 40 × 26
Inv. 1912 n. 162

Jacopo Bassano
*Adamo ed Eva*
Olio su tavola, cm 53 × 76
Inv. 1912 n. 170

Leandro Bassano
*Scena pastorale*
Olio su tela, cm 51 × 73
Inv. 1912 n. 177

Bonifacio de' Pitati
*Mosè salvato dalle acque*
Olio su tavola, cm 31 × 111
Inv. 1912 n. 161

Annibale Carracci
*Testa virile*
Olio su tela, cm 46 × 37
Inv. 1912 n. 166

Correggio (copia da)
*Putto della Madonna di San Sebastiano*
Tavola, cm 31,6 × 27,9
Inv. 1912 n. 153

Carlo Dolci
*Ritratto di Vittoria della Rovere in vesti vedovili*
Olio su tela, cm 84 × 57
Inv. 1912 n. 404

Carlo Dolci
*Santa Rosa da Lima*
Olio su tela, cm 33 × 25
Inv. 1912 n. 155

Carlo Dolci
*Il sonno di san Giovannino*
Olio su tela, cm 45 × 58
Inv. 1912 n. 154

Jacopo da Empoli
*Ritratto di Giovan Battista Gambetti*
Tavola, cm 96 × 72
Inv. 1890 n. 2124

Fra' Bartolomeo
*Cristo come "Salvator Mundi"*
1516
Olio su tavola, cm 282 × 204
Inv. 1912 n. 159

Giovanni da San Giovanni
*Madonna col Bambino*
Olio su tela, cm 50 × 68
Inv. 1912 n. 396

Guercino
*San Pietro*
Olio su tela, cm 47 × 36
Inv. 1912 n. 168

Guercino
*San Sebastiano*
Olio su tela, cm 253 × 169
Inv. 1912 n. 490

Pier Francesco Mola
*Ritratto di un poeta*
Olio su tela, cm 72 × 86
Inv. 1912 n. 181

Francesco Montemezzano
*Ritratto di donna in nero*
Olio su tela, cm 75 × 58
Inv. 1912 n. 37

Pietro Perugino
*Compianto sul Cristo morto*
1495
Olio su tavola, cm 214 × 195
Inv. 1912 n. 164

Pietro Perugino (scuola di)
*Madonna col Bambino e due sante*
Olio su tavola, cm 77 × 61
Inv. 1912 n. 340

Domenico Puligo
*Sacra Famiglia*
Olio su tavola, cm 79 × 58
Inv. 1912 n. 169

Raffaello
*Madonna col Bambino ("Madonna del Granduca")*
1506 ca
Olio su tavola, cm 84,5 × 55,9
Inv. 1912 n. 178

Raffaello
*Madonna col Bambino e san Giovannino ("Madonna della seggiola")*
1516 ca
Olio su tavola, diam. cm 71
Inv. 1912 n. 151

Raffaello
*Madonna in trono col Bambino e santi ("Madonna del baldacchino")*
1508 ca
Olio su tavola, cm 297 × 217
Inv. 1912 n. 165

Raffaello
*Ritratto del cardinal Bibbiena*
Olio su tela, cm 86 × 66
Inv. 1912 n. 158

Raffaello
*Ritratto di Agnolo Doni*
1505-06
Olio su tavola, cm 65 × 45,7
Inv. 1912 n. 61

Raffaello
*Ritratto di Maddalena Doni*
1505-06
Olio su tavola, cm 65 × 45,7
Inv. 1912 n. 59

Raffaello
*Ritratto di Tommaso Inghirami ("Fedra Inghirami")*
1510 ca
Olio su tavola, cm 89,5 × 62,3
Inv. 1912 n. 171

Raffaello
*Visione di Ezechiele*
1518 ca
Olio su tavola, cm 47,7 × 29,5
Inv. 1912 n. 174

Andrea Schiavone
*Sansone uccide un Filisteo*
Olio su tela, cm 216 × 188
Inv. 1912 n. 152

Scuola fiorentina del XVI secolo
*Ritratto di gentildonna*
Tavola, cm 99 × 72
Inv. 1912 n. 439

Scuola fiorentina del XVI secolo
*Ritratto di uno scultore*
Olio su tela, cm 107 × 88
Inv. 1912 n. 447

Scuola veneta
*Ritratto di dama con libro*
Olio su tela, cm 87 × 65
Inv. 1912 n. 414

Sebastiano del Piombo
*Martirio di sant'Agata*
1520
Olio su tavola, cm 127 × 178
Inv. 1912 n. 179

Sodoma (scuola del)
*Ecce Homo*
Olio su tavola, cm 60 × 47
Inv. 1912 n. 374

Giusto Suttermans
*Ritratto del canonico Pandolfo Ricasoli*
Olio su tela, cm 116 × 86
Inv. 1912 n. 401

Giusto Suttermans
*Ritratto di dama*
Olio su tela, cm 68 × 51
Inv. 1912 n. 323

Giusto Suttermans
*Testa di Madonna*
Olio su tela, cm 38 × 24
Inv. 1912 n. 160

Alessandro Tiarini
*Adamo ed Eva piangono Abele ucciso*
Olio su tela, cm 249 × 167
Inv. 1912 n. 488

## JUPITER ROOM

Francesco Albani
*Apparizione di Gesù alla Vergine*
Rame, cm 43 × 57
Inv. 1912 n. 173

Francesco Albani
*Sacra Famiglia con due angeli*
Olio su tela, cm 56 × 43
Inv. 1912 n. 175

Andrea del Sarto
*Annunciazione*
1528
Olio su tavola, cm 182 × 184
Inv. 1912 n. 124

Andrea del Sarto
*Madonna in gloria e quattro santi ("Pala Poppi")*
Olio su tavola, cm 308 × 208
Inv. 1912 n. 123

Andrea del Sarto
*San Giovannino*
1523 ca
Olio su tavola, cm 94 × 68
Inv. 1912 n. 272

Federico Barocci
*Il Redentore*
Olio su tela, cm 61 × 49
Inv. 1912 n. 101

Paris Bordone
*Ritratto di dama*
Olio su tela, cm 107 × 83
Inv. 1912 n. 109

Borgognone
*Battaglia*
Olio su tela, cm 233 × 350
Inv. 1912 n. 112

Bronzino
*Ritratto di Guidobaldo
della Rovere*
1531-32
Olio su tavola, cm 114 × 86
Inv. 1912 n. 149

Angelo Caroselli (attr.)
*Sant'Agnese (La Mansuetudine)*
Olio su tela, cm 75 × 61
Inv. 1912 n. 420

Annibale Carracci
*Madonna col Bambino
e san Giovannino*
Olio su tela, cm 27 × 20
Inv. 1912 n. 425

Niccolò Cassana
*La Congiura di Catilina*
Olio su tela, cm 155 × 187
Inv. 1912 n. 111

Cigoli
*Ritratto di giovane gentiluomo*
Olio su tela, cm 78 × 62
Inv. 1912 n. 226

Carlo Dolci
*Ritratto di un giovane
di casa Bardi*
1631
Olio su tela, cm 58 × 46
Inv. 1890 n. 316

Carlo Dolci
*San Pietro in lacrime*
Olio su tela, cm 175 × 125
Inv. 1912 n. 91

Fra' Bartolomeo
*Pietà*
1511-12 ca
Olio su tavola, cm 158 × 199
Inv. 1912 n. 64

Fra' Bartolomeo
*San Marco Evangelista*
Olio su tela, cm 350 × 215
Inv. 1912 n. 125

Cesare Gennari
*Sacra Famiglia*
Olio su tela, cm 56 × 71
Inv. 1912 n. 332

Giorgione
*Le tre età dell'uomo*
1500 ca
Olio su tavola, cm 62 × 77
Inv. 1912 n. 110

Guercino
*Madonna della rondinella*
Olio su tela, cm 120 × 88
Inv. 1912 n. 156

Guercino
*Mosè*
Olio su tela, cm 65 × 55
Inv. 1912 n. 103

Guercino
*Sacra Famiglia*
Olio su tela, cm 156 × 85
Inv. 1912 n. 132

Giovanni Lanfranco
*Estasi di santa Margherita
da Cortona*
1622
Olio su tela, cm 230 × 185
Inv. 1912 n. 318

Lorenzo Lippi
*Santa Caterina*
Olio su tela, cm 79 × 56
Inv. 1890 n. 802

Lorenzo Lippi
*Sant'Agata*
Olio su tela, cm 79 × 56
Inv. 1890 n. 803

Pietro Perugino
*Madonna in adorazione del
Bambino ("Madonna del Sacco")*
Olio su tavola, cm 88 × 86
Inv. 1912 n. 219

Frans Pourbus il Giovane
*Ritratto di Giovane*
Olio su tela, cm 85 × 65
Inv. 1912 n. 244

Raffaello
*Ritratto di dama ("La Velata")*
1516 ca
Olio su tela, cm 82 × 60,5
Inv. 1912 n. 245

Guido Reni
*Sant'Elisabetta*
Olio su tela, cm 51 × 39
Inv. 1912 n. 395

Peter Paul Rubens
*Ninfe e satiri*
Tela, cm 206 × 401
Inv. 1912 n. 141

Peter Paul Rubens
*Sacra Famiglia con sant'Elisabetta
("Madonna della cesta")*
Tavola, cm 114 × 88
Inv. 1912 n. 139

Francesco Salviati
*Le tre Parche*
Tavola, cm 61 × 83
Inv. 1912 n. 113

Bartolomeo Schedoni
*Sacra famiglia*
Tavola, cm 63 × 46
Inv. 1912 n. 304

Scuola fiorentina del XVI secolo
*Ritratto di un uomo e di una
donna (già Andrea del Sarto
e la moglie)*
Tavola, cm 86 × 62
Inv. 1912 n. 118

Scuola tedesca del XVI secolo
*Ritratto di Jacobina Vogekort*
Olio su tavola, cm 59 × 47
Inv. 1912 n. 33

Scuola veneta del XVI secolo
*Ritratto d'uomo*
Olio su tela, cm 59 × 48
Inv. 1912 n. 390

Giusto Suttermans
*Ritratto di Elia, sopracòmito
delle galere*
Tela, cm 69 × 56
Inv. 1912 n. 119

Giusto Suttermans
*Ritratto di Ferdinando II de' Medici
col turbante*
Olio su tela, cm 64 × 50
Inv. 1890 n. 2334

Giusto Suttermans
*Ritratto di Galileo Galilei*
1636
Olio su tela, cm 56 × 48
Inv. 1912 n. 106

Giusto Suttermans
*Ritratto di Simone Paganucci*
Olio su tela, cm 117 × 88
Inv. 1912 n. 117

Giusto Suttermans
*Ritratto di un vecchio*
Olio su tela, cm 99 × 78
Inv. 1890 n. 419

Verrocchio
*San Girolamo*
Tempera su tavola, cm 40 × 26
Inv. 1912 n. 370

Giuseppe Vignali
*Estasi di san Francesco*
Olio su tela, cm 20 × 21
Inv. 1912 n. 356

## MARS ROOM

Andrea del Sarto
*Annunciazione
("Pala di San Godenzo")*
Tela, cm 184 × 175
Inv. 1912 n. 97

Andrea del Sarto
*Storie di Giuseppe Ebreo*
Olio su tavola, cm 98 × 135
Inv. 1912 n. 87

Andrea del Sarto
*Storie di Giuseppe Ebreo*
Olio su tavola, cm 98 × 135
Inv. 1912 n. 88

Bronzino
*Ritratto dell'ingegnere
Luca Martini*
Tavola, cm 101 × 79
Inv. 1912 n. 434

Guido Cagnacci
*La Maddalena portata in cielo*
Olio su tela, cm 192 × 139
Inv. 1912 n. 75

Cigoli
*Il Sacrificio di Isacco*
1604-05
Olio su tela, cm 175 × 132
Inv. 1912 n. 95

Cigoli
*Santa Maria Maddalena*
Olio su tela, cm 173 × 124
Inv. 1912 n. 98

Carlo Dolci
*Santa Margherita*
Olio su tela, cm 77 × 59
Inv. 1912 n. 227

Fra' Bartolomeo
*Sacra Famiglia con santa
Elisabetta*
Olio su tavola, cm 102 × 90
Inv. 1912 n. 256

Luca Giordano
*L'Immacolata Concezione*
Olio su tela, cm 243 × 153
Inv. 1912 n. 104

Antiveduto Gramatica
*La buona ventura*
Olio su tela, cm 97 × 134
Inv. 1912 n. 6

Guercino
*San Sebastiano*
Olio su tela, cm 174 × 122
Inv. 1912 n. 99

Bartolomé Estaban Murillo
*Madonna col Bambino*
1650 ca
Olio su tela, cm 157 × 107
Inv. 1912 n. 63

Bartolomé Estaban Murillo
*Madonna col bambino
("Madonna del Rosario")*
Olio su tela, cm 165 × 109
Inv. 1912 n. 56

Domenico Puligo
*Madonna col Bambino e san
Giovannino*
Olio su tavola, cm 105 × 88
Inv. 1912 n. 242

Guido Reni
*San Pietro in lacrime*
Olio su tela, cm 184 × 135
Inv. 1912 n. 78

Peter Paul Rubens
*Le conseguenze della guerra*
1637-38
Olio su tela, cm 206 × 345
Inv. 1912 n. 86

Peter Paul Rubens
*I quattro filosofi*
1611-12
Olio su tavola, cm 164 × 139
Inv. 1912 n. 85

Ventura Salimbeni
*Sacra Famiglia*
Olio su tela, cm 148 × 173
Inv. 1912 n. 45

Giovanni Andrea Sirani
*Rebecca al pozzo*
Olio su tela, cm 265 × 221
Inv. 1912 n. 100

Tintoretto
*Ritratto di Alvise Cornaro*
1560-65 ca
Olio su tela, cm 113 × 85
Inv. 1912 n. 83

Tiziano Vecellio
*Ritratto del medico Andrea Vesalio*
Olio su tela, cm 130 × 98
Inv. 1912 n. 80

Tiziano Vecellio
*Ritratto di Ippolito de' Medici*
1533
Olio su tela, cm 139 × 107
Inv. 1912 n. 201

Jan van den Hoecke
*Madonna col Bambino,
san Giovannino e santa
Elisabetta*
Olio su tela, cm 145 × 94
Inv. 1912 n. 235

Adrien van der Werff
*Ritratto di John Churchill
duca di Marlborough*
Olio su tela, cm 131 × 107
Inv. 1912 n. 76

Antonie van Dyck
*Ritratto del cardinale Guido
Bentivoglio*
1625 ca
Olio su tela, cm 195 × 147
Inv. 1912 n. 82

Pieter van Mol
*San Francesco in estasi*
Olio su tela, cm 146 × 103
Inv. 1912 n. 93

Paolo Veronese
*Ritratto di gentiluomo
con pelliccia*
1550-60 ca
Olio su tela, cm 140 × 107
Inv. 1912 n. 216

## APOLLO ROOM

Cristofano Allori
*L'ospitalità di san Giuliano*
Olio su tela, cm 259 × 202
Inv. 1912 n. 41

Cristofano Allori
*Ritratto di un uomo in nero*
Olio su tela, cm 55 × 62
Inv. 1912 n. 301

Andrea del Sarto
*Compianto sul Cristo morto
("Pietà di Luco")*
1523-25
Olio su tavola, cm 238 × 198
Inv. 1912 n. 58

Andrea del Sarto
*Madonna col Bambino, santa
Elisabetta e san Giovannino
("Sacra Famiglia Medici")*
1529
Olio su tavola, cm 140 × 104
Inv. 1912 n. 81

Andrea del Sarto
*Ritratto di giovane uomo*
Olio su tela, cm 70 × 53
Inv. 1912 n. 66

Andrea del Sarto
*Sacra Famiglia*
Olio su tavola, cm 129 × 105
Inv. 1912 n. 62

Simone Cantarini
*Sant'Andrea*
Olio su tela, cm 99 × 68
Inv. 1912 n. 48

Niccolò Cassana
*Ritratto di un guerriero*
Olio su tela, cm 136 × 98
Inv. 1912 n. 218

Cigoli
*Deposizione dalla croce*
1600-08
Tavola, cm 321 × 206
Inv. 1912 n. 51

Gaspard de Crayer
*Sacra Famiglia*
Olio su tela, cm 149 × 120
Inv. 1890 n. 733

Cornelius de Vos
*Ritratto di donna con ventaglio*
Olio su tela, cm 98 × 72
Inv. 1912 n. 440

Carlo Dolci
*Diogene*
Olio su tela, cm 88 × 72
Inv. 1912 n. 53

Carlo Dolci
*San Casimiro, principe di Colina*
Olio su tela, cm 95 × 79
Inv. 1912 n. 392

Carlo Dolci
*San Giovanni Evangelista*
Olio su tela, cm 94 × 78
Inv. 1912 n. 397

Dosso Dossi
*Ninfa e satiro*
Olio su tela, cm 57 × 53
Inv. 1912 n. 147

Dosso Dossi
*San Giovanni Battista*
Tavola, cm 73 × 56
Inv. 1912 n. 380

Garofalo
*Augusto e la Sibilla Tiburtina*
Olio su tavola, cm 63 × 41
Inv. 1912 n. 122

Guercino
*San Pietro risuscita Tabita*
Olio su tela, cm 132 × 159
Inv. 1912 n. 50

Giambattista Langetti
*Ritratto di uomo*
Olio su tela, cm 53 × 41
Inv. 1912 n. 300

Jacopo Ligozzi
*Giuditta*
1602
Olio su tela, cm 97 × 79
Inv. 1912 n. 444

Carlo Maratta
*La Madonna appare
a san Filippo Neri*
1675 ca
Olio su tela, cm 343 × 197
Inv. 1912 n. 71

Domenico Mazza
*Sacra Conversazione*
Olio su tela, cm 130 × 164
Inv. 1912 n. 52

Ludovico Mazzolino
*Cristo e l'adultera*
Olio su tavola, cm 63 × 42
Inv. 1912 n. 129

Palma il Vecchio (scuola di)
*La cena di Emmaus*
Olio su tela, cm 153 × 204
Inv. 1912 n. 38

Guido Reni
*Cleopatra*
1638-39 ca
Olio su tela, cm 122 × 96
Inv. 1912 n. 270

Peter Paul Rubens
*Ritratto di Gerard Schoppius*
Olio su tela, cm 116 × 88
Inv. 1912 n. 198

Peter Paul Rubens
*Ritratto di Isabella Clara Eugenia
governatrice dei Paesi Bassi*
Tela, cm 116 × 96
Inv. 1890 n. 4263

Sebastiano del Piombo
*Ecce Homo*
Olio su tavola, cm 70 × 52
Inv. 1912 n. 322

Giusto Suttermans
*Ritratto di Francesco Maria
de' Medici bambino*
Tela, cm 112 × 85
Inv. 1912 n. 344

Giusto Suttermans
*Ritratto di Vittoria della Rovere
come vestale Tuccia*
Olio su tela, cm 98 × 80
Inv. 1912 n. 116

Giusto Suttermans (scuola di)
*Ritratto di uomo in armatura*
Olio su tela, cm 67 × 52
Inv. 1912 n. 314

Tintoretto
*Ritratto di Vincenzo Zeno*
Olio su tela, cm 86 × 110
Inv. 1912 n. 131

Tiberio Titi
*Ritratto del principe Leopoldo
de' Medici bambino*
Olio su tela, cm 59 × 74
Inv. 1912 n. 49

Tiziano Vecellio
*La Maddalena*
1535 ca
Olio su tavola, cm 84 × 69
Inv. 1912 n. 67

Tiziano Vecellio
*Ritratto virile ("L'uomo
dagli occhi grigi" o "L'Inglese")*
1545 ca
Olio su tela, cm 111 × 96
Inv. 1912 n. 92

Tiziano Vecellio (scuola di)
*Madonna della Misericordia*
Olio su tela, cm 154 × 144
Inv. 1912 n. 484

Antonie van Dyck
*Ritratto di Carlo I d'Inghilterra e
di Enrichetta Maria di Francia*
Olio su tela, cm 66 × 82
Inv. 1912 n. 150

Alessandro Vitali
*Federico Ubaldo della Rovere
neonato*
Olio su tela, cm 60 × 73
Inv. 1912 n. 55

Jacob Ferdinand Voet
*Ritratto di donna Olimpia
Aldobrandini*
Olio su tela, cm 72 × 58
Inv. 1912 n. 34

## VENUS ROOM

Francesco Bassano il Giovane
*Il martirio di santa Caterina*
1622-23
Olio su tela, cm 329 × 213
Inv. 1912 n. 11

Giovanni Bilivert
*Apollo e Marsia*
Olio su tela, cm 181 × 173
Inv. 1912 n. 22

Giovanni Bilivert
*Sant'Isidoro*
Olio su tela, cm 75 × 62
Inv. 1912 n. 25

Bonifacio de' Pitati
*Sacra Conversazione*
Olio su tavola, cm 107 × 143
Inv. 1912 n. 84

Antonio Canova
*Venere italica*
1810-11
Marmo di Carrara, h. cm 172
Inv. n. 878

Cigoli
*La terza apparizione di Gesù
a Pietro*
Olio su tela, cm 366 × 236
Inv. 1912 n. 27

Francesco Curradi
*Narciso al fonte*
1622
Olio su tela, cm 180 × 207
Inv. 1912 n. 10

Guercino
*Apollo e Marsia*
Olio su tela, cm 186 × 205
Inv. 1912 n. 8

Guercino
*San Giuseppe*
Olio su tela, cm 84 × 70
Inv. 1912 n. 29

Rutilio Manetti
*La morte di santa Maria
Maddalena*
Olio su tela, cm 130 × 162
Inv. 1912 n. 23

Rutilio Manetti
*Ruggero e Alcina (Riunione
di sposi)*
1622-23
Olio su tela, cm 182 × 203
Inv. 1912 n. 12

Bartolomeo Passarotti
*Ritratto di Guidobaldo II
della Rovere*

Olio su tela, cm 99 × 81
Inv. 1912 n. 138

**Pietro da Cortona**
*Santa Martina rifiuta
di adorare gli idoli*
Olio su tela, cm 102 × 79
Inv. 1912 n. 21

**Guido Reni**
*Ritratto di un vecchio*
Olio su tela, cm 77 × 62
Inv. 1912 n. 24

**Salvator Rosa**
*Marina al tramonto*
1645 ca
Olio su tela, cm 234 × 395
Inv. 1912 n. 4

**Salvator Rosa**
*Marina con vascelli e galere*
Olio su tela, cm 233 × 395
Inv. 1912 n. 15

**Salvator Rosa**
*La menzogna*
Olio su tela, cm 136 × 96
Inv. 1912 n. 2

**Mattero Rosselli**
*Il trionfo di David*
Olio su tela, cm 203 × 201
Inv. 1912 n. 13

**Peter Paul Rubens**
*Il ritorno dei contadini dai campi*
1640 ca
Olio su tavola, cm 121 × 194
Inv. 1912 n. 14

**Peter Paul Rubens**
*Ulisse nell'isola dei Feaci*
Olio su tavola, cm 128 × 207
Inv. 1912 n. 9

**Scuola emiliana del XVI secolo**
*Ritratto di Torquato Tasso*
Tavola, cm 103 × 81
Inv. 1890 n. 3143

**Scuola fiorentina del XVII secolo**
*Ritratto di Pietro Francavilla*
Olio su tela, cm 70 × 58
Inv. 1890 n. 774

**Scuola veneta del XVI secolo**
*Madonna col Bambino
e due angeli*
Olio su tela, cm 67 × 60
Inv. 1912 n. 483

**Sebastiano del Piombo**
*Ritratto di Baccio Valori*
Lavagna, cm 80 × 66
Inv. 1890 n. 409

**Giusto Suttermans**
*Ritratto di Alessandro Farnese*
Tela, cm 77 × 64
Inv. 1890 n. 2203

**Giusto Suttermans**
*Ritratto di bambino*
Olio su tela, cm 112 × 85
Inv. 1890 n. 2404

**Giusto Suttermans**
*Ritratto di Giacinto Talducci*
Olio su tela, cm 79 × 61
Inv. 1890 n. 4271

**Giusto Suttermans**
*Ritratto di uno scultore*
Olio su tela, cm 59 × 46
Inv. 1890 n. 781

**Giusto Suttermans**
*Ritratto di Vittoria della Rovere
come sant'Orsola*
Olio su tela, cm 61 × 47
Inv. 1890 n. 5169

**Giusto Suttermans**
*Ritrovo di cacciatori*
Olio su tela, cm 149 × 204
Inv. 1912 n. 137

**Tintoretto**
*Venere, Amore e Vulcano*
Olio su tela, cm 85 × 197
Inv. 1912 n. 3

**Tiziano Vecellio**
*Il concerto*
1510-12
Olio su tela, cm 86,5 × 123,5
Inv. 1912 n. 185

**Tiziano Vecellio**
**(copia da Raffaello)**
*Ritratto del papa Giulio II*
Olio su tavola, cm 99 × 82
Inv. 1912 n. 79

**Tiziano Vecellio**
*Ritratto di gentildonna
("La Bella")*
1636 ca
Olio su tela, cm 89 × 75,5
Inv. 1912 n. 18

**Tiziano Vecellio**
*Ritratto di Pietro Aretino*
1545
Olio su tela, cm 96,7 × 76,6
Inv. 1912 n. 54

**Tiziano Vecellio (bottega di)**
*Ecce Homo*
Olio su tela, cm 71 × 54
Inv. 1912 n. 31

**Francesco Vanni**
*Sposalizio mistico
di santa Caterina*
1602
Olio su tela, cm 67 × 60
Inv. 1912 n. 32

# Modern Art Gallery
# list of works

## ROOM 1

**Pompeo Girolamo Batoni**
*Ercole al bivio*
1742
Olio su tela, cm 93,5 × 73
Inv. 1890 n. 8547

**Pompeo Girolamo Batoni**
*Ercole bambino che strozza
i serpenti*
1743
Olio su tela, cm 94 × 72,5
Inv. 1890 n. 8548

**Pietro Benvenuti**
*Ritratto dell'architetto Nicolò
Mathas*
Olio su tela, cm 73 × 58
Inv. 1890 n. 8401

**Wilhelm A. Berczy**
*Ritratto della famiglia granducale*
1781-82
Gouache su pergamena su tavola,
cm 55,6 × 64,2
Inv. O.D.A. Petraia n. 141

**Filippo Hackert**
*La foresta di Camaldoli*
1802
Olio su tela, cm 78 × 61
C.g. n. 503

**Filippo Hackert**
*Paesaggio classico*
Olio su tela, cm 78 × 61
C.g. n. 507

**Ignoto**
*Testa di Medusa*
Marmo, h. cm 38
Inv. O.D.A. n. 1911/1741 rosso

**Carlo Labruzzi**
*Ritratto di Teresa Pichler Monti*
1807
Olio su tela, cm 87 × 68
Inv. 1890 n. 4671

**Gaspero Landi**
*Le tre Marie e l'angelo al sepolcro
di Cristo*
Olio su tela, cm 209 × 307
C.g. n. 38

**Gaspero Landi**
*Vetruria ai piedi di Coriolano*
Olio su tela, cm 210 × 297
Inv. 1890 n. 3847

**Giuseppe Macpherson (attr.)**
*Scena di conversazione*
1772-78 ca
Olio su tela, cm 50 × 64
Inv. 1890 n. 3404

**Anton Raphael Mengs**
*Ritratto di Carlo III di Borbone*
Olio su tela, cm 129 × 97,5
Inv. 1890 n. 2938

**Anton Raphael Mengs**
*Ritratto di Carlos de Borbon*
1770 ca
Olio su tela, cm 127 × 95
Inv. 1890 n. 2813

**Anton Raphael Mengs**
*Ritratto di Don Gabriel de Borbon*
1763
Olio su tela, cm 127,5 × 95,5
Inv. 1890 n. 2811

**Anton Raphael Mengs**
*Ritratto di Don Pascual
de Borbon*
Olio su tela, cm 128 × 97
Inv. 1890 n. 2812

**Stefano Ricci**
*Apollo e Giacinto*
Marmo di Carrara, h. cm 154
Inv. Dep. 621

**Pietro Tenerani**
*Psiche abbandonata*
1816-17
Marmo, h. cm 118
Gl. n. 2472

**Stefano Tofanelli**
*Ritratto di Francesco Belluomini*
1801
Olio su tela, cm 47 × 38
C.g. n. 15

**Stefano Tofanelli**
*Ritratto di Luigi Mansi*
1802
Olio su tela, cm 101 × 73
Inv. 1890 n. 9440

**Stefano Tofanelli**
*Ritratto di Margherita Belluomini
Poggi (bozzetto)*
1801
Olio su tela, cm 33 × 25,5
C.g. n. 13

## ROOM 2

**Lorenzo Bartolini**
*Busto di George Gordon Byron*
post 1822
Marmo, h. cm 63,5
Gl. n. 2703

**Pietro Benvenuti**
*Il giuramento dei Sassoni
a Napoleone*
Olio su tela, cm 380 × 480
C.g. n. 3

**Pietro Benvenuti**
*Ritratto di Elena Mastiani
Brunacci*
1809
Olio su tela, cm 133 × 167
C.g. n. 8

**Pietro Benvenuti**
*Ritratto di Vittorio Fossombroni*
Olio su tela, cm 58 × 49
Inv. 1890 n. 3322

**Giuseppe Bezzuoli**
*Ritratto di Elisa Baciocchi
e della figlia Elisa Napoleone*
1814 ca
Olio su tela, cm 88 × 71,5
Gl. n. 5643

**Giuseppe Bezzuoli (attr.)**
*Clizia*
Olio su tela, cm 79 × 62,5
Inv. 1890 n. 5863

**Nicolas Didier Boguet**
*Paesaggio con pastori*
1792
Olio su tela, cm 175 × 249
Inv. 1890 n. 571

**Vincenzo Camuccini**
*Ritratto di Maria Luisa di
Borbone duchessa di Lucca*
Olio su tela, cm 212 × 163
Inv. O.D.A. n. 1430

**Antonio Canova**
*Calliope*
1812
Marmo, h. cm 46
C.g. n. 632

**Canova (copia da)**
*Testa colossale di Napoleone*
Marmo, h. cm 77
C.g. n. 624

**Salomon-Guillame Counis**
*Autoritratto*
1839
Olio su tela, cm 67 × 55
Inv. 1890 n. 2111

**François-Xavier Fabre**
*Ritratto di Antonio Santarelli*
1812
Olio su tela, cm 70,5 × 54
Inv. 1890 n. 3304

**Louis Gauffier**
*Autoritratto con la moglie
e i due figli*
Olio su tela, cm 72,5 × 54,5
Inv. 1890 n. 8404

**Louis Gauffier (attr.)**
*Alessandro posa il sigillo
sulla bocca di Efestione*

Olio su tela, cm 95 × 73
Inv. 1890 n. 9370

**Ignoto**
*Ritratto di Napoleone*
1807-10
Olio su tela, diam. cm 50
Inv. n. 1679 nero

**Ignoto del XIX secolo**
*La partenza di Attilio Regolo*
Olio su tela, cm 38 × 46
Gl. n. 4731

**Giovan Battista Lampi jr.**
*Ritratto di Maria Beatrice d'Este*
1817
Olio su tela, cm 90 × 79
Gl. n. 2479

**Manifattura di Sèvres**
*Busto di Maria Luisa d'Asburgo
d'Austria*
Biscuit, h. cm 64,5
Inv. O.D.A. n. 212

**Manifattura di Sèvres**
*Busto di Napoleone*
Biscuit, h. cm 52
Inv. O.D.A. n. 486

**Pietro Pedroni**
*Ritratto di padre Francesco
Raimondo Adami*
1774
Olio su tela, cm 70 × 53
Inv. 1890 n. 2653

**Demetrio Pescatori**
*Busto di Maria Luisa d'Asburgo*
Marmo, diam. cm 35
Inv. O.D.A. n. 1740

**Francesco Pozzi**
*Testa ideale*
Marmo, h. cm 39,5
Inv. O.D.A. n. 489

**Giovanni Antonio Santarelli**
*Due plateaux con cere*
Cera, diam. cm 7,5
Inv. O.D.A. n. 74-99

**Scuola toscana degli inizi
del XIX secolo**
*Ritratto di Ludovico di Borbone
re d'Etruria*
Olio su tela, cm 98 × 78
Inv. 1890 n. 2832

**Vincenzo Segarelli**
*Bagno alla Villa reale di Marlia
presso Lucca*
1832
Olio su tela, cm 57 × 75
Inv. O.D.A. n. 1294

Vincenzo Segarelli
*Villa reale di Marlia*
1831
Olio su tela, cm 57 × 75
Inv. O.D.A. n. 1350

Jean Baptiste Tierce
*Cascata di Tivoli*
1782
Olio su tela, cm 124 × 173
Inv. 1890 n. 556

Jean Baptiste Wicar (?)
*Ritratto di Luigi Bonaparte,
re d'Olanda*
1817
Olio su tela, cm 170 × 120,5
Inv. 1890 n. 3561

Michaele Wutky
*Veduta delle cascate di Tivoli*
1785
Olio su tela, cm 136 × 120,5
Inv. 1890 n. 5456

## ROOM 3

Lorenzo Bartolini
*Busto di Carlo Ludovico
di Borbone*
1825
Marmo, h. cm 50
C.g. n. 626

Giuseppe Bezzuoli
*Ritratto di Maria Antonietta
di Toscana*
Olio su tela, cm 86 × 70,5
Gl. n. 2338

Vincenzo Bonelli
*Busto di Ferdinando III di Toscana*
Marmo, h. cm 68
Inv. O.D.A. n. 362

Vincenzo Consani
*Bassorilievo con il ritratto
di Maria Luisa di Borbone*
1840
Marmo, cm 48,5 × 38,5
C.g. n. 717

Vincenzo Consani
*Busto di Maria Teresa di Savoia*
1840
Marmo, h. cm 46
C.g. n. 627

François-Xavier Fabre
*Ritratto di Maria Luisa di
Borbone, regina d'Etruria*
1801-04
Olio su tela, cm 58 × 45,5
Inv. 1890 n. 5200

Galleria dei lavori su disegno
di Carlo Carlieri
*Centro tavola di Elisa Baciocchi*
1807-16
Lapislazzuli con mosaici di
calcedoni, perle e finiture in bronzo
dorato, cm 298 e 73
Inv. A.S.E. n. 79

Vincenzo Giannini (attr.)
*Ritratto di Maria Teresa di Toscana*
Olio su tela, cm 96 × 76
Inv. 1890 n. 4249

Ottaviano Giovannozzi
*Busto di Leopoldo II di Toscana*
1843

Marmo, h. cm 68
Inv. O.D.A. n. 361

Ottaviano Giovannozzi
*Busto di Maria Antonietta
di Toscana*
1842
Marmo. h. cm 72
Inv. O.D.A. n. 321

Wilhelm Görner
(da J. Schwind)
*Ritratto di Francesco I
imperatore d'Austria*
Litografia colorata, cm 57,5 × 40,5
Inv. O.D.A. n. 1602

Ignoto del XIX secolo
*Carlo III di Borbone nel giardino
della Villa reale di Marlia*
Olio su tela, cm 64 × 50
Inv. O.D.A. n. 1181

Ignoto del XIX secolo
*La granduchessa Marianna*
Marmo, h. cm 65
Inv. O.D.A. n. 241

Gaspero Martellini (attr.)
*Ritratto di Marianna Carolina
di Toscana*
1821 ca
Olio su tela, cm 110,5 × 87
Inv. M.P.P. 1846 n. 27025

Luigi Pampaloni
*Busto di Augusta Ferdinanda*
1844 ca
Marmo, h. cm 68
Inv. O.D.A. n. 360

Vincenzo Spinazzi
*Busto di Pietro Leopoldo*
Marmo, h. cm 73
Inv. Acc. n. 303

Ferdinand Stephanje
*Ritratto di Ferdinando I d'Austria*
1814
Vetro dorato, graffito e dipinto,
cm 58 × 45
Inv. 1890 n. 5113

## ROOM 4

Lorenzo Bartolini
*Modello del monumento
a Nicola Demidoff*
Marmo, h. cm 200
Gl. n. 2364

Giuseppe Bezzuoli
*Autoritratto*
1852
Olio su tela, cm 87,5 × 72,5
Gl. n. 921

Giuseppe Bezzuoli
*Morte di Zerbino e pianto
di Isabella*
1852
Olio su tela, cm 98 × 140
Gl. n. 4879

Giuseppe Bezzuoli
*Ritratto di Vincenzo Consani*
Olio su tela, cm 76 × 66
Inv. 1890 n. 3350

Giuseppe Bezzuoli
*Trasporto di Cristo al sepolcro*
1843 ca

Olio su tela, cm 99 × 122
Gl. 5283

Bottega carrarese degli inizi
del XIX secolo
*Busto di Gerolamo Bonaparte*
Marmo, h. cm 53
Gl. 2256

Bottega carrarese
*Busto di Maria Luisa d'Asburgo
Austria*
1810 ca
Marmo, h. cm 76
Inv. O.D.A. n. 208

Ida Botti Scifoni
*Autoritratto*
1839
Olio su tela, cm 60 × 47
Inv. 1890 n. 1938

Karl Pavlovic Brjullov
*Ritratto di Anatolio Demidoff
a cavallo*
Olio su tela, cm 315 × 230
Gl. n. 2365

Aristodemo Costoli
*Autoritratto*
Olio su tela, cm 46,5 × 38
Inv. 1890 n. 1968

Pio Fedi
*Bassorilievo con l'autoritratto
di profilo*
1860 ca
Gesso, diam. cm 58,5
Gl. n. 2828

Giuseppe Girometti
*Busto di Paolo Demidoff*
1829
Marmo, h. cm 49
Gl. n. 2477

Ignoto
*Altorilievo con il ritratto di Anatolio
Demidoff*
Gesso, h. cm 66
Gl. n. 2954

Ignoto
*Altorilievo con il ritratto di Nicola
Demidoff*
Gesso, h. cm 63
Gl. n. 2953

Ignoto del XIX secolo
*Busto di Napoleone Bonaparte*
Marmo, h. cm 60
Inv. G.A.A. n. 341

Hiram Powers
*Busto di Eva*
1860 ca
Marmo, h. cm 70
Gl. n. 2947

Hiram Powers
*Busto di giovane schiava greca*
Marmo, h. cm 54
Gl. n. 5613

Hiram Powers
*Proserpina*
Gesso, h. cm 62
Gl. n. 2280

Hiram Powers (stile di)
*Busto di giovinetto*

Marmo, h. cm 54,5
Gl. n. 2948

Ary Scheffer
*Ritratto della principessa Matilde
Bonaparte Demidoff*
1844
Olio su tela, cm 176 × 89,5
Gl. n. 2366

Ary Scheffer
*Ritratto di Giuseppe Montanelli*
1855 ca
Olio su tela, cm 87 × 60,5
C.g. n. 153

Scultore romano
*Busto idealizzato di Nicola
Demidoff*
Marmo, h. cm 59
Gl. n. 2478

## ROOM 5

Giovanni Bastianini
*Busto di giovane donna*
1855 ca
Gesso, h. cm 57
C.g. n. 724

Giovanni Bastianini
*Busto di giovane donna*
1851
Gesso, h. cm 51
C.g. n. 725

Giuseppe Bezzuoli
*Caino*
1844-46
Olio su tela, cm 117 × 88,5
Gl. n. 303

Giuseppe Bezzuoli
*L'entrata di Carlo VIII a Firenze*
1827-29
Olio su tela, cm 290 × 356
C.g. n. 22

Giuseppe Bezzuoli
*Follia che guida il carro di Amore*
1848
Olio su tela, cm 102 × 113,5
Gl. n. 5282

Giuseppe Bezzuoli
*Giovanni dalle Bande Nere
al passaggio dell'Adda*
1852
Olio su tela, cm 375 × 592
Gl. n. 5563

Amos Cassioli
*La battaglia di Legnano*
1870
Olio su tela, cm 370 × 640
C.g. n. 20

Francesco Coghetti
*Cristo deposto*
1848
Olio su tela, cm 122 × 95
Gl. n. 5657

Vincenzo Consani
*Testa di Battista in un bacile*
1840
Marmo, h. cm 41
C.g. n. 706

Giovanni Dupré
*Abele morente*
1846-51
Bronzo, lungh. cm 192
C.g. n. 634

Giovanni Dupré
*Caino*
1849
Bronzo, h. cm 190
C.g. n. 635

Francesco Hayez
*I due Foscari*
1852 ca
Olio su tela, cm 121 × 167,5
C.g. n. 17

Francesco Hayez
*Sansone*
1842
Olio su tela, cm 210 × 162
Gl. n. 309

Giovanni Mochi
*Dante che presenta Giotto
a Guido Novello da Polenta*
1855
Olio su tela, cm 84 × 108
Inv. Acc. n. 349

Francesco Sabatelli
*Aiace d'Oileo*
Olio su tela, cm 210 × 148
C.g. n. 4

Salvino Salvini
*La Ehma*
Gesso, h. cm 150
C.g. n. 732

## Room 6

Giuseppe Abbati
*Chiostro*
Olio su cartone, cm 19,3 × 25,2
C.g. n. 175

Cristiano Banti
*Torquato Tasso ed Eleonora
d'Este (bozzetto)*
Olio su cartone, cm 21 × 30
Gl. n. 1165

Giovanni Bastianini
*Busto di giovane donna*
1855
Gesso, h. cm 53,5
C.g. n. 722

Giovanni Bastianini
*Busto di giovane donna
(Piccarda Donati?)*
Marmo, h. cm 57
Gl. n. 5398

Odoardo Borrani
*L'estasi di santa Teresa*
1883
Olio su tavola, cm 56,4 × 42,3
Inv. S.m. Il Re n. 317

Odoardo Borrani
*Medioevo*
1864
Olio su tela, cm 145 × 121
C.g. n. 19

Vincenzo Cabianca
*I novellieri fiorentini*
Olio su tela, cm 76 × 100
C.g. n. 300

Vincenzo Cabianca
*Pia de' Tolomei condotta
al castello di Maremma*
1860-70 ca

Olio su tela, cm 57 × 75
Gl. n. 4873

Bernardo Celentano
*A Pompei*
Olio su tela, cm 28,7 × 36
Gl. n. 1945

Bernardo Celentano
*Autoritratto*
Olio su tela, cm 46,5 × 34
Gl. n. 1946

Bernardo Celentano
*Interno con figura: la modella
travestita*
Olio su tela, cm 44 × 30,5
Gl. n. 1947

Vincenzo Dattoli
*Muzio Attendolo Sforza strappa
gli stendardi all'alfiere Alfonso
d'Aragona*
1861
Olio su tela, cm 74 × 77
Inv. O.D.A. n. 1443

Dionigi Faconti
*Passatempo d'estate*
1861
Olio su tela, cm 60 × 48
Inv. O.D.A. n. 1400

Pio Fedi
*Bozzetti*
1855-60 ca
Argilla, misure varie
Gl. nn. 2348-2357

Domenico Morelli
*I funerali di san Francesco*
Olio su tela, cm 61 × 23
C.g. n. 96

Domenico Morelli
*Ritratto di Giacomo Tofano,
magistrato napoletano*
Olio su tela, cm 62 × 51
C.g. n. 107

Filippo Palizzi
*La famiglia reale di Napoli
a caccia*
Olio su tela, cm 88 × 130
C.g. n. 103

Giovacchino Toma
*Natura morta con frutta*
Olio su carta su tela, cm 27 × 41,5
Gl. n. 1948

Giovacchino Toma
*Natura morta con frutta*
Olio su tela, cm 28 × 41,5
Gl. n. 1949

Giovacchino Toma
*Natura morta con frutta*
Olio su tela, cm 29,5 × 42
Gl. n. 1950

Giovacchino Toma
*Natura morta con frutta*
Olio su carta su tela, cm 29,5 × 42
Gl. n. 2006

Stefano Ussi
*Ritratto di Linda Ussi*
1855 ca
Olio su tela, cm 61 × 48
C.g. n. 52

Stefano Ussi
*Il supplizio del Savonarola
(bozzetto)*
Olio su vetro, cm 41 × 45
C.g. n. 66

## Room 7

Giovanni Bastianini
*Busto del senatore Filippo Antonio
Gualtiero*
1863
Terracotta, h. cm 60
Gl. n. 4871

Antonio Ciseri
*Ritratto di Antonio Tommasi*
Olio su tela, cm 130 × 88
C.g. n. 28

Antonio Ciseri
*Ritratto di Caterina Ciseri
Curadossi, figlia dell'artista*
Olio su tela, cm 34 × 28
Gl. n. 749

Antonio Ciseri
*Ritratto di Domenico Guerrazzi*
Olio su tela, cm 69 × 56
Inv. 1890 n. 3306

Antonio Ciseri
*Ritratto di Egisto Sarri*
1870
Olio su tela, cm 52 × 41
C.g. n. 29

Antonio Ciseri
*Ritratto di Felice Ciantelli*
1873 ca
Olio su tela, cm 72,9 × 58,5
Gl. n. 5374

Antonio Ciseri
*Ritratto di Gaetano Bianchi*
Olio su tela, cm 47 × 37
C.g. n. 32

Antonio Ciseri
*Ritratto di Gino Capponi*
1880
Olio su tela, cm 60,5 × 50
C.g. n. 27

Antonio Ciseri
*Ritratto di Giovanni Dupré*
Olio su tela, cm 67 × 54
Inv. 1890 n. 3305

Antonio Ciseri
*Ritratto di Giuseppe Ricci*
1856
Olio su tela, cm 59 × 46
Gl. n. 2158

Antonio Ciseri
*Ritratto di Luigi Paganucci*
Olio su tela, cm 57,5 × 44,5
Inv. 1890 n. 8338

Antonio Ciseri
*Ritratto di Maurizio Bufalini*
Olio su tela, cm 60,5 × 51
C.g. n. 30

Antonio Ciseri
*Ritratto di medico spagnolo*
1864
Olio su tela, cm 47 × 37
C.g. n. 33

Antonio Ciseri
*Ritratto di Raffaello Lambruschini*
1873
Olio su tela, cm 60 × 49
Inv. 1890 n. 3316

Antonio Ciseri
*Ritratto di signora (bozzetto)*
Olio su tela, cm 31 × 27
C.g. n. 36

Antonio Ciseri
*Ritratto di Vincenzo Ciseri*
Olio su tela, cm 47 × 39
C.g. n. 37

Antonio Ciseri
*Ritratto di Vittoria Avila Altoviti
Toscanelli (bozzetto)*
Olio su tavola, cm 32 × 22
C.g. n. 34

Antonio Ciseri
*Studio di testa femminile*
Olio su tela, cm 56 × 37
C.g. n. 26

Antonio Ciseri
*Studio per il ritratto di Caterina
Ciseri, madre dell'artista*
Olio su tela, cm 42 × 39
Gl. n. 747

Giovanni Dupré
*Busto del padre*
1878
Terracotta, h. cm 52
Inv. Dep. n. 547

Pio Fedi
*Busto del principe Chatoriski*
1840 ca
Marmo, h. cm 67
Gl. n. 2358

Michele Gordigiani
*Ritratto di Andrea Maffei*
1870-79
Olio su tela, cm 71,5 × 57
Inv. 1890 n. 3310

Michele Gordigiani
*Ritratto di Lorenzo Bartolini*
1873
Olio su tela, cm 59,5 × 48
Inv. 1890 n. 3301

Gerolamo Induno
*Ritratto di Giuseppe Garibaldi*
Olio su tela, cm 73,5 × 60
Inv. Dep. n. 552

Silvestro Lega
*David che placa l'ira di Saul
(bozzetto)*
Olio su tela, cm 23,5 × 29,5
Gl. n. 4812

Adeodato Malatesta
*Ritratto di signora*
1880
Olio su tavola, cm 31 × 20,5
Gl. n. 1940

Gaetano Marinelli
*Studio di testa maschile*
Olio su tela, cm 22 × 18,5
Gl. n. 5372

Gaetano Marinelli
*Studio di testa maschile*

Olio su tela, cm 21,5 × 16
Gl. n. 5373

**Luigi Mussini**
*Autoritratto*
Olio su tela, cm 64 × 51,5
Inv. 1890 n. 1999

**Luigi Mussini**
*Ritratto di Pio Fedi*
1842
Olio su lastra metallica, cm 38 × 32
Gl. n. 2347

**Antonio Puccinelli**
*Ritratto di Pietro Tincolini*
1891
Olio su tela, cm 77 × 63
Inv. 1890 n. 3261

**Emilio Santarelli**
*Busto di Giuseppe Bezzuoli*
Gesso, h. cm 60
Gl. n. 2481

**Raffaello Sorbi**
*Ritratto dello scultore
Emilio Zocchi*
1868
Olio su tela, cm 51,5 × 39,5
C.g. n. 137

**Raffaello Sorbi**
*Ritratto di Oronzo Lelli*
1868
Olio su tela, cm 51 × 39,5
Inv. 1890 n. 3262

**Stefano Ussi**
*Bozzetto di scena medievale*
Olio su tavola, cm 34 × 44,5
Inv. Acc. Dis. n. 76

**Stefano Ussi**
*Bozzetto di scena medievale*
Olio su tavola, cm 37 × 47,5
Inv. Acc. Dis. n. 87

**Stefano Ussi**
*Bozzetto per la cacciata
del duca d'Atene*
1884
Olio su cartone, cm 26 × 34
Gl. n. 1784

**Stefano Ussi**
*Bozzetto per il Niccolò
Machiavelli*
Olio su tavola, cm 25 × 19
Inv. Dep. n. 570

**Stefano Ussi**
*Ritratto di Giovanbattista Niccolini*
1864
Olio su tela, cm 74 × 68
C.g. n. 65

**BALLROOM**

**Aristodemo Costoli**
*Meneceo (gladiatore morente)*
1830
Gesso, h. cm 178
C.g. n. 736

**Giovanni Dupré**
*Bacchino della crittogama*
1859
Marmo, h. cm 115
Gl. n. 2709

**Giovanni Dupré**
*Bacchino festante*
1861
Marmo, h. cm 114
Gl. n. 2710

**Odoardo Fantacchiotti**
*Susanna*
1872
Marmo, h. cm 136
C.g. n. 636

**Pio Fedi**
*San Sebastiano*
1844
Gesso, h. cm 163
C.g. n. 737

**Ignoto austriaco**
*Ritratto di Maria Luisa di Borbone*
1765 ca
Olio su tela, cm 250 × 180
Gl. n. 2927

**Carlo Morelli**
*Ritratto di Leopoldo II,
granduca di Toscana*
1848
Olio su tela, cm 292 × 200
Gl. n. 2705

**Carlo Morelli**
*Ritratto di Maria Antonietta,
granduchessa di Toscana*
Olio su tela, cm 292 × 200
Gl. n. 2706

**Scuola austriaca**
*Ritratto di Pietro Leopoldo,
granduca di Toscana*
1765 ca
Olio su tela, cm 250 × 180
Gl. n. 2926

**Giuseppe Sogni**
*Ritratto di Elisabetta,
imperatrice d'Austria*
1854 ca
Olio su tela, cm 250 × 170
Inv. 1890 n. 8421

**Giuseppe Sogni**
*Ritratto di Francesco Giuseppe
Imperatore d'Austria*
1854 ca
Olio su tela, cm 250 × 170
Inv. 1890 n. 3581

**ROOM 8**

**Joseph Matthaus Aigner**
*Ritratto della nobildonna
Carolina Nugent*
Olio su tela, cm 65 × 53
Gl. n. 2724

**Giovanni Bastianini**
*Busto di donna*
1859
Gesso, h. cm 70
Gl. n. 235

**Giovanni Bastianini**
*La danza*
1856
Gesso, h. cm 147
C.g. n. 727

**Giovanni Bastianini**
*Pescatorello*
1858 ca
Gesso, h. cm 179
C.g. n. 728

**Giovanni Boldini**
*Ritratto della contessa Giulia
Tempestini Kennedy-Lawrie*
1862 ca
Olio su tela, cm 115 × 79
Gl. n. 251

**Giovanni Boldini**
*Ritratto virile*
Olio su tela, cm 41 × 31
C.g. n. 319

**Josephine Calamatta**
*Ritratto di Luigi Calamatta*
Olio su tela, cm 91 × 70
Inv. 1890 n. 3948

**Amos Cassioli**
*Ritratto del pittore Augusto Betti*
1869
Olio su tela, cm 112 × 90
Inv. 1890 n. 3379

**Vito D'Ancona**
*Ritratto di Gioacchino Rossini*
1874
Olio su tela, cm 85 × 66
Inv. 1890 n. 3300

**Vito D'Ancona**
*Testa di donna*
Olio su tela, cm 44,5 × 36,6
C.g. n. 235

**Marcelin Desboutin**
*Maternità*
1855 ca
Olio su tela, cm 112 × 86,5
Gl. n. 1714

**Giovanni Fattori**
*Autoritratto*
1854
Olio su tela, cm 59 × 47
Gl. n. 875

**Giovanni Fattori**
*Ritratto della signora Biliotti*
1870 ca
Olio su tela, cm 64 × 53
Gl. n. 1826

**Giovanni Fattori**
*Ritratto di giovane*
1865 ca
Olio su tela, cm 59 × 47
Gl. n. 1685

**Michele Gordigiani**
*Ritratto del cavaliere Orazio Hall*
1862
Olio su tela, cm 137 × 110
Inv. Acc. n. 669

**Michele Gordigiani**
*Ritratto dello scultore
Giovanni Bastianini*
1875
Olio su tela, cm 80 × 68
Gl. n. 241

**Michele Gordigiani**
*Ritratto di Elettra Bianchi Conti
bambina*
1868
Olio su tela, cm 88 × 65
C.g. 158

**Alessandro Ossani**
*Ritratto della contessa
Giulia Fabbricotti*
1869
Olio su tela, cm 220 × 127
Inv. Dep. n. 231

**Antonio Puccinelli**
*Ritratto della nobildonna
Morrocchi*
1855-60
Olio su tela, cm 104 × 86
Gl. n. 191

**Antonio Puccinelli**
*Ritratto di Emilio Donnini*
1847
Olio su tela, cm 43,2 × 34,9
Inv. 1890 n. 9510

**Emanuele Trionfi**
*Dopo il ballo*
1868
Olio su tela, cm 75 × 100
Inv. Acc. n. 433

**Stefano Ussi**
*Le gioie materne*
1880-85 ca
Olio su tela, cm 81 × 69
C.g. n. 40

**Ignazio Villa**
*Busto femminile*
1848
Marmo, h. cm 78
Gl. n. 2279

**Angelo Visconti**
*Ritratto di Ulisse de Matteis*
1857
Olio su tela, cm 87 × 66
Gl. n. 4682

**Francesco Saverio
Winterhalter**
*Ritratto della principessa
Lina Gagarine*
1857
Olio su tela, cm 75 × 56
C.g. n. 622

**ROOM 9**

**Bartolomeo Ardy**
*Paesaggio*
Olio su tela, cm 44 × 89
Inv. O.D.A. n. 1632

**Federico Cortese**
*La campagna romana
presso Terracina*
1865
Olio su tela, cm 79 × 156
Inv. Acc. n. 419

**Serafino De Tivoli**
*Una pastura (Vacche nel bosco)*
Olio su tela, cm 102 × 73
C.g. n. 169

**Emilio Donnini**
*Fornaci in val d'Arno*
1862
Olio su tela, cm 44 × 63
Inv. O.D.A. n. 260

**Emilio Donnini**
*Marina dell'isola d'Elba*
1860
Olio su tela, cm 83,5 × 112,5
Inv. Acc. n. 452

**Emilio Donnini**
*Marina presso Rio*
1862
Olio su tela, cm 75 × 115
Inv. O.D.A. n. 1370

Emilio Donnini
*Veduta di paese lungo il Serchio*
Olio su tela, cm 83 × 115
Inv. Acc. n. 448

Giovanni Dupré
*La Flora*
1869
Marmo, h. cm 82,5
Gl. n. 4881

Antonio Fontanesi
*Dopo la pioggia*
Olio su tela, cm 128 × 192
C.g. n. 82

Antonio Fontanesi
*Lungarno a Santa Trinita*
Olio su tela, cm 69 × 105
C.g. n. 81

Andrea Markò
*Bivacco di pastori*
1862
Olio su tela, cm 53 × 74
C.g. n. 88

Andrea Markò
*Carbonai*
1861
Olio su tela, cm 116 × 155
C.g. n. 76

Andrea Markò
*Il guado*
1861
Olio su tela, cm 78 × 103
Inv. Acc. n. 450

Andrea Markò
*Monte Forato nelle Alpi Apuane*
1871
Olio su tela, cm 121 × 116
C.g. n. 90

Andrea Markò
*Paesaggio (cascine di Pisa)*
1861
Olio su tela, cm 50 × 50
C.g. n. 75

Andrea Markò
*Temporale*
Olio su tela, cm 46 × 66
C.g. n. 74

Carlo Markò jr.
*Castiglion del Lago*
1870
Olio su tela, cm 44 × 123
C.g. n. 91

Carlo Markò jr.
*Motivo di San Marziale
verso Colle Val d'Elsa*
1863
Olio su tela, cm 76 × 74
Inv. Acc. n. 434

J.P. Mene
*Lotta di tre cani*
Bronzo
Inv. n. 199 rosso

Curio Nuti
*Motivo del Chianti*
1863
Olio su tela, cm 36 × 54
Inv. O.D.A. n. 1634

Giuseppe Palizzi
*Interno di una foresta*

1845
Olio su tela, cm 89 × 115
C.g. n. 87

Luigi Paoletti
*Interno di una foresta*
1860
Olio su tela, cm 132 × 107
Inv. Acc. n. 311

Luisa Silei
*Paesaggio*
Olio su tela, cm 67 × 92
Inv. Acc. n. 449

Alfonso Simonetti
*Una Maremma*
1866
Olio su tela, cm 50 × 75
Inv. O.D.A. n. 1297

## ROOM 10

Giuseppe Abbati
*Monaco*
Olio su tela, cm 49 × 19
Gl. n. 1664

Francesco Saverio Altamura
*Profilo di donna*
1852
Olio su tela, cm 39 × 29
Gl. n. 1642

Cristiano Banti
*Boscaiole (Le predone)*
Olio su tavola, cm 20 × 40
C.g. n. 253

Cristiano Banti
*Boscaiole (Le predone)*
1881 ca
Olio su tela, cm 62,5 × 135,5
Gl. n. 1668

Cristiano Banti
*Bozzetto storico*
Olio su tela, cm 71 × 49
Gl. n. 1656

Cristiano Banti
*Cinque bozzetti*
Olio su tavole, misure varie
Inv. 1890 n. 3397

Cristiano Banti
*Confidenze*
Olio su tela, cm 28 × 40
C.g. n. 249

Cristiano Banti
*Ritratto di Alaide in giardino*
Olio su tavola, cm 20 × 25
Gl. n. 1654

Cristiano Banti
*Riunione di contadine*
1861
Olio su tela, cm 31,3 × 46,4
C.g. n. 252

Cristiano Banti
*Signora che lavora sul terrazzo*
Olio su tavola, cm 30,5 × 15
Gl. n. 1674

Cristiano Banti
*Tre contadine*
Olio su tavola, cm 64 × 31,5
Gl. n. 1644

Cristiano Banti
*Tre contadine*
Olio su tavola, cm 73 × 34
Gl. n. 1657

Cristiano Banti
*Tre contadine a passeggio*
Olio su tavola, cm 56 × 31,5
Gl. n. 1645

Giovanni Boldini
*Alaide Banti al pianoforte*
1885 ca
Olio su tavola, cm 27 × 18
Gl. n. 1673

Giovanni Boldini
*L'amatore delle arti*
1865 ca
Olio su tela, cm 32 × 22,5
Gl. n. 1659

Giovanni Boldini
*Autoritratto*
Olio su tela, cm 57 × 37
Gl. n. 1658

Giovanni Boldini
*Autoritratto*
1892
Olio su tela, cm 45 × 40
Gl. n. 1667

Giovanni Boldini
*Bovi (bozzetto)*
1885
Olio su tavola, cm 15 × 26
Gl. n. 1670

Giovanni Boldini
*Bovi al carro*
1885
Olio su tavola, cm 17,5 × 25,5
Gl. n. 1663

Giovanni Boldini
*Ritratto della marchesa
Adelaide Ristori del Grillo*
Olio su tela, cm 55,5 × 40
Gl. n. 1669

Giovanni Boldini
*Ritratto del marchese del Grillo*
Olio su tela, diam. cm 71
Gl. n. 1676

Giovanni Boldini
*Ritratto di Alaide Banti*
1885 ca
Olio su tavola, cm 28 × 14,5
Gl. n. 1666

Giovanni Boldini
*Ritratto di Alaide Banti*
Olio su tavola, cm 20 × 32,5
Gl. n. 1671

Giovanni Boldini
*Ritratto di Alaide Banti (bozzetto)*
Olio su tavola, cm 18 × 27
Gl. n. 1678

Giovanni Boldini
*Ritratto di Alaide Banti
al caminetto*
1885
Olio su tavola, cm 62 × 28
Gl. n. 1662

Giovanni Boldini
*Ritratto di Alaide Banti
in abito bianco*
1866

Olio su tavoletta, cm 42,5 × 23
Gl. n. 1660

Giovanni Boldini
*Ritratto di Alaide in grigio*
Olio su tavola, cm 37 × 23
Gl. n. 1665

Giovanni Boldini
*Ritratto di Cristiano Banti*
1865-66 ca
Olio su tela, cm 57 × 33,5
Gl. n. 1641

Giovanni Boldini
*Ritratto di Cristiano Banti*
1885
Olio su tavola, cm 29 × 12
Gl. n. 1677

Giovanni Boldini
*Ritratto di Leonetto Banti*
1866
Olio su tela, cm 44 × 22,5
Gl. n. 1680

Giovanni Boldini
*Testa di bambino*
Olio su tela, cm 44,5 × 35
Gl. n. 1643

Giovanni Boldini
*La zingara*
Olio su tela, cm 57 × 46
Gl. n. 1672

Adriano Cecioni
*Busto della marchesa Vettori*
Terracotta, h. cm 48
Gl. n. 1682

Giuseppe De Nittis
*Le anatrine*
Olio su tavola, cm 14 × 28
Gl. n. 1675

Oscar Ghiglia
*Ritratto di Alaide Banti*
1926
Olio su tela, cm 130 × 90
Gl. n. 1647

Michele Gordigiani
*Ritratto di Alaide Banti*
1872
Olio su tela, cm 136 × 98
Gl. n. 1648

Michele Gordigiani
*Ritratto di Leopolda Banti Redi*
Olio su tela, diam. cm 80
Gl. n. 1655

Michele Gordigiani (attr.)
*Ritratto di Leopolda Redi Banti*
Olio su tela, diam. cm 73
Gl. n. 1649

Ignoto
*Calco della mano di Adriano
Cecioni*
Gesso
Gl. n. 1683

Ignoto del XV secolo
*Vestizione di una santa giovinetta*
Tavola, cm 40 × 55

Maniera del Ghirlandaio
*Madonna con Bambino*
XIV secolo

Tavola, cm 38 × 30
Inv. 1890 n. 7401

**Telemaco Signorini**
*Casolari rustici con orticello*
Olio su tavola, cm 12 × 21
Gl. n. 1681

**Telemaco Signorini**
*Paesaggio nuvoloso*
Olio su tavola, cm 12 × 22
Gl. n. 1661

## ROOM 11

**Giuseppe Abbati**
*Castiglioncello*
Olio su tavola, cm 10 × 30
C.g. n. 171

**Giuseppe Abbati**
*Collina maremmana*
Olio su tela, cm 13 × 27
C.g. n. 170

**Giuseppe Abbati**
*Il cortile del Bargello*
Olio su tela, cm 16,5 × 20
C.g. n. 164

**Giuseppe Abbati**
*Ritratto di signora in grigio*
Olio su tavola, cm 26 × 14
C.g. n. 188

**Giuseppe Abbati**
*Ritratto di Teresa Martelli*
Olio su tela, cm 59 × 38
C.g. n. 190

**Giuseppe Abbati**
*Strada di paese*
Olio su cartone, cm 18 × 21
C.g. n. 165

**Giuseppe Abbati**
*Veduta di Castiglioncello*
Olio su tavola, cm 10 × 86
C.g. n. 172

**Giuseppe Benassai**
*Pecore con pastore*
1865
Olio su tela, cm 31 × 80
C.g. n. 591

**Giovanni Boldini**
*Caricatura di Guglielmo Pampana*
ante 1871
Olio su tela, cm 23 × 17
C.g. n. 318

**Giovanni Boldini**
*Ritratto di Diego Martelli*
post 1867
Olio su tela, cm 15 × 18
C.g. n. 317

**Giovanni Boldini**
*Ritratto di Leopoldo Pisani*
1863-64 ca
Olio su tavola, cm 30 × 13
C.g. n. 314

**Odoardo Borrani**
*Castiglioncello*
Olio su tavola, cm 12,7 × 29
C.g. n. 325

**Vincenzo Cabianca**
*Le bagnanti*
1868

Olio su tela, cm 82 × 151
C.g. n. 242

**Vincenzo Cabianca**
*Casale rustico*
Olio su cartone, cm 26,5 × 16,5
C.g. n. 251

**Cesare Ciani**
*La malata*
1895
Olio su tavola, cm 20,4 × 10,8
C.g. n. 344

**Giovanni Fattori**
*Assalto alla Madonna della scoperta (bozzetto)*
Olio su tela, cm 52 × 83
C.g. n. 193

**Giovanni Fattori**
*Bovi al pascolo*
Olio su tela, cm 27 × 52
C.g. n. 202

**Giovanni Fattori**
*Lanciere in vedetta*
1880-90 ca
Olio su tela, cm 27 × 52
C.g. n. 199

**Giovanni Fattori**
*Maiali al pascolo*
1890-1900 ca
Olio su tela, cm 71 × 46
C.g. n. 206

**Giovanni Fattori**
*Perché non dirlo?*
Olio su tavola, cm 12 × 22
C.g. n. 493

**Giovanni Fattori**
*Plotone di cavalleria (bozzetto)*
1870-80
Olio su tavola, cm 20 × 32
C.g. n. 198

**Giovanni Fattori**
*Riposo (barocci romani)*
1873 ca
Olio su tavola, cm 21 × 32
C.g. n. 194

**Giovanni Fattori**
*Vallospoli (Fauglia)*
1875 ca
Olio su tavola, cm 32,5 × 18,8
C.g. n. 215

**Francesco Gioli**
*Paesaggio*
Olio su tavola, cm 10 × 17
C.g. n. 514

**Luigi Gioli**
*Paese*
Olio su tavola, cm 11 × 19
C.g. n. 516

**Salvatore Grita**
*Il voto contro natura*
1860-70
Gesso, h. cm 65,5
C.g. n. 702

**Silvestro Lega**
*Giovane contadina (studio)*
Olio su tavola, cm 40 × 26
C.g. n. 174

**Silvestro Lega**
*In villa*

Olio su tavola, cm 13 × 33
C.g. n. 185

**Silvestro Lega**
*Paesaggio*
Olio su tela, cm 16,5 × 24,5
C.g. n. 183

**Silvestro Lega**
*La passeggiata in giardino*
Olio su tela, cm 35 × 22,5
C.g. n. 178

**Silvestro Lega**
*La visita allo studio*
Olio su tavola, cm 44 × 35
C.g. n. 182

**Camille Pissarro**
*Paesaggio (L'approssimarsi della tempesta)*
Olio su tela, cm 60 × 74
C.g. n. 269

**Camille Pissarro**
*La tosatura della siepe*
Olio su tela, cm 46,5 × 55,5
C.g. n. 266

**Raffaello Sernesi**
*Monelli*
1862 ca
Olio su tavola, cm 18,2 × 13,5
C.g. n. 177

**Raffaello Sernesi**
*Sull'aia*
Olio su tela, cm 19 × 51
C.g. n. 168

**Telemaco Signorini**
*La Piagentina*
Olio su cartone, cm 14 × 22
C.g. n. 276

**Telemaco Signorini**
*Settignano (Impressioni di campagna)*
Olio su cartone, cm 13 × 22
C.g. n. 275

**Ettore Ximenes**
*Busto di Giuseppe Garibaldi*
Terracotta, h. cm 68
C.g. n. 690

**Federico Zandomeneghi**
*A letto (fanciulla dormiente)*
1878
Olio su tela, cm 60,5 × 73,5
C.g. n. 261

**Federico Zandomeneghi**
*Al pianoforte*
Olio su tavola, cm 29 × 34
C.g. n. 267

**Federico Zandomeneghi**
*Bastimento sullo scalo*
1869
Olio su tela, cm 41 × 96
C.g. n. 270

**Federico Zandomeneghi**
*Luna di miele (A pesca sulla Senna)*
Olio su tavola, cm 16 × 29
C.g. n. 263

**Federico Zandomeneghi**
*Ritratto di Diego Martelli*
1879

Olio su tela, cm 72 × 90
C.g. n. 230

**Federico Zandomeneghi**
*Ritratto di Diego Martelli*
1870
Olio su tela, cm 63 × 41
C.g. n. 265

## ROOM 11 BIS

**Virginia Boggi**
*Ritratto di Ernestina Martelli Mocenni*
Miniatura su avorio, cm 3,8 × 3
C.g. n. 585

**Bregiotti**
*Testa di donna*
Miniatura su avorio, cm 5,5 × 4,4
C.g. n. 584

**Cesare Fantacchiotti**
*Busto di Diego Martelli*
Bronzo, h. cm 64
C.g. n. 645

**Garagalli (copia da François-Xavier Fabre)**
*Ritratto di Ugo Foscolo*
Olio su tela, cm 19,5 × 16,5
Inv. Com. n. 1

**Ignoto**
*Ritratto di Diego Martelli a diciotto anni*
Olio su cartone, cm 12 × 15
C.g. n. 577

**Ignoto**
*Ritratto di donna*
Miniatura su avorio, diam. 4,7
C.g. n. 582

**Ignoto**
*Ritratto di Giulio Foscolo*
Olio su tela, cm 17 × 13
C.g. n. 578

**Ignoto**
*Ritratto di Quirina Mocenni Maggiotti*
Acquerello su carta, cm 16 × 15
Inv. Com. n. 8

**Ignoto**
*Ritratto di Quirina Mocenni Maggiotti*
Olio su tela, cm 98,5 × 77,5
Inv. Com. n. 100

**Ignoto**
*Ritratto virile*
Miniatura su avorio, cm 4,2 × 3,7
C.g. n. 583

**Ignoto**
*Ritratto virile (Fabrizio Morosini)*
1847
Matita su carta, cm 6 × 5
C.g. n. 1107

## ROOM 12

**Giuseppe Abbati**
*Cappella nel Palazzo Pretorio di Firenze*
Olio su tela, cm 49 × 67
C.g. n. 163

Giuseppe Abbati
*L'orazione*
Olio su tela, cm 57 × 42
C.g. n. 187

Federico Andreotti
*Savonarola che scaccia dalla sua cella i due sicari inviatigli dalla Bentivoglio (bozzetto)*
Olio su tela, cm 18 × 25
Gl. n. 1150

Odoardo Borrani
*Ritratto giovanile di Adriano Cecioni*
Olio su tela, cm 35 × 26
Inv. Acc. n. 613

Carlo Brazzini
*Interno di San Miniato al Monte alle Croci*
Olio su tela, cm 70 × 56
Inv. 1890 n. 3478

Ferdinando Buonamici
*Benvenuto Cellini convalescente*
Olio su tela, cm 102 × 129
Gl. n. 5593

Ferdinando Buonamici
*Veduta del colle di Fiesole*
1868
Olio su tela, cm 88 × 119
Gl. n. 4869

Adriano Cecioni
*Bambino con gallo*
1868
Gesso, h. cm 79
Inv. Acc. n. 324

Adriano Cecioni
*Primi passi*
1869 ca
Gesso, h. cm 73
Gl. n. 5612

Adriano Cecioni
*Ritratto della moglie*
1867-70
Olio su tela, cm 38,5 × 36
C.g. n. 184

Adriano Cecioni
*Una visita al sepolcro*
1865
Gesso, cm 155 × 113
C.g. n. 719

Adriano Cecioni
*L'uscita del padrone*
1880 ca
Bronzo, h. cm 44
Gl. n. 2387

Gaetano Chierici
*Le gioie di una madre*
1866
Olio su tela, cm 70 × 95
C.g. n. 136

Giuseppe Ciaranfi
*Benedetto Varchi che legge l'Istoria fiorentina a Cosimo de' Medici*
Olio su tela, cm 99 × 123
Inv. Acc. n. 403

Enrico Fanfani
*Milton cieco detta il suo poema alle figlie*
1856

Olio su tela, cm 64 × 80,5
Inv. Acc. n. 353

Enrico Fanfani
*Scena della sommossa fiorentina del 27 aprile 1859*
1860
Olio su tela, cm 108 × 92
Inv. 1890 n. 3481

Giovanni Fattori
*Maria Stuarda al campo di Crookstone*
1861
Olio su tela, cm 76 × 108
C.g. n. 229

Ferdinando Folchi
*Accademia musicale nel salone dei Cinquecento*
1845
Olio su tela, cm 88 × 118
Inv. Acc. n. 480

Frullani
*Interno della chiesa di Santa Croce*
Olio su tela, cm 65 × 57
Inv. O.D.A. n. 1689

Annibale Gatti
*Monna Chita presenta il figlio alla Signoria di Firenze*
1861
Olio su tela, cm 35 × 70
Inv. Acc. n. 343

Annibale Gatti
*Studio per una scena storica*
Olio su tela, cm 21,5 × 16,5
Gl. n. 3688

Lorenzo Gelati
*Refettorio di San Domenico*
Olio su tela, cm 56 × 70
Inv. n. 20472

Bartolomeo Giuliano
*L'aspettativa*
Olio su tela, cm 42 × 53
C.g. n. 108

Ignoto
*Veduta del Monte alle Croci*
Olio su tela, cm 45 × 60
Inv. O.D.A. n. 1635

Domenico Induno
*L'antiquario (L'usuraio)*
Olio su tela, cm 81 × 55
C.g. n. 93

Silvestro Lega
*Il canto dello stornello*
Olio su tela, cm 158 × 98
Gl. n. 4683

Silvestro Lega
*La visita alla balia*
1873
Olio su tela, cm 56 × 93
C.g. n. 181

Adolfo Malevolti
*Interno della chiesa di Santo Spirito*
Olio s tela, cm 75 × 63
Inv. 1890 n. 3487

Federico Moja
*La cappella del Rosario a Venezia dopo l'incendio del 1867*

Olio su tela, cm 75 × 60
C.g. n. 78

Giuseppe Moricci
*Benvenuto Cellini detta la sua vita a un fanciullo*
Olio su tela, cm 98 × 75
Inv. Acc. n. 453

Giuseppe Moricci
*Il mercato vecchio a Firenze*
1860
Olio su tela, cm 84 × 74
Inv. 1890 n. 3488

Francesco Giovanni Pezzini
*Interno della chiesa di San Miniato al Monte*
1862
Olio su tela, cm 110 × 90
Inv. 1890 n. 3486

Giovanni Pezzini
*Interno del Duomo di Firenze*
1861
Olio su tela, cm 112 × 92
Inv. O.D.A. n. 1452

G. Planeta
*Dante Alighieri di fronte a Santa Maria Novella*
1866
Olio su tela, cm 57 × 28,5
Gl. n. 4845

Ludovico Raymond
*Avelli di Santa Maria Novella*
1862
Olio su tela, cm 57 × 105
Inv. O.D.A. n. 1458

Pietro Saltini
*L'elemosina*
1870 ca
Olio su tela, cm 57 × 46
Gl. n. 4893

Pietro Saltini
*Frate in cantina*
Olio su tela, cm 54 × 87
Gl. n. 4894

Ettore Ximenes
*Le marmiton*
1880 ca
Terracotta, h. cm 61
Gl. n. 4681

## ROOM 13

Carlo Ademollo
*Anna Cuminello trovata morta il giorno dopo la battaglia di San Martino*
1861 ca
Olio su tela, cm 114 × 146
Gl. n. 2967

Carlo Ademollo
*Episodio della battaglia di San Martino*
Olio su tela, cm 86 × 116
Dep. M. Ris.

Carlo Ademollo
*Pasquale Cova alla battaglia di Varese*
Olio su tela, cm 152 × 135
Inv. 1890 n. 8534

Ignazio Affanni
*Partenza del garibaldino dalla famiglia nel 1859*
1861
Olio su tela, cm 96 × 68
Inv. Acc. n. 361

Ignoto lombardo
*Ritratto del patriota Angelo Brunetti, detto Ciceruacchio*
1847-49 ca
Olio su tela, cm 47 × 36,5
Gl. n. 2936

Luigi Bechi
*Il marchese Fadini salva a Montebello il generale De Sonnaz*
1859-62
Olio su tela, cm 174 × 232
Inv. Acc. n. 364

Ferdinando Buonamici
*Artisti volontari toscani alla caserma di Modena*
1885
Olio su tela, cm 85 × 102
Inv. M. Ris. n. 389

Vincenzo Cabianca
*Garibaldi a Caprera*
Olio su tela, cm 71 × 86,5
Gl. n. 1083

Eurisio Capocci
*Gesta brigantesa*
1867
Olio su tela, cm 126 × 152
Inv. O.D.A. n. 259

Adriano Cecioni
*Busto di Giuseppe Mazzini*
1878-79 ca
Gesso, h. cm 60
Inv. Acc. n. 817

Cosimo Conti
*L'eccidio della famiglia Cignoli*
1861
Olio su tela, cm 174 × 231
Inv. Acc. n. 380

Giovanni Fattori
*Battaglia (bozzetto)*
1862 ca
Olio su tela, cm 35 × 56
C.g. n. 200

Giovanni Fattori
*Battaglia (bozzetto)*
1860 ca
Olio su tela, cm 40,5 × 61
C.g. n. 203

Giovanni Fattori
*Il campo italiano dopo la battaglia di Magenta*
Olio su tela, cm 232 × 348
Inv. Acc. n. 444

Giovanni Fattori
*Difesa della Porta Capuana a Santa Maria di Capua*
1860 ca
Olio su tela, cm 59 × 100
Inv. M. Ris. n. 114

Giovanni Fattori
*Gli eccidi di Mantova*
1855 ca

Olio su tavola, cm 18 × 26
C.g. n. 214

Vincenzo Giani
*Busto del conte Francesco Verasis di Castiglione*
1868
Marmo, h. cm 86
Inv. M.P.P. n. 1834

Michele Gordigiani
*Ritratto di Leopoldo Montucchielli*
1859
Olio su tela, cm 72 × 58
Inv. 1890 n. 9150

Ignoto
*Ritratto di Giuseppe Mazzini*
Pastello su cartone, 88,5 × 74,5
Inv. Dep. n. 573

Alessandro Lanfredini
*I coscritti italiani del reggimento Sigismondo dopo la battaglia di Magenta*
1859-62
Olio su tela, cm 173 × 232
Inv. Acc. n. 367

Silvestro Lega
*Episodio della guerra del 1859 (ritorno di bersaglieri italiani da una ricognizione)*
1861
Olio su tela, cm 57,5 × 95
Inv. Acc. n. 413

Giuseppe Moricci
*Lettera del volontario dal campo alla sua famiglia*
1861
Olio su tela, cm 115 × 142
Inv. Acc. n. 307

Antonio Puccinelli
*Ritratto di volontario toscano*
1849
Olio su tela, cm 31 × 24
Inv. M. Ris. n. 13

Edoardo Raimondi
*La fornace di Palestro, il mattino dopo la battaglia (guerra del 1859)*
1868
Olio su tela, cm 54 × 105
Inv. Acc. n. 389

Augusto Rivalta
*Il ritorno dalla posta*
Bronzo, h. cm 114
C.g. n. 714

Telemaco Signorini
*Entrata degli zuavi francesi e degli artiglieri toscani a Rubera*
Olio su tela, cm 29 × 57
Inv. M. Ris. n. 208

### ROOM 14

Amos Cassioli
*Offerta a Venere*
Olio su tela, cm 39 × 60
Inv. Acc. n. 346

Gabriele Castagnola
*L'episodio di Filippo Lippi e la monaca Buti*

Olio su tela, cm 223 × 159
Inv. Acc. n. 386

Antonio Ciseri
*Ecce Homo*
1891
Olio su tela, cm 292 × 380
C.g. n. 31

Antonio Ciseri
*Trasporto di Cristo al sepolcro*
Olio su tela, cm 89 × 136
C.g. n. 35

Thomas Couture
*Ritratto di Anselm Feuerbach*
1851-53 ca
Olio su tela, cm 60 × 50
Inv. Dep. n. 600

Achille D'Orsi
*I parassiti*
1877
Bronzo, cm 115 × 185 × 95
C.g. n. 637

Emilio Franceschi
*Opimia*
Gesso, h. cm 110
Inv. Acc. n. 509

Louis Gallait
*David e Golia*
Olio su tela, cm 34 × 18,7
Gl. n. 4687

Annibale Gatti
*Ambasciata di fronte a un pontefice*
Olio su tela, cm 63 × 46
Gl. n. 3689

Ignoto del XIX secolo
*Martire con leopardo*
Olio su tela, cm 236 × 164
Inv. Dep. n. 598

Narciso Malatesta
*Cacciagione*
1867
Olio su tela, cm 80 × 100
Inv. O.D.A. n. 267

Giacomo Martinetti
*Bambina dormiente*
1864
Olio su tela, cm 86 × 115
Inv. Acc. n. 369

Rodolfo Morgari
*Raffaello morente*
Olio su tela, cm 250 × 200
Inv. Acc. n. 337

Pietro Saltini
*Angelo in adorazione*
Terracotta, h. cm 19
Gl. n. 5419

Pietro Saltini
*Angelo musicante*
Terracotta, h. cm 23
Gl. n. 5420

Pietro Saltini
*Busto di giovane donna*
Terracotta, h. cm 19
Gl. n. 5418

Alcide Segoni
*Il ritrovamento del corpo*

*di Catilina dopo la battaglia di Pistoia*
1871
Olio su tela, cm 136 × 174
C.g. n. 18

Raffaello Sorbi
*Scena storica*
1864
Olio su tela, cm 32,5 × 26,5
Gl. n. 4846

Scipione Vannutelli
*Maria Stuarda che si avvia al patibolo*
1861
Olio su tela, cm 110 × 82
C.g. n. 23

### ROOM 15

Carlo Ademollo
*Un cane salva un bambino empolese dalle acque dell'Arno*
1870 ca
Olio su tela, cm 36 × 44
Gl. n. 3696

Francesco Barzaghi
*Fanciullo a cavallo di una scopa*
1875
Marmo, h. cm 121
Gl. n. 4680

Arturo Faldi
*Il superstite della grande armata*
1882
Olio su tela, cm 66 × 56
Inv. S.m. Il Re n. 308

Annibale Gatti
*I funerali di santa Verdiana (bozzetto)*
1865 ca
Olio su tela, cm 46,5 × 39
Gl. n. 3687

Annibale Gatti
*Il trionfo della musica*
Olio su tela, cm 64 × 82
C.g. n. 133

Enrico Pestellini
*La sorella maggiore (Amore filiale)*
1887
Olio su tela, cm 99 × 132
Gl. n. 5654

Egisto Sarri
*Corradino di Svevia ascolta la sua condanna*
Olio su tela, cm 177 × 135
Inv. 1890 n. 3267

Egisto Sarri
*Scena di interno*
Olio su tela, cm 35 × 25,5
Gl. n. 4842

Gabriele Smargiassi
*Buonconte da Montefeltro morto in battaglia*
Olio su tela, cm 213 × 300
Inv. O.D.A. n. 1352

Raffaello Sorbi
*Il granduca Pietro Leopoldo nella campagna toscana*
1913

Olio su tela, cm 46 × 65
C.g. n. 134

Stefano Ussi
*Bozzetti con costumi africani*
Olio su tavola, misure varie
C.g. nn. 60-64

Stefano Ussi
*Bozzetti con scene africane*
Olio su tavola e su tela, misure varie
C.g. nn. 41-48

Stefano Ussi
*Bozzetti con scene africane*
Olio su tavola, misure varie
C.g. nn. 53-58

Stefano Ussi
*Bozzetti con scene africane*
Olio su tavola, misure varie
C.g. nn. 67-72

Stefano Ussi
*La cacciata del Duca d'Atene*
1860
Olio su tela, cm 320 × 452
C.g. n. 59

Stefano Ussi
*Cammelli nel deserto*
Olio su tela, cm 42 × 62
Inv. Dep. n. 571

Stefano Ussi
*Ritratto di Carlo Levi*
1887
Olio su tela, cm 64 × 51
C.g. n. 73

Stefano Ussi
*Ritratto di Gaetano Bianchi*
1860 ca
Olio su tela, cm 42 × 34
C.g. n. 39

Santo Varni
*Laura al bagno*
1858
Marmo bianco, cm 46 × 80 × 30
Gl. n. 5596

José Villegas y Cordero
*Uomo sdraiato*
Olio su tela, cm 52 × 71,5
Inv. Dep. n. 285

### ROOM 16

Carlo Ademollo
*L'ultimo assalto alla battaglia di San Martino*
Olio su tela, cm 291 × 558
Inv. 1890 n. 8528

Giuseppe Baldini
*Allegoria della Vittoria*
1864
Olio su tela, cm 87 × 65
Inv. O.D.A. n. 1606

Cesare Bartolena
*Lettera per la mamma*
1880 ca
Olio su tela, cm 49 × 59
Inv. S.m. Il Re n. 286

Cesare Bartolena
*La madre del coscritto*
1878 ca
Olio su tela, cm 63 × 51
Inv. S.m. Il Re n. 277

Cesare Bartolena
*Manovre*
1870-80 ca
Olio su tela, cm 33,5 × 48
Gl. n. 490

Boncinelli
*Emanuele Filiberto a cavallo*
1886
Commesso in pietre dure, legno,
cm 56 × 69
Inv. S.m. Il Re n. 315

Dugoni
*Ritratto di Vittorio Emanuele II*
1866
Olio su tela, cm 142 × 80
Inv. M.P.P. n. 28153

Giovanni Fattori
*Alt!*
1890-1900 ca
Olio su tavola, cm 29 × 57
C.g. n. 213

Giovanni Fattori
*Carica di cavalleria*
1873
Olio su tela, cm 128 × 235
C.g. n. 180

Vincenzo Gemito
*Busto di Giuseppe Verdi*
1873
Bronzo, h. cm 50
C.g. n. 648

Michele Gordigiani
*Ritratto di Francesco Silvio
Orlandini*
1860
Olio su tela, cm 73 × 59
Inv. 1890 n. 3213

Emilio Lapi
*La battaglia di Palestro*
1862
Olio su tela, cm 236 × 351
Inv. Acc. n. 313

Giuseppe Michelacci
*Monumento a Vittorio Emanuele
II (bozzetto)*
Acquerello su carta, cm 69 × 126
Inv. O.D.A. n. 1265

Alessandro Monteneri,
Guglielmo Ciani,
Domenico Bruschi
*Stipo per la corona del re d'Italia*
1860 ca
Mogano intarsiato, acero
e madreperla, h. cm 327
Inv. S.m. Il Re n. 357

Raffaello Pagliaccetti
*Busto della principessa
Margherita*
1868
Gesso, h. cm 72
Inv. M.P.P. n. 2787

Ludovico Papi
*Medaglione con ritratto
di Vittorio Emanuele II*
Legno, cm 69 × 55
Inv. M.P.P. n. 21815

Enrico Pestellini
*Regina Angelorum ora pro nobis*
1884

Olio su tela, cm 250 × 165
Gl. n. 5653

Carlo Pittarra
*Vittorio Emanuele II a caccia*
Olio su tela, cm 37 × 60
Gl. n. 1933

Raffaele Pontremoli
*Sua Altezza Reale il principe
Umberto al quadrato
di Villafranca*
Olio su tela, cm 137 × 238
Inv. O.D.A. n. 882

Egisto Sarri
*Ritratto di Niccolò Tommaseo*
1877
Olio su tela, cm 62,5 × 52
Inv. 1890 n. 3298

Pietro Senno
*Il principe Amedeo a Custoza*
Olio su tela, cm 48 × 80
Inv. 1890 n. 8533

## ROOM 17

Federico Andreotti
*Figura di donna di profilo (studio)*
Pastello su cartone, cm 79,5 × 63
C.g. n. 141

Federico Andreotti
*Ritratto di Giulia Rosai Tricca*
1891 ca
Olio su tela, cm 158,5 × 89,5
Gl. n. 2261

Federico Andreotti
*Ritratto di Ida Luisi*
1880-90
Olio su tela, cm 65,8 × 48,5
Gl. n. 1417

Adolfo Belimbau
*Momento di riposo (Un pisolino)*
1878
Olio su tavola, cm 34,6 × 22,3
C.g. n. 140

Adriano Cecchi
*Nudo di adolescente (la modella
di Pitti)*
1900 ca
Olio su tela su cartone, cm 26 × 19,5
Gl. n. 3707

Adriano Cecioni
*Busto di giovane donna*
Terracotta, h. cm 51
Gl. n. 1915

Adriano Cecioni
*Napoleone Giotti*
1882 ca
Terracotta, h. cm 27,8
Gl. n. 306

Adriano Cecioni
*Signora che si abbottona
un guanto*
1881 ca
Terracotta, h. cm 41,2
Gl. n. 1102

Charles Chaplin
*Les lilas*
1880 ca
Olio su tela, cm 78 × 55
Gl. n. 2750

Charles Chaplin
*Ritratto della principessa Ratzwill*
1883
Olio su tela, cm 81,5 × 65
Inv. 1890 n. 9509

Tito Conti
*Autoritratto*
1892
Olio su tela, cm 81 × 56,5
Gl. n. 2497

Vittorio Corcos
*Ritratto della figlia di Jack
la Bolina*
1888 ca
Olio su tela, cm 139 × 105
Gl. n. 1580

Vittorio Corcos
*Ritratto della signora Trentanove*
1890
Olio su tela, cm 121 × 71
Inv. 1890 n. 9231

Vittorio Corcos
*Ritratto del violinista Federico
Consolo*
1892
Olio su tela, cm 168 × 140
C.g. n. 159

Vito D'Ancona
*Nello studio*
1875 ca
Olio su cartone, cm 28 × 21
C.g. n. 233

Carolus Duran
*Ritratto della contessa Berta
Vandal De Heckeren*
1878
Olio su tela, cm 225 × 145
Gl. n. 308

Edoardo Gelli
*Ritratto con berretto rosso*
Olio su tela, cm 54 × 67
Inv. Dep. n. 553

Edoardo Gelli
*Ritratto del conte Luigi Pisani*
Olio su tela, cm 70 × 56
Gl. n. 1269

Carmelo Giarrizzo
*Ritratto di Elisa Huber,
moglie dell'artista*
1891 ca
Olio su tela, cm 57,5 × 40,5
Gl. n. 912

Francesco Gioli
*Ritratto di Diego Martelli*
1888
Olio su tela, cm 134 × 80
Inv. Dep. n. 608

Michele Gordigiani
*La moglie del pittore Gabriella
Coujère*
Olio su tela, cm 45 × 34
Gl. n. 1591

Michele Gordigiani
*Ritratto del conte Luigi Pisani*
1884
Olio su tela, cm 62 × 52
Gl. n. 1270

Michele Gordigiani
*Ritratto della contessina Pisani*
1880

Olio su tela, cm 60 × 42
Gl. n. 1268

Michele Gordigiani
*Ritratto della figlia Giulietta*
1890 ca
Olio su tela, cm 74,5 × 52
Gl. n. 1593

Michele Gordigiani
*Ritratto delle contessine Bianca
e Amelia Pisani*
1877
Olio su tela, cm 91 × 70
Gl. n. 1227

Michele Gordigiani
*Ritratto di Gabriella Coujère,
moglie del pittore*
1880 ca
Olio su tela, cm 72 × 58
C.g. n. 155

Ulvi Liegi
*La modellina*
1889
Olio su tela, cm 48 × 40,5
C.g. n. 359

Riccardo Nobili
*In birreria*
1885
Olio su tela, cm 66 × 142
Gl. n. 829

Giacomo Papini
*Il casto Giuseppe*
1882
Terracotta, h. cm 30
Gl. n. 2392

Augusto Rivalta
*Bozzetto per il monumento
a Luigi Pisani*
Bronzo, h. cm 48,2
Gl. n. 1267

Augusto Rivalta
*Ninfa in groppa a un centauro*
Bronzo, h. cm 55
C.g. n. 639

Augusto Rivalta
*Sacra famiglia*
Gesso. h. cm 38
C.g. n. 711

Augusto Rivalta
*Satiro che lotta con una ninfa*
1895-1910
Gesso, h. cm 33
C.g. n. 709

Tony Robert-Fleury
*Ritratto di Maria Bashkirteff*
Olio su tavola, cm 55 × 38
Inv. 1890 n. 3408

Raffaello Romanelli
*Ritratto dell'avvocato
Alfredo Ambrosiano*
1892
Bronzo, h. cm 56
Gl. n. 741

Raffaello Romanelli
*Ritratto virile*
Bronzo, h. cm 58
C.g. n. 647

Filadelfo Simi
*Bice: iridescente della madreperla*

Olio su tela, cm 60 × 178
C.g. n. 123

**Gaetano Trentanove**
*Busto della moglie*
1890
Marmo, h. cm 73
Gl. n. 2378

**Gaetano Trentanove**
*Ritratto di Victor Hugo*
Marmo, h. cm 122,5
Gl. n. 831

**Francesco Vinea**
*Testa virile (studio)*
1864
Olio su tela, cm 38,5 × 32,5
C.g. n. 127

**Francesco Vinea**
*Visita allo studio*
Olio su tela, cm 71 × 59
C.g. n. 128

**Franz Xavier Winterhalter**
*Ritratto di Eugenie de Montijo*
1870
Pastello ovale su carta, cm 73 × 59,5
Gl. n. 4283

## ROOM 18

**Giorgio Belloni**
*Cervino*
Olio su tela, cm 35 × 56,5
Gl. n. 1983

**Giorgio Belloni**
*Crepuscolo*
1912
Olio su tela, cm 105 × 150
C.g. n. 369

**Giorgio Belloni**
*Sturla*
Olio su cartone, cm 40 × 61
Gl. n. 1941

**Bartolomeo Bezzi**
*Pescarenico*
Olio su tela, cm 55 × 90
C.g. n. 366

**Odoardo Borrani**
*Renaioli sul Mugnone*
1880
Olio su tela, cm 142 × 112
C.g. n. 326

**Vincenzo Cabianca**
*Effetto di sole*
Olio su tavola, cm 31 × 20,5
C.g. n. 240

**Vincenzo Cabianca**
*Nettuno*
1872
Olio su tavola, cm 27 × 18,5
C.g. n. 239

**Adriano Cecioni**
*La madre*
1878-97 ca
Gesso, h. cm 182
C.g. n. 718

**Giuseppe Ciardi**
*Sul limitare*
1911
Olio su tela, cm 70 × 59
C.g. n. 365

**Guglielmo Ciardi**
*Paese*
1903 ca
Olio su tavola, cm 35,5 × 56
Gl. n. 1928

**Guglielmo Ciardi**
*San Giorgio*
Olio su tela, cm 60 × 82
C.g. n. 367

**Vito D'Ancona**
*Portico*
1861 ca
Olio su tavola, cm 15,5 × 23,3
C.g. n. 234

**Giovanni Fattori**
*Barca sulla spiaggia*
1870 ca
Olio su tavola, cm 14,1 × 21,4
C.g. n. 196

**Giovanni Fattori**
*Bovi al carro*
Olio su tela, cm 42,8 × 103,5
C.g. n. 204

**Giovanni Fattori**
*Il cavallo bianco*
1903
Olio su tela, cm 43 × 58
C.g. n. 216

**Giovanni Fattori**
*Libecciata*
Olio su tavola, cm 19,2 × 32,2
C.g. n. 210

**Giovanni Fattori**
*La libecciata*
Olio su tavola, cm 28,5 × 68
C.g. n. 221

**Giovanni Fattori**
*Mare in burrasca*
1892-1900
Olio su tavola, cm 13 × 23
C.g. n. 218

**Giovanni Fattori**
*Maremma toscana*
Olio su tela, cm 74,5 × 202,8
C.g. n. 201

**Giovanni Fattori**
*Maremma toscana*
Pastello su cartone, cm 35,4 × 68,5
C.g. n. 222

**Giovanni Fattori**
*Pioppi*
1890-1900 ca
Olio su tavola, cm 25 × 17
C.g. n. 219

**Giovanni Fattori**
*Ritratto della figliastra*
Olio su tela, cm 71 × 55
C.g. n. 217

**Giovanni Fattori**
*La rotonda di Palmieri*
1866
Olio su tavola, cm 12 × 35
C.g. n. 220

**Giovanni Fattori**
*Lo staffato*
Olio su tela, cm 90 × 130
C.g. n. 166

**Giovanni Fattori**
*Tramonto sul mare*
1890-1900 ca
Olio su tavola, cm 19,1 × 32,2
C.g. n. 224

**Pietro Fragiacomo**
*Le armonie del silenzio*
Olio su tela, cm 63 × 103
C.g. n. 394

**Pietro Fragiacomo**
*Il traghetto*
1914
Olio su tavola, cm 128 × 197
Inv. Dep. n. 3

**Giuseppe Mentessi**
*Paese*
1921
Olio su tavola, cm 30 × 40
Gl. n. 1939

**Telemaco Signorini**
*Arcola*
Olio su cartone, cm 18 × 33
C.g. n. 280

**Telemaco Signorini**
*Bagno penale a Portoferraio*
1894
Olio su tela, cm 56 × 80
C.g. n. 283

**Telemaco Signorini**
*Bambini al sole*
1860
Olio su cartone, cm 13 × 20
C.g. n. 298

**Telemaco Signorini**
*Bath: Cornwell Place*
Olio su cartone, cm 13 × 21,5
C.g. n. 286

**Telemaco Signorini**
*Bath: una strada di città*
Olio su cartone, cm 12,5 × 21,5
C.g. n. 287

**Telemaco Signorini**
*Colline settignanesi*
Olio su cartone, m cm 15 × 27
C.g. n. 279

**Telemaco Signorini**
*Cornwell Row*
1881 ca
Olio su tela, cm 30 × 18
C.g. n. 284

**Telemaco Signorini**
*Donna seduta (Vecchia che cuce)*
Olio su tela su cartone, cm 16 × 10
C.g. n. 289

**Telemaco Signorini**
*Donne sedute*
Olio su tela su cartone, cm 12 × 21
C.g. n. 290

**Telemaco Signorini**
*Pietramala*
Olio su cartone, cm 24 × 35
C.g. n. 297

**Telemaco Signorini**
*Ragazza seduta*
Olio su tela, cm 28 × 17
C.g. n. 291

**Telemaco Signorini**
*Ragazzi seduti*
Olio su tela su cartone, cm 12 × 17
C.g. n. 296

**Telemaco Signorini**
*Settignano*
Olio su cartone, cm 23 × 35
C.g. n. 285

**Telemaco Signorini**
*Testa di giovinetto*
Olio su tela su cartone, cm 16 × 10
C.g. n. 294

**Telemaco Signorini**
*Tetti a Riomaggiore*
1892-94
Olio su tela, cm 79 × 55
C.g. n. 277

**Ettore Tito**
*Le dune*
1907
Olio su tela, cm 54 × 66
C.g. n. 370

**Vittorio Zanetti Zilla**
*Casa di pescatori*
Olio su cartone, cm 91,5 × 66,7
C.g. n. 372

## ROOM 19

**Giuseppe Abbati**
*Scogli a Castiglioncello*
Olio su cartone, cm 24 × 34
Gl. n. 1152

**Giuseppe Abbati**
*Via di campagna con cipressi
(Strada toscana)*
Olio su tela, cm 28 × 38
Gl. n. 1185

**Giovanni Boldini**
*Paese*
Olio su cartone, cm 15 × 26
Gl. n. 1162

**Odoardo Borrani**
*Alture*
Olio su tela, cm 14 × 46
Gl. n. 1155

**Odoardo Borrani**
*Ragazzo*
Olio su tela, cm 15 × 12
Gl. n. 1156

**Vincenzo Cabianca**
*Monaca*
Olio su tavola, cm 35 × 30
Gl. n. 1163

**Vincenzo Cabianca**
*Paese*
1861
Olio su tela, cm 21 × 26
Gl. n. 1164

**Michele Cammarano**
*Veduta con gondola*
Olio su tela, cm 30,7 × 43,3
Gl. n. 1957

**Giovanni Carpanetto**
*Autoritratto*
1885
Olio su tela, cm 34,8 × 27,4
Gl. n. 2004

Eugenio Cecconi
*Nebbia sui monti*
1867-75 ca
Olio su tela su cartone,
cm 26,5 × 48,3
Gl. n. 1166

Adriano Cecioni
*L'incontro per le scale*
1884-86 ca
Marmo, h. cm 116
Gl. n. 3666

Adriano Cecioni
*Il suicida*
1865-67
Gesso, h. cm 217
C.g. n. 720

Adriano Cecioni
*Veduta di Napoli*
1865-67 ca
Olio su tela, cm 9 × 57
Gl. n. 1161

Vito D'Ancona
*Ritratto di cane*
1874
Olio su tela, cm 60 × 46,5
Gl. n. 1160

Vito D'Ancona
*Ritratto di signora*
Olio su tela su cartone, cm 24 × 24
Gl. n. 1158

Giuseppe De Nittis
*Alaide Banti con ombrellino*
Olio su tela, cm 50 × 40
Gl. n. 4725

Lorenzo Delleani
*Al Valentino*
Olio su tavola, cm 38 × 26,5
Gl. n. 1932

Lorenzo Delleani
*Paese*
1895
Olio su tavola, cm 32 × 44,7
Gl. n. 1930

Giovanni Fattori
*Carro con buoi*
Olio su tavola, cm 18 × 32,5
Gl. n. 1140

Giovanni Fattori
*Cavalleggeri in avanscoperta*
1887 ca
Olio su tela, cm 28,5 × 39,5
Gl. n. 1138

Giovanni Fattori
*Diego Martelli a cavallo*
Olio su tela, cm 23 × 30
Gl. n. 1139

Giovanni Fattori
*Ritratto della cugina Argia*
Olio su cartone, cm 36,2 × 29
Gl. n. 1135

Giovanni Fattori
*Ritratto della seconda moglie*
1889
Olio su tela, cm 100 × 70
Gl. n. 1136

Giovanni Fattori
*Soldato a cavallo*

Olio su tavola, cm 24 × 13
Gl. n. 4780

Giovanni Fattori
*Sosta in Maremma*
1880-1900 ca
Olio su tavola, cm 28 × 42
Gl. n. 1137

Ignoto del XIX secolo
*Veduta di un edificio romano in rovina*
Olio su tela su cartone, cm 27 × 20
Gl. n. 4797

Silvestro Lega
*Contadinella sulla scala*
Olio su tavola, cm 38 × 30
Gl. n. 1148

Silvestro Lega
*La padrona del giardino*
1887 ca
Olio su tavola, cm 26 × 36
C.g. n. 179

Silvestro Lega
*Paese*
Olio su tavola, cm 15 × 25
Gl. n. 1147

Silvestro Lega
*Ritratto di giovane*
Olio su tela, cm 28 × 21
Gl. n. 1149

Silvestro Lega
*Ritratto di Ludovico Tommasi*
1883 ca
Olio su tavola sui cartone, cm 37,5 × 29,5
Gl. n. 1917

Silvestro Lega
*Signora che cuce*
Olio su tavola, cm 45 × 25
Gl. n. 1146

Antonio Mancini
*Autoritratto nello studio*
1875-78 ca
Olio su tavola, cm 21,5 × 31,5
Gl. n. 1952

Antonio Mancini
*Doppio ritratto*
1870 ca
Olio su tela, cm 43 × 33,5
Gl. n. 1951

Antonio Mancini
*Interno*
1875 ca
Olio su tela, cm 35 × 24
Gl. n. 1953

Francesco Paolo Michetti
*Guardiana di tacchini*
Olio su tela, cm 28 × 64,5
Gl. n. 1961

Francesco Paolo Michetti
*Ritratto virile*
1883
Olio su tela, cm 51,8 × 39,6
Gl. n. 2426

Francesco Netti
*Nello studio (Interno con figure: i fidanzati)*
Olio su carta, cm 31 × 24
Gl. n. 1964

Francesco Netti
*Studio di paesaggio*
1889
Olio su tavola, cm 29,5 × 19,5
Gl. n. 4836

Filippo Palizzi
*Grano maturo*
Olio su tela, cm 16 × 24,7
Gl. n. 1954

Teofilo Patini
*Bozzetto per il quadro Bestie da soma*
1886 ca
Olio su tela, cm 44 × 64,5
Gl. n. 1959

Salvatore Petruolo
*Saragozza*
1889
Olio su tela su cartone, cm 36 × 30
Gl. n. 1989

Antonio Puccinelli
*Ritratto di soldato*
Olio su tela su cartone, cm 55,5 × 33,5
Gl. n. 4759

Raffaello Sernesi
*Colli fiorentini*
Olio su tavola, cm 14 × 18
Gl. n. 1153

Telemaco Signorini
*Alberi: Settignano, dintorni di Firenze*
Olio su tela su tavola, cm 27,5 × 17
Gl. n. 1542

Telemaco Signorini
*Casale a Coverciano*
Olio su tavola, cm 13 × 18
Gl. n. 1145

Telemaco Signorini
*Casetta a Quincy*
Olio su cartone, cm 10 × 16
Gl. n. 1143

Telemaco Signorini
*Giardino a Careggi*
Olio su tela, cm 36 × 24
Gl. n. 1142

Telemaco Signorini
*Leith*
1881 ca
Olio su tela, cm 45 × 41,5
C.g. n. 282

Telemaco Signorini
*Muro e giardino*
Olio su tela, cm 11 × 20
Gl. n. 4762

Telemaco Signorini
*Paesaggio*
Olio su tavola, cm 15,3 × 10
Inv. Dep. n. 456

Telemaco Signorini
*Paese (bozzetto)*
Olio su tela su cartone, cm 12 × 21
Gl. n. 2408

Telemaco Signorini
*Pascolo a Pietramala*
Olio su tela, cm 120 × 175
Gl. n. 1141

Telemaco Signorini
*Studio presso Spezia*
1859
Olio su cartone, cm 13 × 15
Gl. n. 1543

Raffaello Sorbi
*Casa colonica*
Olio su tavola, cm 6 × 8,5
Gl. n. 1175

Raffaello Sorbi
*Soggetto storico (bozzetto)*
Olio su tavola, cm 12 × 10
Gl. n. 1177

Raffaello Sorbi
*Veduta di un bosco con un uomo che cavalca*
Olio su tavola, cm 7,5 × 5,5
Gl. n. 4776

Francesco Vinea
*Ritratto di signora*
1866
Olio su tavola, cm 23 × 20
Gl. n. 1170

Francesco Vinea
*Ritratto di signora*
Olio su tela, cm 36,5 × 25
Gl. n. 4734

Francesco Vinea
*Ritratto maschile*
Olio su tela, cm 32 × 23
Gl. n. 4754

**ROOM 20**

Stefano Bruzzi
*Pecore al pascolo*
Olio su tela, cm 55 × 85
C.g. n. 364

Niccolò Cannicci
*Effetto di luna*
1905
Olio su tela, cm 121 × 67
C.g. n. 328

Adriano Cecioni
*La madre (bozzetto)*
Gesso, h. cm 105,5
Gl. n. 293

Giovanni Fattori
*Il salto delle pecore*
1887
Olio su tela, cm 89,5 × 174
Gl. n. 1824

Giovanni Fattori
*Mercato in Maremma*
1887 ca
Olio su tela, cm 91 × 176
Gl. n. 1825

Egisto Ferroni
*Ai campi*
1881
Olio su tela, cm 121 × 200
C.g. n. 357

Egisto Ferroni
*Alla fontana*
Olio su tela, cm 275 × 165
C.g. n. 342

Egisto Ferroni
*Il boscaiolo*

1885 ca
Olio su tela, cm 121 × 89
C.g. n. 320

**Ruggero Focardi**
*Vita campagnola*
Olio su tela, cm 198 × 150
C.g. n. 445

**Valmore Gemignani**
*Giovanni Fattori*
Bronzo, h. cm 56
C.g. n. 652

**Francesco Gioli**
*Fiori di campo*
1896
Olio su tela, cm 152 × 76,8
C.g. n. 313

**Luigi Gioli**
*Nel bosco*
1905
Pastello su tela, cm 63,3 × 78
Inv. 1890 n. 3283

**Ruggero Panerai**
*Il cavallo malato*
1887
Olio su tela, cm 186 × 290
C.g. n. 350

**Telemaco Signorini**
*Fine d'agosto a Pietramala*
Olio su tela, cm 58 × 64
C.g. n. 255

**Telemaco Signorini**
*Mattina di settembre
a Settignano*
1883-90
Olio su tela, cm 58,5 × 64
C.g. n. 271

**Ludovico Tommasi**
*Paese toscano*
Olio su tela, cm 55,5 × 70,3
C.g. n. 437

**Fosco Tricca**
*Busto di Giovanni Fattori*
1899
Terracotta, h. cm 47
C.g. n. 653

## ROOM 21

**Enrico Banti**
*Sole di ottobre*
Olio su tela, cm 60 × 100
Inv. S.m. Il Re n. 330

**Adolfo Belimbau**
*Una fonte a Livorno*
1888
Olio su tela, cm 109 × 142
Inv. S.m. Il Re n. 326

**Niccolò Cannicci**
*Autoritratto*
Olio su tela, cm 40 × 31
Gl. n. 329

**Niccolò Cannicci**
*Nel bosco*
1892
Olio su tela, cm 110 × 200
C.g. n. 329

**Niccolò Cannicci**
*Sete nei campi*

Olio su tela, cm 54 × 45
C.g. n. 331

**Eugenio Cecconi**
*La caccia al cinghiale nel padule
di Burano*
1886 ca-1903
Olio su tela, cm 255 × 540
C.g. n. 162

**Arturo Faldi**
*Studio di paese*
Olio su tela, cm 68 × 88
C.g. n. 142

**Francesco Gioli**
*All'ovile*
1913
Olio su cartone, cm 42,5 × 71,5
C.g. n. 310

**Francesco Gioli**
*Il Palazzo Comunale a Volterra*
1884 ca
Olio su tavola, cm 39 × 23,2
C.g. n. 309

**Luigi Gioli**
*Barroccio pisano*
1885
Olio su tela, cm 49,5 × 60,4
C.g. n. 340

**Alfonso Hollaender**
*Boboli*
Olio su cartone, cm 35 × 23
Gl. n. 255

**Alfonso Hollaender**
*La gondola*
Olio su cartone, cm 36 × 23
Gl. n. 256

**Alfonso Hollaender**
*Pini sul mare*
Olio su cartone, cm 35 × 23
Gl. n. 257

**Urbano Lucchesi**
*Il cantastorie*
Terracotta, h. cm 52
Gl. n. 310

**Urbano Lucchesi**
*Il rosario*
Terracotta, h. cm 46
Gl. n. 311

**Enrico Markò**
*Donne che lavano sull'Ema*
1879
Olio su cartone, cm 31 × 23
Inv. S.m. Il Re n. 278

**Filadelfo Simi**
*Studio di paese*
Acquerello su tavola, cm 30 × 22
C.g. n. 335

**Alfonso Testi**
*L'Arno in piena*
Olio su tela, cm 65 × 112
C.g. n. 338

**Adolfo Tommasi**
*Giornata invernale*
Olio su tela, cm 73,8 × 117
C.g. n. 349

**Adolfo Tommasi**
*Primavera*

Olio su tela, cm 150 × 200
C.g. n. 323

**Angelo Tommasi**
*Maternità*
Olio su tela, cm 174 × 100
C.g. n. 363

**Ludovico Tommasi**
*Sul lago di Massaciuccoli*
1896
Olio su tela, cm 138 × 248
Inv. S.m. Il Re n. 365

## ROOM 22

**Niccolò Cannicci**
*Gioie materne*
1887
Olio su tela, cm 147 × 120
Gl. n. 1582

**Eugenio Cecconi**
*Autoritratto*
1860-70 ca
Olio su tela, cm 18,5 × 14,5
Gl. n. 102

**Federico Cortese**
*Il bosco di Capodimonte*
1878
Olio su tela, cm 166 × 106
C.g. n. 106

**Giuseppe De Nittis**
*Pioggia di cenere*
1872
Olio su tavola, cm 45 × 30
C.g. n. 118

**Giuseppe De Nittis**
*Sulle rive dell'Ofanto*
Olio su tela, cm 25 × 100
C.g. n. 116

**Egisto Ferroni**
*Il ballo*
1885
Olio su tavola, cm 26 × 20
Gl. n. 766

**Ruggero Focardi**
*Il gioco delle bocce*
1882
Olio su tela, cm 74 × 121
Inv. Com. n. 220

**Francesco Gioli**
*Passa il viatico*
1878
Olio su tela, cm 120 × 201
Gl. n. 5608

**Francesco Gioli**
*Un incontro*
1874
Olio su tela, cm 82,8 × 137
C.g. n. 311

**Pio Joris**
*Paesaggio*
Olio su tela, cm 30 × 42
Gl. n. 1975

**Pio Joris**
*Paesaggio con figura (Passeggiata)*
1865
Olio su tela, cm 32 × 54
Gl. n. 1970

**Pio Joris**
*La venditrice di frutta*

1893
Olio su tavola, cm 23,5 × 18,5
Gl. n. 1973

**Antonio Mancini**
*Maschera*
Olio su tela, cm 63 × 48
C.g. n. 111

**Francesco Paolo Michetti**
*Pastorelle*
1872
Olio su tavola, cm 37 × 28
C.g. n. 114

**Domenico Morelli**
*Ritrovo in un cimitero
di Costantinopoli*
1894
Olio su tela, cm 46,2 × 71,5
Gl. n. 307

**Filippo Palizzi**
*Monelli*
1872
Olio su tela, cm 35 × 50
C.g. n. 105

**Filippo Palizzi**
*Pastorella*
1874
Olio su tela, cm 35 × 50
Inv. Dep. n. 91

**Alberto Pasini**
*Carovana presso il mar Rosso*
1864
Olio su tela, cm 39 × 66
C.g. n. 89

**Giuseppe Raggio**
*Butteri*
Olio su cartone, cm 27,5 × 26
Gl. n. 1979

**Giuseppe Raggio**
*Mandria di bufali*
Olio su tela, cm 85 × 145
C.g. n. 102

**Augusto Rivalta**
*Orante*
Gesso, h. cm 40
C.g. n. 713

**Augusto Rivalta**
*Ritorno dalla posta*
Gesso, h. cm 114
C.g. n. 714

**Luigi Serra**
*I coronari a San Carlo a' Catinari*
Olio su tela, cm 56 × 128
C.g. n. 98

**Gioacchino Toma**
*La pioggia di cenere dal Vesuvio*
1880
Olio su tela, cm 93 × 150
C.g. n. 94

**Achille Vertunni**
*Il torrente la Nera presso Narni*
Olio su tela, cm 157 × 103
C.g. n. 92

**Alberto Zardo**
*Tramonto autunnale*
1918
Olio su tela, cm 123 × 110
Inv. Com. n. 280

Torello Ancillotti
*Etude de salon orientale*
1889 ca
Olio su tavola, cm 49 × 61
Gl. n. 2994

Adolfo De Carolis
*Nudo di donna*
1905
Olio su tela, cm 70 × 158
Gl. n. 1727

Henri De Groux
*Giulio Cesare a cavallo avanza
fra le sue legioni*
Olio su tela, cm 60 × 62
Gl. n. 135

Roberto Pio Gatteschi
*Ritratto della moglie*
Olio su tela, cm 220 × 180
Gl. n. 2702

Edoardo Gelli
*Ritratto di Bruna Pagliano*
1904
Olio su tela, cm 170,5 × 126
Gl. n. 2395

Philip Alexius Lazlo de Lombos
*Ritratto dell'abate mitrato
di San Martino*
1906
Olio su cartone, cm 79 × 51,5
Inv. 1890 n. 8555

Franz Lenbach
*Ritratto del marchese Giovanni
di Montagliari*
1885 ca
Olio su tavola, cm 68 × 55
C.g. n. 154

Franz Lenbach
*Ritratto di Giulia Cioni contessa
di Villeneuve*
1884 ca
Olio su tela, cm 109 × 65,5
C.g. n. 146

Franz Lenbach
*Ritratto di Giulia Cioni contessa
di Villeneuve*
1884
Olio su tavola, cm 75 × 59,3
C.g. n. 156

Ernest Friedrich von Liphart
*Ritratto di Karl Edward
von Liphart*
1883
Olio su tavola, cm 33,5 × 42
Inv. 1890 n. 9439

Giacomo Martinetti
*Dianora de' Castracani rinviene
Castruccio fanciullo nella vigna*
1873
Olio su tela, cm 125 × 93
Gl. n. 4679

Sidney Paget
*Lancillotto ed Elena*
Olio su tela, cm 106 × 156
Gl. n. 5615

John Singer Sargent
*Ritratto del pittore Ambrogio
Raffaele*

Olio su tela, cm 68 × 88
C.g. n. 143

Kurt Stoeving
*Allegoria della vita*
Olio su tavola, cm 170 × 244
Gl. n. 5652

Sirio Tofanari
*Carezza*
1909
Bronzo, cm 24 × 63 × 62
C.g. n. 658

Domenico Trentacoste
*Caino*
1903 ca
Gesso, h. cm 32
Gl. n. 4608

Domenico Trentacoste
*Figura femminile allegorica
per la torre del Parlamento*
Gesso, h. cm 165
Gl. n. 4514

Domenico Trentacoste
*Figura femminile allegorica
per la torre del Parlamento*
Gesso, h. cm 165
Gl. n. 4515

Domenico Trentacoste
*Figura femminile allegorica
per la torre del Parlamento*
Gesso, h. cm 155
Gl. n. 4517

Domenico Trentacoste
*Figura femminile allegorica
per la torre del Parlamento*
Gesso, h. cm 155
Gl. n. 4518

Domenico Trentacoste
*Saffo*
Gesso, h. cm 25,3
Gl. n. 4607

Angiolo Vannetti
*Auriga disgraziato*
1909
Bronzo, cm 40 × 60 × 50
C.g. n. 692

Otto Vermehren
*Autoritratto in costume*
Olio su tela, cm 74 × 52
Gl. n. 3709

Otto Vermehren
*Copia dalla Flora di Tiziano
agli Uffizi*
Olio su tela, cm 87 × 63
Gl. n. 3658

Otto Vermehren
*Paolo e Francesca*
Olio su tela, cm 152,5 × 97
Gl. n. 3659

Otto Vermehren
*Promontorio marino*
Olio su tela, cm 73,5 × 92,5
Gl. n. 3657

Otto Vermehren
*Ritratto di Margherita Papini,
moglie dell'artista*
1890 ca
Olio su tela, cm 55,5 × 38,7
Gl. n. 3711

Benvenuto Benvenuti
*Frate fuoco*
Olio su tela, cm 62 × 75
Gl. n. 262

Antonio Calcagnadoro
*In chiesa (Vecchi in preghiera)*
1899
Olio su tela, cm 70 × 128
Gl. n. 3663

Adolfo De Carolis
*Sulla foce*
Tempera su carta, cm 43 × 68
Gl. n. 1728

Antonio Antony De Witt
*Ruscello*
1891
Olio su tela, cm 65 × 66
C.g. n. 528

Carlo Fornara
*Paesaggio*
Olio su tavola, cm 24,5 × 30
Gl. n. 2005

Vittore Grubicy
*Gruppo di pecore presso
una siepe (Terzetto tenue)*
1896-1917
Olio su tela, cm 27 × 45
C.g. n. 391

Vittore Grubicy
*Inverno in montagna
(Terzetto tenue)*
Olio su tela, cm 37 × 37
C.g. n. 390

Vittore Grubicy
*Mattino delicato (Terzetto tenue)*
1872-89
Olio su tela, cm 38 × 33
C.g. n. 392

Vittore Grubicy
*Il pastore antico*
1887-1914
Olio su tela, cm 30 × 50
C.g. n. 393

Giorgio Kienerk
*Sorge la luna (Sera, campagna
toscana)*
1897
Olio su tela, cm 164 × 248
Gl. n. 5617

Ulvi Liegi
*Sulla terrazza del casolare –
Roncegno*
Olio su cartone, cm 53 × 70
C.g. n. 361

Ulvi Liegi
*Veduta in Valsesia*
1924
Olio su tela, cm 48 × 64,5
Gl. n. 1181

Llewelyn Lloyd
*Fiori in vaso (trittico)*
1907
Olio su tela, cm 77 × 44
C.g. n. 450/3

Llewelyn Lloyd
*Giardino fiorito (trittico)*
1907

Olio su tela, cm 72 × 52
C.g. n. 450/2

Llewelyn Lloyd
*Il giardino in fiore (trittico)*
1907
Olio su tela, cm 77 × 44
C.g. n. 450/1

Amedeo Lori
*Padule d'Arnino (Bocca d'Arno)*
1900 ca
Olio su tela, cm 47 × 94
C.g. n. 356

Vittorio Meoni
*Colle Val d'Elsa "ai Frati"*
Olio su cartone, cm 39 × 52
C.g. n. 348

Vittorio Meoni
*Oasi nelle crete senesi*
1912 ca
Olio su tela, cm 47 × 38
C.g. n. 347

Angelo Morbelli
*Mi ricordo quand'ero fanciulla*
1903 ca
Olio su tela, cm 45 × 69,5
C.g. n. 385

Plinio Nomellini
*Bacchino*
Olio su tela, cm 121 × 94
C.g. n. 451

Plinio Nomellini
*Incidente in fabbrica*
Olio su tela, cm 95 × 133
Gl. n. 5402

Plinio Nomellini
*Il primo compleanno (la famiglia)*
1914
Olio su tela, cm 305 × 285
Inv. Dep. n. 4

Plinio Nomellini
*Ritratto di Lorenzo Viani*
1902 ca
Olio su tela, cm 61 × 48
Gl. n. 2939

Gaetano Previati
*Nel prato*
1880-90
Olio su tela, cm 61 × 55
C.g. n. 368

Gino Romiti
*I giardini del mare*
Olio su tela, cm 170 × 156
C.g. n. 455

Medardo Rosso
*Bambino alle cucine economiche*
1893
Bronzo, h. cm 35
C.g. n. 661

Medardo Rosso
*Donna che ride*
1891
Bronzo, h. cm 59
C.g. n. 677

Medardo Rosso
*La portinaia*
Cera e gesso, h. cm 36, h. cm 58
C.g. n. 664

Medardo Rosso
*Uomo che legge*

1894
Bronzo, h. cm 41
C.g. n. 659

**Giulio Aristide Sartorio**
*Fienile*
Pastello su carta, cm 55 × 75
C.g. n. 113

**Adolfo Tommasi**
*Veduta del parco della Villa reale di Marlia*
Secondo decennio del XX secolo
Olio su tela, cm 78,5 × 87,5
Gl. n. 5637

**Domenico Trentacoste**
*La minestra*
Gesso, h. cm 103
Gl. n. 4610

**Alberto Zardo**
*Terreni inondati*
Olio su tela, cm 65 × 85
C.g. n. 139

## ROOM 25

**Giuseppe Abbati**
*Paesaggio fiesolano*
Tela, cm 14 × 30
Gagliardini

**Giuseppe Abbati**
*Il prato dello strozzino*
Tavola, cm 14 × 38
Gagliardini

**Giuseppe Abbati**
*Signora nella cripta di San Miniato*
Tela, cm 40 × 29
Gagliardini

**Cristiano Banti**
*Le guardianelle*
Tavola, cm 17 × 35
Gagliardini

**Odoardo Borrani**
*La luttuosa notizia (Il dispaccio del 9 gennaio 1878)*
Olio su tela, cm 110 × 138
Gagliardini

**Odoardo Borrani**
*Interno di oratorio*
1875
Tavola, cm 71 × 104
Gagliardini

**Odoardo Borrani**
*Paesaggio di San Marcello pistoiese*
Tela, cm 14 × 39
Gagliardini

**Vincenzo Cabianca**
*Case in Liguria*
Tela, cm 25,5 × 19
Gagliardini

**Vincenzo Cabianca**
*Luci e ombre a Palestrina*
1859
Tela, cm 63 × 51
Gagliardini

**Niccolò Cannicci**
*Il mercato dei bovi a San Gimignano*

Tela, cm 21,5 × 31,5
Gagliardini

**Bernardo Celentano**
*Il consiglio dei dieci (studio)*
Tela, cm 73 × 22
Gagliardini

**Giovanni Costa**
*Giornata di scirocco*
Tela, cm 88 × 193
Gagliardini

**Giovanni Costa**
*Paesaggio con ruderi*
Tela, cm 13,5 × 44
Gagliardini

**Vito D'Ancona**
*Paesaggio*
Tavola, cm 18 × 29
Gagliardini

**Serafino De Tivoli**
*Lavandaia sulla riva della Senna*
Tela, cm 54 × 79
Gagliardini

**Giovanni Fattori**
*Autoritratto*
Tela, cm 48 × 39
Gagliardini

**Giovanni Fattori**
*Carabiniere sulla neve*
Tavola, cm 34 × 25
Gagliardini

**Giovanni Fattori**
*Cavalli nella pineta di Tombolo*
1866-67
Olio su tela, cm 85 × 174
Gagliardini

**Giovanni Fattori**
*La libecciata*
Tavola, cm 27 × 67
Gagliardini

**Giovanni Fattori**
*Riflessioni*
Tela, cm 46 × 36
Gagliardini

**Giovanni Fattori**
*Ritratto del signor Mazzoli*
Tela, cm 24 × 16
Gagliardini

**Giovanni Fattori**
*La sosta*
Tela, cm 99 × 66
Gagliardini

**Giovanni Fattori**
*Sotto la tenda*
Tavola, cm 11 × 22
Gagliardini

**Giovanni Fattori**
*Lo staffato (studio)*
Tavola, cm 38,5 × 66
Gagliardini

**Silvestro Lega**
*Imboscata di bersaglieri italiani in Lombardia*
Tela, cm 56 × 94
Gagliardini

**Silvestro Lega**
*In villa*
1880

Cartone, cm 47 × 64
Gagliardini

**Silvestro Lega**
*Pergolato*
1864
Olio su tavola, cm 20 × 26
Gagliardini

**Silvestro Lega**
*Portone colonico*
Gagliardini

**Silvestro Lega**
*Le rose della primavera*
Tela, cm 60 × 50
Gagliardini

**Silvestro Lega**
*Lo studio del pittore*
1895
Olio su tavola, cm 29 × 38
Gagliardini

**Antonio Puccinelli**
*In pittore in sagrestia*
Tela, cm 31,5 × 40
Gagliardini

**Raffaello Sernesi**
*Paesaggio*
Tela, cm 10 × 29
Gagliardini

**Telemaco Signorini**
*Cacciata degli austriaci dalla borgata di Solferino*
1859-61
Olio su tela, cm 61,5 × 120
Gagliardini

**Telemaco Signorini**
*Il ponte sull'Affrico a Piagentina*
Tavola, cm 22 × 30
Gagliardini

**Telemaco Signorini**
*Il Ponte Vecchio a Firenze*
Tavola, cm 39 × 32,5
Gagliardini

**Telemaco Signorini**
*Interno di palazzo veneziano*
Gagliardini

**Telemaco Signorini**
*La mungitura*
Tela, cm 39 × 33
Gagliardini

## ROOM 26

**Giovanni Bartolena**
*La bottiglia di maraschino*
Tavola, cm 62 × 43
Gagliardini

**Giovanni Boldini**
*Cavalli al tombarello*
Tela, cm 70 × 100
Gagliardini

**Giovanni Boldini**
*Signora in bianco*
Tela, cm 130 × 97
Gagliardini

**Oscar Ghiglia**
*Composizione*
Tela, cm 66 × 85
Gagliardini

**Oscar Ghiglia**
*Lo specchio*

Tela, cm 48 × 49
Gagliardini

**Plinio Nomellini**
*Mezzogiorno*
Olio su tela, cm 198 × 198
Gagliardini

**Elisabeth Chaplin**
*Autoritratto con scialle rosso*
1912 ca
Olio su tela, cm 104,5 × 74
Gl. n. 2738

**Elisabeth Chaplin**
*Il fratello Jean Jacques soldato*
1916-18 ca
Tempera su tela, cm 120 × 90
Gl. 2776

**Elisabeth Chaplin**
*L'ora di studio*
1910
Olio su tela, cm 170 × 108
Gl. n. 2777

**Elisabeth Chaplin**
*La villa "il Treppiede"*
post 1940
Olio su cartone, cm 68 × 75,5
Gl. n. 2785

**Elisabeth Chaplin**
*Nausicaa con gli uccellini*
1925
Olio su tela, cm 51,5 × 45,5
Gl. n. 2770

**Elisabeth Chaplin**
*Nenette che sale le scale*
1913-15 ca
Olio su tela, cm 191 × 113
Gl. n. 2725

**Elisabeth Chaplin**
*Ritratto del fratello*
1914 ca
Olio su tela, cm 120 × 70
Gl. n. 2784

**Elisabeth Chaplin**
*Ritratto della signorina Ida Capecchi*
1910 ca
Olio su tela, cm 220 × 125
Gl. n. 2034

**Elisabeth Chaplin**
*Ritratto del padre*
1926
Olio su tela, cm 77 × 63
Gl. n. 2783

**Elisabeth Chaplin**
*Ritratto di famiglia in esterno*
1906 ca
Olio su tela, cm 230 × 200
Gl. n. 2749

**Elisabeth Chaplin**
*Ritratto di famiglia in interno*
1910 ca
Olio su tela, cm 150 × 200
Gl. n. 2768

**Elisabeth Chaplin**
*Ritratto di Robert con cane e automobilina*
1930-31 ca
Olio su tela, cm 67 × 43,5
Gl. n. 2742

Elisabeth Chaplin
*Robert con il cane*
1930 ca
Olio su tela, cm 50 × 44,5
Gl. n. 2747

Marguerite Chaplin Bavier
Chafour
*Busto di Elisabeth*
Marmo, h. cm 31
Gl. n. 2810

Marguerite Chaplin Bavier
Chafour
*Nenette con cappello*
1904-05 ca
Gesso h. cm 37
Gl. n. 2812

Domenico Trentacoste
*Nudo femminile*
Gesso, h. cm 185 × 115
Gl. n. 4609

## ROOM 27

Vincenzo Cabianca
*Mattutino*
1902
Acquerello su carta, cm 43 × 100
C.g. n. 262

Felice Carena
*Nudo di donna*
1912
Tecnica mista su cartone, cm 79 × 65
Gl. n. 1507

Fabio Casanuova
*Ritratto di vecchia*
Olio su tela, cm 87 × 61
Gl. n. 1200

Arturo Checchi
*La coperta rossa*
1912
Olio su tela, cm 60 × 78,5
C.g. n. 404

Umberto Coromaldi
*La madre contenta*
Olio su tela, cm 125 × 116
C.g. n. 388

Giovanni Costetti
*La pensierosa*
1921
Olio su cartone su tavola,
cm 100 × 69
C.g. n. 453

Adolfo De Carolis
*Ritratto della figlia Adriana*
1909 ca
Olio su tela su cartone, cm 50 × 35,5
Gl. n. 1729

Antonio Antony De Witt
*Autoritratto con sfondo di case
di Lucca*
1916
Olio su tavola, cm 60,5 × 43,5
Gl. n. 4120

Guido Ferroni
*Sensazioni pittoriche (Marina)*
Olio su cartone, cm 39 × 45
C.g. n. 486

Emilio Gallori
*Nerone vestito da Etera*
Inv Dep. Acc. Arti del Disegno

Oscar Ghiglia
*Autoritratto*
1920
Olio su tela, cm 80 × 80
Gl. n. 2283

Oscar Ghiglia
*Camelie*
Olio su tavola, cm 42 × 31,5
Gl. n. 1922

Oscar Ghiglia
*Ritratto di Giovanni Papini*
Olio su tela, cm 66 × 57
Gl. n. 2282

Adolf Hildebrand
*Busto di Carlo Placci*
1909 ca
Bronzo, h. cm 40,5
Gl. n. 785

Fillide Levasti Giorgi
*Il giardino della Fortezza
da Basso*
1930-35 ca
Olio su tavola, cm 62 × 76
Gl. n. 2830

Fillide Levasti Giorgi
*Natura morta*
1920 ca
Olio su tela, cm 75 × 100
Gl. n. 2829

Fillide Levasti Giorgi
*Natura morta con vasi*
1918
Olio su tela, cm 57 × 45
Gl. n. 5605

Alfredo Müller
*Paesaggio toscano*
1914
Olio su tela, cm 91 × 84
C.g. n. 396

Alfredo Müller
*Riviera ligure*
1931
Olio su tela, cm 60 × 60
C.g. n. 441

Plinio Nomellini
*Autoritratto*
1906-16
Olio su tela, cm 70 × 58
Gl. n. 1248

Armando Spadini
*Confidenze*
1919-22 ca
Olio su tela, cm 107 × 100
Gl. n. 4684

Armando Spadini
*Ritratto della moglie Pasqualina*
ante 1924
Olio su tela, cm 41,5 × 35,5
C.g. n. 399

Armando Spadini
*Signora in giardino*
1913
Olio su tela, cm 66,5 × 47
C.g. n. 398

Armando Spadini
*Le tre chiocce*
ante 1925

Olio su tela, cm 50 × 65
C.g. n. 397

Domenico Trentacoste
*La derelitta*
Gesso, h. cm 82
Gl. n. 4314

Giacinto Trussardi
*Ritratto dello scultore
Emilio Gallori*
1913
Olio su tela, cm 100 × 75
Inv. Com. n. 605

## ROOM 28

Beatrice Ancillotti Goretti
*Ritratto di Giovanni Costetti*
Olio su tela, cm 47,5 × 39
Gl. n. 3073

Augusto Bastianini
*Renaioli sull'Arno*
Olio su tela, cm 220 × 150
Gl. n. 1581

Pietro Bernardini
*Ritratto di fanciulla*
Tempera su tela, cm 93 × 87
C.g. n. 428

Aldo Carpi
*Dopo cena*
Olio su tela, cm 90 × 130
C.g. n. 379

Mario Cavaglieri
*La mascherata*
1918
Olio su tela, cm 120 × 116
Gl. n. 4886

Galileo Chini
*La fede*
1912
Olio su tela, cm 200 × 127
C.g. n. 442

Galileo Chini
*L'indolenza*
1912
Olio su tela, cm 200 × 126
Gl. n. 1629

Galileo Chini
*La pace*
1911-14
Olio su tela, cm 199 × 126,5
Gl. n. 1628

Massimiliano Corcos
*Ritratto di Pietro Milani*
1914
Olio su tela, cm 47 × 39
C.g. n. 449

Giovanni Costetti
*Donna con bicchiere*
1915 ca
Olio su cartone, cm 49,5 × 34,5
Gl. n. 2836

Giovanni Costetti
*Nudo con ombrellino verde*
1918-20 ca
Olio su cartone, cm 33,5 × 24
Gl. n. 2834

Giovanni Costetti
*Ragazza al balcone
(Alla terrazza)*

Olio su cartone, cm 50 × 33
Gl. n. 2842

Raffaello Gambogi
*Antignano*
1912
Olio su tela, cm 76 × 120
C.g. n. 339

Elin Gambogi Danielson
*Interno*
Olio su tela, cm 52 × 44
C.g. n. 520

Giulio Cesare Giachetti
*Educande*
1915
Olio su cartone, cm 38 × 122
C.g. n. 403

Beatrice Ancillotti Goretti
*Autoritratto*
1904 ca
Olio su tela, cm 59 × 50
Gl. n. 3619

Giorgio Kienerk
*Occhi pensosi*
1915
Pastello su carta, cm 56 × 46
C.g. n. 129

Guido Marussig
*L'albero magico*
1914 ca
Olio su tela, cm 131 × 130
C.g. n. 427

Alfredo Müller
*Paese fiorentino*
1915
Olio su tela, cm 74 × 87
Gl. n. 2114

Emilio Notte
*I vecchi*
Olio su tela, cm 101 × 172
C.g. n. 433

Giuseppe Rossi
*Il renaiolo*
Bronzo, h. cm 81
C.g. n. 682

Filadelfo Simi
*Ritratto della madre*
Olio su tela, cm 42 × 34
C.g. n. 124

Salvino Tofanari
*Ritratto di Galileo Chini*
1906
Olio su tela, cm 175 × 105
Gl. n. 2396

Ludovico Tommasi
*Siesta*
1912
Olio su tela, cm 70 × 55,5
C.g. n. 436

Ada van de Schalk
*Figura di contadina*
Olio su tela, cm 45 × 40
C.g. n. 521

Lorenzo Viani
*Autoritratto*
1910-12 ca
Olio su tela, cm 98 × 67
Gl. n. 430

Giuseppe Viner
*La mina*
Olio su tela, cm 128 × 143
Gl. n. 1024

## ROOM 29

Felice Carena
*Autoritratto nello studio*
1933
Olio su tela, cm 236 × 278
Gl. n. 1197

Giovanni Costetti
*Abiti arancio*
1915 ca
Olio su cartone, cm 49 × 33
Gl. n. 2843

Giovanni Costetti
*Autoritratto*
1941
Olio su cartone, cm 76,5 × 62
Gl. n. 1262

Giovanni Costetti
*Autoritratto con l'allievo
Domenico Candia*
1922 ca
Olio su cartone, cm 70 × 58
Gl. n. 2840

Giovanni Costetti
*Il buon sorriso (La francese)*
1903 ca
Olio su tela, cm 120 × 95
Gl. n. 2847

Giovanni Costetti
*La domanda*
1930
Olio su cartone, cm 77,5 × 62
Gl. n. 2838

Giovanni Costetti
*Donna con la veletta*
1926
Olio su cartone, cm 58 × 47
Gl. n. 2860

Giovanni Costetti
*May con la madre*
1926
Olio su tela, cm 200 × 100
Gl. n. 2844

Giovanni Costetti
*Nudo accovacciato*
1930 ca
Olio su faesite, cm 57,5 × 46
Gl. n. 2856

Giovanni Costetti
*Il passeggio*
1913-14 ca

Olio su cartone, cm 31 × 22
Gl. n. 2846

Giovanni Costetti
*Ritratto dell'allievo Domenico
Candia*
Olio su cartone, cm 40 × 34,5
Inv. Dep. n. 529

Giovanni Costetti
*Ritratto del pittore Carlo Socrate*
Olio su cartone, cm 60 × 45,5
Inv. Dep. n. 528

Giovanni Costetti
*Ritratto del pittore Onofrio
Martinelli*
Olio su tela, cm 58 × 47,5
Inv. Dep. n. 534

Giovanni Costetti
*Ritratto di Augusto Hermet*
Olio su tela, cm 46 × 38
Inv. Dep. n. 541

Giovanni Costetti
*Ritratto di May in giallo*
1938
Olio su cartone, cm 43 × 33
Gl. n. 2855

Giovanni Costetti
*Ritratto di pittore svedese*
Olio su cartone, cm 50 × 40
Inv. Dep. n. 531

Giovanni Costetti
*Ritratto di signora*
Olio su cartone, cm 71 × 44
C.g. n. 454

Giovanni Costetti
*Ritratto di Ugo Dettore*
Olio su cartone, cm 66 × 48
Inv. Dep. n. 535

Giuseppe Graziosi
*Testa di Felice Carena*
1931
Bronzo, h. cm 35
Gl. n. 782

Romano Romanelli
*Ritratto di Ardengo Soffici*
1928
Bronzo, h. cm 40
Gl. n. 1639

Domenico Trentacoste
*Il ciccaiolo*
1900
Gesso, h. cm 167
Gl. n. 4323

## ROOM 30

Baccio Maria Bacci
*Ritratto di Domenico Trentacoste*
1923
Olio su tavola, cm 47 × 46
Gl. n. 129

Baccio Maria Bacci
*La valle della Mensola*
1920
Olio su tela, cm 60 × 70
C.g. n. 415

Evaristo Boncinelli
*Busto del suocero*
Bronzo, h. cm 48
C.g. n. 668

Evaristo Boncinelli
*La cieca*
1916-17 ca
Gesso patinato, h. cm 48
Gl. n. 2047

Evaristo Boncinelli
*L'idiota*
1919
Gesso patinato, h. cm 40
Gl. n. 2044

Evaristo Boncinelli
*Il suocero*
1916-17 ca
Gesso patinato, h. cm 50
Gl. n. 2054

Evaristo Boncinelli
*Testa di vecchio*
Marmo, h. cm 32
Gl. n. 2042

Evaristo Boncinelli
*Testa di vecchio*
Gesso, h. cm 33
Gl. n. 2050

Galileo Chini
*Licata*
1931
Olio su tavola, cm 48 × 68
Gl. n. 301

Galileo Chini
*Natura morta*
1914
Olio su tela, cm 45 × 80
C.g. n. 409

Raffaele De Grada
*Sant'Ellero*
1927
Olio su tela, cm 68 × 83
C.g. n. 400

Guido Ferroni
*Vita umile*
1920 ca
Olio su cartone, cm 40 × 45
C.g. n. 424

Francesco Franchetti
*Natura morta*
1922
Olio su cartone, cm 40 × 49,5
Gl. n. 1599

Giulio Cesare Giachetti
*Cavalli*
1922 ca
Olio su cartone, cm 34 × 34
Gl. n. 2122

Giuseppe Graziosi
*La zia Luigia*
Olio su tela, cm 98 × 100
C.g. n. 418

Renato Natali
*Borgata (via Buontalenti)*
Olio su tela, cm 190 × 150
C.g. n. 402

Mario Puccini
*Fiori in vaso e libellula*
Olio su tela, cm 50 × 33
C.g. n. 420

Antonio Rizzi
*Madonna della Pace*
Olio su tela, cm 212 × 146
C.g. n. 421

Giovanni Romagnoli
*Riflesso di sole*
Olio su tela, cm 51 × 61
C.g. n. 383

Ottone Rosai
*Piazza del Carmine*
1922
Olio su tela, cm 50 × 72
Gl. n. 795

Ardengo Soffici
*Colle toscano*
1925
Olio su tela, cm 70 × 70
C.g. n. 465

Giuseppe Viner
*Cave di marmo*
1906
Olio su tela, cm 65 × 81
Gl. n. 305

Giuseppe Viner
*Fecondazione (la sementa)*
1903
Olio su cartone, cm 31 × 71
C.g. n. 446

# Palatine Gallery: index of artists and works

# Modern art gallery: index of artists and works

printed in October 2001
by Genesi - Città di Castello
for
s i l l a b e